Living
Witness

Living Witness

Explorations in missional ethics

WIPF & STOCK · Eugene, Oregon

Wipf and Stock Publishers
199 W 8th Ave, Suite 3
Eugene, OR 97401

Living Witness
Explorations in Missional Ethics
By Draycott, Andy and Rowe, Jonathan
Copyright©2012 InterVArsity Press - UK
ISBN 13: 978-1-62032-891-0
Publication date 1/15/2013
Previously published by InterVarsity Press - UK, 2012

For
Chris and Lizzie (J. R.)
and
Lindsay and Jane (A. D.)

CONTENTS

	Acknowledgments	9
	Contributors	11
1.	What is missional ethics? *Jonathan Rowe*	13

Part 1: Foundations

2.	Trinity *Christopher J. H. Wright*	35
3.	Creation *Brian Brock*	57
4.	Hope *Grant Macaskill*	79
5.	Church *Matt Jenson*	93
6.	Preaching *Andy Draycott*	114

Part 2: Issues

7. Packaging — 137
   Sarah E. Ruble

8. Families — 156
   Joshua Hordern

9. Friendship — 178
   Guido de Graaff

10. Politics — 198
    Jonathan Chaplin

11. Servanthood — 217
    Nathan John Moser

12. Money — 240
    Sean Doherty

13. Immigration — 258
    M. Daniel Carroll R.

14. Conclusion — 278
    Andy Draycott and Jonathan Rowe

Index of Scripture references — 283
Index of names — 289

ACKNOWLEDGMENTS

Like many good things, this project had its origins over a meal in Cambridge, when we first met for a seminar organized by the Kirby Laing Institute for Christian Ethics. We discovered that each of us had both taught Christian ethics and been involved in mission on the Iberian Peninsula, experiences that had convinced us there were important things to be said about 'missional ethics'. We would like to thank our fellow contributors for the convivial manner in which our explorations were discussed at conferences in California and Cambridge. Particular thanks are due to Jonathan Chaplin and Guido de Graaff, respectively Chairman and Secretary of the Tyndale Fellowship's Ethics and Social Theology Study Group, who allowed us to take 'missional ethics' as the theme of the 2011 gathering. And Pedro Zamora of the Fundación Federico Fliedner, Madrid, and Dennis Dirks, Dean of Talbot School of Theology, Biola University, California, who provided generous assistance that helped defray the costs of the project. Finally, Philip Duce, Senior Commissioning Editor at IVP, oversaw publication of our reflections.

Our prayer is that *Living Witness* will stimulate thinking in the church about how our common life in the Spirit can testify to the goodness of God.

A. D. and J. R.
All Saints' Day 2011

CONTRIBUTORS

Brian Brock (DPhil, King's College, London), Lecturer in Moral and Practical Theology, University of Aberdeen. Author of *Singing the Ethos of God* (Eerdmans) and *Christian Ethics in a Technological Age* (Eerdmans).

M. Daniel Carroll R. (Rodas) (PhD, Sheffield), Distinguished Professor of Old Testament, Denver Seminary. Author and editor of numerous books, most recently *Christians at the Border: Immigration, the Church and the Bible* (Baker).

Jonathan Chaplin (PhD, LSE), Director, Kirby Laing Institute of Christian Ethics, Cambridge; member of Divinity Faculty, University of Cambridge. Author and editor of several books including *Herman Dooyeweerd* (University of Notre Dame), *Multiculturalism* (Theos) and *God and Government* (SPCK).

Guido de Graaff (DPhil, Oxford), Tutor for Christian Doctrine and Ethics, and Director of Studies, Southeast Institute for Theological Education, London. Translator of *Essays in Anthropology: Variations on a Theme* (Cascade).

Sean Doherty (DPhil cand., Oxford), Tutor in Ethics, St Mellitus College. Author of *Foundations for Medical Ethics* (Grove) and co-convenor of the Grove Ethics Group.

Andy Draycott (PhD, Aberdeen), Assistant Professor, Biola University, USA. Editor of *The World in Small Boats* (Eerdmans).

Joshua Hordern (PhD, Edinburgh), Associate Director, Kirby Laing Institute of Christian Ethics; Research Fellow, Wolfson College, Cambridge. Author of *Political Affections* (OUP) and *One Nation but Two Cities: Christianity and the Conservative Party* (Bible Society).

Matt Jenson (PhD, St Andrews), Associate Professor, Torrey Honors Institute, Biola University, USA. Author of *The Gravity of Sin: Augustine, Luther and Barth on 'homo incurvatus in se'* (T. & T. Clark) and (with David Wilhite) *The Church: A Guide for the Perplexed* (T. & T. Clark).

Grant Macaskill (PhD, St Andrews), Lecturer in New Testament, University of St Andrews. Author of *Revealed Wisdom and Inaugurated Eschatology in Ancient Judaism and Early Christianity* (Brill).

Nathan Moser (PhD, Trinity International), Lecturer in Old Testament, Facultad de Teología SEUT and St Louis University, Madrid. Author of 'Isaías', in *Biblia de Estudio Mundo Hispano* (Editorial Mundo Hispano).

Jonathan Rowe (PhD, St Andrews), Tutor and Director of Development, South West Ministry Training Course, Exeter. Author of *Michal's Moral Dilemma: A Literary, Anthropological and Ethical Interpretation* (T. & T. Clark).

Sarah Ruble (PhD, Duke), Assistant Professor, Gustavus Adolphus College. Author of *The Gospel of Freedom and Power: Protestant Missionaries in American Culture After World War II* (UNC Press).

Christopher J. H. Wright (PhD, Cambridge), International Director, Langham Partnership International. Author of many books including *The Mission of God* (IVP) and *Old Testament Ethics for the People of God* (IVP).

1. WHAT IS MISSIONAL ETHICS?

Jonathan Rowe

Because God calls his people to be a living witness to him, morality is mission. Conversely, immorality is 'anti-mission', a failure to give true testimony or witness. This, in a nutshell, is the theme of *Living Witness: Explorations in Missional Ethics*. Our argument is that the whole life of the people of God, not only verbal proclamation, testifies to the church's faith – or lack of faith – in her Lord.

Questions of right living are usually addressed under the rubric of ethics, that is, reflection upon concrete, observable moralities. Ethical concerns include how to live well, what is right and good, virtue and vice, and how all these are both grounded and related to one another. Christian ethics addresses the same matters in the light of God. Starting with his creation of the world and its redemption in Jesus Christ has important consequences for the questions that Christian ethics asks as well as its answers. But it also raises the issue of how ethics relates to mission. Although by no means the only relevant text, Jesus' Great Commission (Matt. 28:18–20) has been considered a missionary mandate for many years. This same Jesus, however, also preached the Sermon on the Mount, often acknowledged as a call for a distinctive Christian ethic. Yet many are startled to see 'mission' and 'ethics' combined in a phrase like 'missional ethics'. Isn't this oxymoronic? Are not mission and ethics separate, even incompatible, because one refers to the good news of God's grace while the other points to rules and regulations? The contributors to this book explain that mission and ethics are intricately and necessarily interwoven. On the following pages we explore why this is so by unpacking the biblical and theological roots of missional ethics, probing its limits and exploring its possibilities.

Although the question 'What is missional ethics?' is answered throughout the volume, the rest of this introduction provides a brief orientation to the issues by sketching the contours of a response and then briefly presenting the essays. By outlining the key characteristics of missional ethics, we hope to offer readers a series of signposts to the subsequent discussion. We shall start at the beginning, with the source of missional ethics.

The source of missional ethics

At the time the word 'missional' was first used in 1907 mission was conceived as an activity of the church undertaken elsewhere by specialists, and missional was simply a synonym for missionary. David Bosch, the twentieth century's pre-eminent missiologist, describes how the influence of Barthian theology led to the church's mission being conceived as a matter of involvement in *God's* primary mission, the *Missio Dei*. According to this view, mission 'is primarily and ultimately, the work of the Triune God, Creator, Redeemer and Sanctifier, for the sake of the world, a ministry in which the church is privileged to participate'.[1]

Affirming that God's mission is the source of the church's mission is not quite the same as saying that it is the source of missional ethics, but a number of scholars have shown how we can arrive at this conclusion. Among ethicists, Oliver O'Donovan argues that Christian ethics is evangelical because living in ways consonant with the created world's moral order witnesses to that order and, therefore, to its Creator. So rather than thinking of ethics as incidental, or something that *follows* proclamation, O'Donovan contends that 'certain ethical and moral judgments belong to the gospel itself'.[2] Several biblical scholars have teased away at how God called a people to bless or be a light to the nations (Gen. 12:1–4; Isa. 49:6), but the most thoroughgoing missional biblical theology is Christopher Wright's *The Mission of God*.[3] Wright's volume

---

1. David Bosch, *Transforming Mission: Paradigm Shifts in Theology of Mission* (New York: Orbis, 1991), p. 392.
2. Oliver O'Donovan, *Resurrection and Moral Order: An Outline for Evangelical Ethics*, 2nd ed. (Leicester: Inter-Varsity Press, 1994), p. 12.
3. Christopher Wright, *The Mission of God: Unlocking the Bible's Grand Narrative* (Downers Grove: InterVarsity Press Academic; Leicester: Inter-Varsity Press, 2006).

demonstrates how the whole Bible can be read in the light of God's mission and, interestingly, he actually uses the phrase 'missional ethics' to describe the role of virtuous living in Israelite and then the church's witness.

One way to explain how missional ethics has its source in God is to ask two questions of the people of God: 'Who are you?' and 'What do you do?'[4] Answers can be found in Peter's first letter to an early Christian community. He tells them they are 'a chosen race, a royal priesthood, a holy nation, God's own people, in order that [they] may proclaim the mighty acts of him who called [them] out of darkness into his marvellous light' (1 Pet. 2:9). The affirmation that Christian communities are a royal priesthood and a holy nation does not come out of thin air, but alludes to an earlier part of Scripture where we read that on Mount Sinai God instructs Moses to tell Israel the following:

> You have seen what I did to the Egyptians, and how I bore you on eagles' wings and brought you to myself. Now therefore, if you obey my voice and keep my covenant, you shall be my treasured possession out of all the peoples. Indeed, the whole earth is mine, but you shall be for me a priestly kingdom and a holy nation. (Exod. 19:4–6)

Notice three things in this passage. First, God is God of all the earth. He chooses a particular people, therefore, for his worldwide, universal purposes. Second, God's choosing a people for himself comes before the demand that they live in a certain way. Before they receive the Ten Commandments, God saves the Israelites from oppressive slavery in Egypt; in other words, 'grace comes first'. Third, there is a very good reason for God's choice. Israel will be God's 'treasured possession out of all the peoples', and because he is concerned for the whole of his creation, this people have a special role as a priestly kingdom. A priest is someone who stands in the middle between two parties as an intermediary, so when God chooses a priestly people he has in mind that they will represent him to the world and the world to him. So, to return to the question 'Who are you?', the people of God are to be God's representatives or ambassadors.

In Romans 15:16 Paul describes his ministry of evangelism in these terms. The Scriptures also insist, however, that the community will fulfil their priestly role in the manner of their living; their morals are part of their mission. This is the significance of the term 'holy nation', which does not mean that Israel will separate itself from other nations but that God's people will reflect in their

---

4. For similar questions see Christopher Wright, *The Mission of God's People: A Biblical Theology of the Church's Mission* (Grand Rapids: Zondervan, 2010).

life together the fact that they *are* his people. Once again, it is worth emphasizing that God's grace comes first, but it is a choice *for* something. This enables us to answer the question 'What do you do?': the people of God witness to God's presence among them by living 'counterculturally'.

Missional ethics, then, has its source in God, because God has a mission. The Old Testament relates how he called into being a priestly people as a means to fulfil his mission and New Testament writers use the same idea to describe the church and its role. We speak of missional ethics, therefore, because right living is central to the church's missionary task.

The scope of missional ethics

While the idea of *Missio Dei* has been widely accepted there is less agreement about what constitutes the church's mission, a debate that is often couched in terms of the relationship between evangelism and social action. Because both feature in the ministry of Jesus (Mark 10:45; John 18:37), John Stott is clear that these 'same two activities constitute the church's mission'.[5] And the recent Cape Town Commitment (2010), emerging from a conference organized by the Lausanne Movement, refers to the Holy Spirit inspiring and empowering 'mission in all its dimensions: evangelism, bearing witness to the truth, discipling, peace-making, social engagement, ethical transformation, caring for creation, overcoming evil powers, casting out demonic spirits, healing the sick, suffering and enduring under persecution' (CTC 5[c]). This approximates to Bosch's claim that the 'missionary task is as coherent, broad and deep as the needs and exigencies of human life'.[6] Such full-orbed visions create a space for morality as part of the gospel, but they also remind us that missional ethics does not encompass the totality of the church's mission. So while, as this book demonstrates, the conjunction of mission and ethics can broach all aspects of life and enable one to affirm that morality is mission, it is not helpful to say the opposite, that is, that all mission is morality. Mission is more than right living, even if the manner of engaging in evangelism, for instance, raises ethical questions.

---

5. John Stott (ed.), *Making Christ Known: Historic Mission Documents from the Lausanne Movement 1974–1989* (Carlisle: Paternoster, 1996), p. 11. The Lausanne Covenant (1974) stated that 'In the church's mission of sacrificial service evangelism is primary' (LC 6), an affirmation that led to much debate. Subsequent evangelical statements either avoid this expression or tie it closely to a view of 'integral mission'.
6. Bosch, *Transforming Mission*, p. 10.

So far we have considered the scope of missional ethics in terms of *what* it includes. A further issue is its scope in terms of *where* it takes place, a question that is related to where God is working. While evangelicals and Roman Catholics tend to answer this question, in their different ways, by affirming that God works through the church, discussion of this issue in ecumenical circles has sometimes viewed the matter rather differently. The emphasis upon the triune God as the source of mission has led some to propose that God's activity in the world is primary and that the church's role is to 'follow God' and discern what he is already doing. The theological justification for this idea is that the Holy Spirit blows where he wills. While evangelicals and Roman Catholics have found difficulties with thoroughgoing versions of the notion for Christological and ecclesiological reasons, respectively, the proposal highlights two important matters. First, God is indeed at work in both the world and the church, and one should not forget that each influences the other. Second, missional ethics must be able to account for good wherever it is to be found as well as be able to explain why Christian ethics derives from God's mission.

To summarize, because the scope of mission is as wide as human life itself, right morality forms a part of what it means to witness to God. Moreover, although missional ethics does not encompass the whole of the church's mission, it raises important questions for how the latter relates to God's concern for, and involvement in, his creation.

The shape of missional ethics

Missional ethics not only arises from a particular source and has a certain scope, but it also possesses specific forms or shapes. So we may say that missional ethics is variously God shaped, story shaped, community shaped, 'other' shaped and, importantly if perplexingly, shaped only in outline and not amenable to precise definition. Let's look, very briefly, at each.

God shaped
We have already examined how missional ethics is God shaped because it derives from God's own mission, yet the trinitarian roots of the *Missio Dei* enable us to say more.[7]

---

7. On not dichotomizing the triune God's being and acts see John Flett, '*Missio Dei*: A Trinitarian Envisioning of a Non-Trinitarian Theme', *Missiology* 37.1 (2009), pp. 5–18.

First, missional ethics is shaped by God as Creator. The world created by God is not only a physical space but also a place in which there are certain patterns or structures to the relations between created things. In other words, creation is not chaotic but ordered. This ordering includes moral goods, so we may speak of a created moral order, and Christian ethics seeks behaviour in harmony with the way that the world was made. Michael Banner has a vivid expression for this, arguing that the task of Christian ethics is to turn the world upside down.[8] Because our fallen condition means that the world is topsy-turvy, Christian ethics is in the business of reversing this situation, of indicating what life would be if it were the right way up.

Second, missional ethics is shaped by God as Redeemer. In 1 Corinthians 1:23 Paul writes that he proclaims Christ crucified. He is very aware that this is a stumbling block to Jews and foolishness to Gentiles, for a crucified Christ according to common thinking was rather like powdered water – simply impossible. Yet the counter cultural incarnation and ministry of Jesus enables us to understand something important about missional ethics. Just as God humbles himself even to death on a cross and then chooses the weak of the world to humble the wise, in the same way, the path of missional ethics is cross shaped. It is a call to live faithfully in the midst of derision, abuse and persecution (1 Pet. 4:1–4).

Third, missional ethics is shaped by God as Spirit. This has at least two implications. First, the Holy Spirit will lead his people into all truth, including moral truth (John 16:13; Phil. 3:15). Second, God himself provides the inspiration and strength to live with the grain of the created order but against the grain of the fallen world. Missional ethics is not only derived from the mission of God, but undergirded and sustained by him. God's grace in the person of the Holy Spirit, therefore, is the assurance that missional ethics will achieve its end.

I will not say more about how missional ethics is God shaped, since this is explained much more fully in Christopher Wright's essay, but it is useful to pause here to highlight one particular implication of God-shaped missional ethics for the church: the people of God must *know God*. One metaphor for church leadership is that of a safari leader. It is not quite as simple as the natural history programmes make it appear because the African savannah is huge, so safari leaders need one very special qualification: they must know the lions. They must know when the animals sleep and when they hunt, where they like

---

8. Michael Banner, *Christian Ethics and Contemporary Moral Problems* (Cambridge: Cambridge University Press, 1999), esp. pp. 1–46.

to go and how to get there, and how to avoid provoking them. If this is a metaphor for the role of a priest, it is also appropriate for a priestly people whose task is to lead others to the Lion of Judah. A prerequisite of any God-shaped missional ethics, therefore, is to *know* the one in whom we have put our trust (2 Tim. 1:12), which means that right at the centre of a God-shaped missional ethics is the worship of God.[9]

Story shaped
Because missional ethics is God shaped, it is informed by God's actions in creation, calling a people and establishing a covenant with them, sending his Son to redeem the world and looking forward to his promised coming again. These actions are often described as the history of God's salvation. Although it is important not to reduce everything to salvation history – to the exclusion of praise, proverb and wisdom – the story of God's dealings with his people has enabled them to understand themselves as living in the light of this history and to make sense of new experiences in its light. In a similar way, missional ethics is shaped by *this* story, which authorizes certain behaviour at the same time as proscribing other actions.

N. T. Wright has outlined how God's dealings, as they are recorded in Scripture, are authoritative for the people of God.[10] He proposes that salvation history is like a series of acts in a play. While each act is different, for we do not see the same thing several times over, they are related to the others. Developments in the plot, a growing idea of the character of each person and some unexpected twists and turns all occur within an overall frame of reference. We do not see completely disconnected and unrelated scenes, but a progression from one to the next and on to the following act. By analogy, the people of God in the Old Testament, the New Testament and the early church are like the previous acts of the play in which we are now actors. Our role is not to re-enact earlier scenes, but to improvise in the light of the play that has already been acted and its finale, which has already been revealed. What has gone before is authoritative for us

---

9. For a statement of the link between mission, ethics and worship see also N. T. Wright, *Virtue Reborn* (London: SPCK, 2010), p. 214. Note, however, that Wright seems to imply that worship is a higher calling than ethics. I think it is unnecessary to suppose that ethical living is not itself worship, cf. 1 Cor. 10:31; Col. 3:17, texts cited by Wright.
10. N. T. Wright, 'How Can the Bible be Authoritative?', in *Vox Evangelica* 21 (1991), pp. 7–32. For an application of the idea to Christian ethics see Samuel Wells, *Improvisation: The Drama of Christian Ethics* (London: SPCK, 2004).

since we have to take it into account and continue in a similar vein. It just will not do to reinvent the wheel, or do something completely out of character, or even start performing a different sort of play. Missional ethics, therefore, is story shaped because it takes seriously the biblical traditions of the church. It attends to these traditions and respects them, attempting to live in such a way that the story is commended to others who do not yet identify with it.

As people live the story it becomes part of them and their ethics becomes 'second nature', that is, they become morally virtuous. N. T. Wright argues that the dynamic of Christian virtue is to point away from itself to God. 'Ultimately, God does not want, and Paul does not suppose that God wants, human beings as perfected individuals, all clean and scrubbed up but with nothing to do. Morality, surprisingly to some, is part of *mission*.'[11]

Community shaped
The Christian life is lived not only by individuals but together with others. In the Old Testament the people of God are called to live in such a way that the surrounding nations remark upon the wise laws they have been given and the nearness of their deity (Deut. 4:5–8). The community addressed by Peter were exhorted to live such good lives that pagans would observe their honourable deeds and glorify God (1 Pet. 2:11–12). And the oft-cited *Letter to Diognetus* shows that the same vision inspired the early church. Missional ethics is necessarily community shaped.

In recent years some writers have used 'missional' in contradistinction to Christendom to denote a particular form of church. They advocate 'missional churches', outward-looking communities able to understand contemporary culture and interpret the gospel to it.[12] Although there may be some similarities between missional ethics and a 'missional church' perspective, they are not identical. The missional church movement has been accused of being a marketing exercise.[13] This may or may not be a fair assessment – and perhaps

---

11. Wright, *Virtue Reborn*, p. 178, emphasis original; see also p. 210.
12. See, e.g., Darrell Guder (ed.), *Missional Church: A Vision for the Sending of the Church in North America* (Grand Rapids: Eerdmans, 1998); Alan Roxburgh, *Missional: Joining God in the Neighborhood* (Grand Rapids: Baker, 2011); Lois Barrett, 'Defining Missional Church', in J. R. Krabill, W. Sawatsky and C. E. Van Engen (eds.), *Evangelical, Ecumenical, and Anabaptist Missiologies in Conversation* (New York: Orbis, 2006), pp. 177–183.
13. Note especially John Milbank, 'Stale Expressions: the Management-Shaped Church', *Studies in Christian Ethics* 21 (April 2008), pp. 117–128.

the charge could also be laid at Paul's own door since he sought to become all things to all people in order to win some to Christ (1 Cor. 9:22) – but the focus of community-shaped missional ethics lies elsewhere.

The moral philosopher Alasdair MacIntyre highlights how communities inhabit ethical traditions.[14] While people may either subvert or nurture their tradition, it enables them to make sense of their world. Like those of other societies the people of God live within a moral tradition, in this case one that is informed by the story of God's dealings with them. Furthermore, this tradition promotes certain virtues and steers people away from particular vices, so that the life of the community is a witness to God. In fact, the reality of a community is itself a witness to the love of God in a fragmented world of broken families and fleeting relationships of all types, and we might start to think about what this could mean for the testimony of our own churches.

A word of caution, however, may be in order. It can be tempting to think that homogeneity is required. The assumption is that there is only one way to live as a Christian: one either hits the bullseye or misses. This, however, is to oversimplify the Christian life, for when Jesus commands his disciples to love God and each other he gives a very general command that can be fulfilled in a multitude of ways. There are, of course, some things that fall outside what it means to love, but this does not stop 'loving' being something open and, if we must think in terms of attaining goodness, the flat expanse of Table Mountain, South Africa, is a better image than the pointed peak of a cartoon mountain. You can still topple off both summits, but in the case of Table Mountain there are many potential ways of responding well to God before one gets to the situation of falling into sin. Naturally, if a common life is a feature of the church's mission, as proposed here, this raises questions about the limits to acceptable moral diversity, something that is particularly challenging in multicultural contexts.

Responding to such questions can be difficult, and because of this there is another important feature of community-shaped missional ethics. Teaching people about the story of which they are part, informing them about biblical injunctions or training them in the practices of prayer are all good, but insufficient for the moral life. We also need to know how to react to the myriad moral goods and evils that we encounter. Moral deliberation, however, does not consist in simply knowing something to be right or wrong. A person must

---

14. Alasdair MacIntyre, *After Virtue: A Study in Moral Theory*, 3rd ed. (London: Duckworth, 2007).

also realize what is happening around her: she must perceive correctly. For example, if Jane has promised to go for a walk with her friend Sarah, she must perceive that Sarah's request to accompany her on a particularly inclement day involves promise-keeping, not just ambling in the hills in the rain. Only then will she be able to begin the process of moral judgment. One ethicist argues that because different people perceive differently and see, or don't see, the moral significance of situations to varying degrees, perception is more difficult for some than for others.[15] Here lies the importance of a community, for in it we can help each other learn how to perceive. Members of a community committed to missional ethics, therefore, can attend to its gospel witness by assisting each other to develop a sense of moral responsibility to love others.

'Other' shaped
'Others', rather obviously, bestow another shape to mission and, therefore, to missional ethics. It should not need saying, although in practice it probably does, that properly ethical mission does not conceive the other as a target, the centre of our efforts to evangelize or care, but as another created being, another person. So while friends, family and enemies may indeed hear the gospel message or experience practical expressions of our love, they are first and foremost other people made in the image of God with whom we share our lives.

Two important questions surrounding other-shaped missional ethics need to be discussed, namely, how to appreciate others' moral goodness without condescension, and the nature of the message that missional ethics seeks to communicate. In order to address these issues we need to take a step backwards to think about how moral goods relate to moral rules, and then how both relate to God. Let's start with the observation that moral goods are more foundational than rules or regulations.[16] This is so because biblical 'law' seeks to promote or protect certain goods, sometimes prioritizing them according to the situations in which they occur. We can think about this in terms of drawing back a curtain to see what is behind it: when we pull back the curtain of moral law we find moral goods. In a canonical context the first 'good' is creation itself. Creation

---

15. Lawrence Blum, *Moral Perception and Particularity* (Cambridge: Cambridge University Press, 1994), p. 30.
16. See Jonathan Rowe, *Michal's Moral Dilemma: A Literary, Anthropological and Ethical Interpretation*, Library of Hebrew Bible/Old Testament Studies 533 (New York: T. & T. Clark, 2011), esp. pp. 37–68; Jonathan Rowe, 'Moral Goods: A Common Denominator for Old Testament Ethics', *Ethics in Brief* 15.1 (Spring 2010).

is not only instrumentally good (good *for* something), but good in the way it has been ordered. So if we were to pull back the curtain of moral goods we would discover the relationship of moral goods to each other, in other words, a moral order of moral goods. What happens if we draw back the curtain of the moral order? Behind the final curtain we find God, Creator and Redeemer. This discovery has important implications. On the one hand, because God is the 'highest good', the notion of the imitation of God is prominent throughout the Bible. On the other hand, although we have drawn back the curtain of rules, we must not abandon them because biblical teaching has the same divine source as creation itself and so reflects a true understanding of the moral order of moral goods.

Understanding this scheme enables us to answer the first of our questions above concerning how Christians can appreciate others' moral goodness. When Amos asks the rhetorical questions 'Do horses run on rocks? Does one plough the sea with oxen?' (Amos 6:12) he assumes that the answer is obvious. This is what gives the following phrase its force: 'But you have turned justice into poison and the fruit of righteousness into wormwood.' The sins enumerated by Amos concern the conversion of evils into goods, and vice versa, a process that is presented as obviously unnatural, a 'cosmic nonsense'.[17] In other words, there is a 'natural morality' in which moral goods are discernible to all. Although not everyone chooses to live this way, the heart of natural morality concerns the possibility of a universal perception of moral goods. It is entirely to be expected, therefore, that others from different cultural and religious traditions can correctly perceive this order because they, too, are created by God and able to respond to him. This offers new vistas for engagement with others, including, for instance, interfaith dialogue, because it is simply not necessary to affirm that Christians possess exclusive insight into ethics. What is more, one can account for moral virtue as a disposition towards morally upright selections of moral goods (and avoidance of evils) wherever it may be found.

But the acceptance of a natural morality is not the end of the matter. In many cases the identification of things as goods or evils, and their prioritization, is either not always obvious or, if it is, people do not behave as they should. This means that the revelation of God must be central to missional ethics. Because both Scripture and natural morality share the same divine source there

---

17. John Barton, 'Natural Law and Poetic Justice in the Old Testament', in *Understanding Old Testament Ethics: Approaches and Explorations* (Louisville: Westminster John Knox Press, 2003), pp. 32–44, quote p. 38.

is, in principle, no need to choose between them.[18] Yet because missional ethics takes Scripture seriously the centrality of the call to repentance in biblical thought and church history cannot be avoided. The Old Testament prophets were insistent that a wayward and recalcitrant people turn to God. The public ministry of Jesus commenced with a call to repentance (Mark 1:15). And Peter's sermon on the day of Pentecost exhorted his listeners to repent (Acts 2:38). The call to repentance, to turn to God, is central to the church's mission and it must be fundamental for missional ethics. This poses a particular challenge when, as is sometimes appropriate or required, the church's witness is 'silent', not drawing attention to its inspiration in the Scriptures and experience of God.

Other-shaped missional ethics, then, accepts the other for who he or she is, finds a place for the other's morally upright behaviour that recognizes it as such, and also maintains that God's revelation of himself demands a response, specifically, repentance.

Shaped only in outline

Having sketched four ways in which missional ethics is shaped, it might seem paradoxical to conclude by affirming that it eludes precise delineation. It is crucial though to realize that we cannot completely describe the form of missional ethics. In a fundamental sense, missional ethics is only an outline that needs to be filled in by believers in their own time and place.

There is a specific sort of missiological and ethical approach to answering the question that forms our title that does not fit well with this notion. Samuel Escobar describes the method of identifying a problem so that it can be 'solved' as 'management missiology'. Similarly, certain sorts of approaches to ethics aim to overcome difficulties in order to leave them behind.[19] Without denying

---

18. And by taking moral goods as more basic than 'law', wisdom or narrative, one can avoid collapsing any one genre into the other – for example, to take a popular misconception, by assuming that narrative is merely illustrative of 'law'. In fact, as we sing God's praises, read the history books, use biblical wisdom and meditate upon 'laws' our lives are (re)orientated, that is, our understanding of the correct order of moral goods is renewed: Scripture becomes part of us and we live in its *habitus* rather than standing outside looking in. See Brian Brock, *Singing the Ethos of God: On the Place of Christian Ethics in Scripture* (Grand Rapids: Eerdmans, 2007).
19. Samuel Escobar, 'Evangelical Missiology: Peering into the Future', in W. D. Taylor (ed.), *Global Missiology for the 21st Century: The Iguassu Dialogue* (Pasadena: William Carey Library, 1999), pp. 101–122; see also the management and therapeutic models of ethics in MacIntyre, *After Virtue*.

the utility of management *per se*, Michael Hanby contrasts our management orientation with the practice of prayer.[20] Prayer is not an attempt to manipulate God to achieve a desired end, but an abandoning of any pretension to god-like control of our environment. In prayer we realize that we are weak and powerless with respect to our futures; we need God to be involved. This has important implications for missional ethics, for we do not seek to define an activity, approach or vision in order to apply it as some sort of technique, a recipe for assured success. By avoiding the temptation to create a neat theological, missiological or philosophical construct we may gain something much more valuable, namely, a missional ethics that is both truly moral and essentially missional because it connects with reality. Michael Banner criticizes some moral philosophy for being divorced from moral practice and challenges moral theologians to ensure their reflection is adequately grounded, engaged with lived moralities rather than simply an artificial scheme to which real life is then enjoined to be moulded.[21] By taking seriously the contexts of God's mission, the community of faith and the lives of others, missional ethics is well placed to respond to this challenge. Because it is contextualized, it will both influence and be influenced.[22] On the one hand, this means that missional ethics is necessarily an ongoing work, as faith seeks moral understanding in the midst of life's vicissitudes. It never 'arrives', is never definitive, but is always in some sense provisional even though we know the direction in which we wish to travel. On the other hand, because missional ethics occurs in the messy matrix of life rather than presuming to adopt a 'supracultural' perspective, it can be challenged and critiqued by those alongside us who take other views. So there is a proper place for all sorts of liberationist perspectives, but also the theoretical space for these claims themselves to be contested.

There is another reason why missional ethics can be described in outline only. I have already mentioned that there exists a wide variety of ways in which moral goods might be configured and remain ethically acceptable, whether this be in decisions or a virtuous life. In addition, we must acknowledge that God gives to each person a unique vocation. Although there may be similarities in

---

20. Michael Hanby, 'Interceding: Giving Grief to Management', in S. Hauerwas and S. Wells (eds.), *The Blackwell Companion to Christian Ethics* (Oxford: Blackwell, 2006), pp. 237–249.
21. Michael Banner, 'Moral Philosophy: The Moral Philosophy of What?', *Studies in Christian Ethics* 24 (May 2011), pp. 232–241.
22. See Andrew Walls, 'The Gospel as Prisoner and Liberator of Culture', in *The Missionary Movement in Christian History* (New York: Orbis, 1996), pp. 3–15.

the ways in which people respond to God's grace in creation and redemption, as the people of God improvise their ethical and missional roles in the light of the hope set before them they are called to one thing or another according to their vocation. It is not possible, therefore, to prescribe particular shapes to the moral or missional life applicable to all. We may only say that the idea of missional ethics encourages Christian believers to take seriously their specific calling and their place in the moral community called to witness to our Lord.

Explorations in missional ethics

Reflecting upon the addresses at the 2010 Edinburgh Mission conference, Vinoth Ramachandra laments that 'we have been blinded by the neat divisions we have been [sic] drawn between theology, ethics and mission'.[23] This volume's focus upon missional ethics is an answer to his call that these boundaries be deconstructed. Each contributor brings his or her own particular expertise and experience to the task. Some will have noticed, however, a preponderance of white males; perhaps the only thing missing is the pith helmet of yore? It is true that we have avoided tokenism, but two observations are in order. On the one hand, virtually all have significant cross-cultural experience and are accustomed to crossing boundaries and viewing the world alongside 'others', being changed in the process. On the other hand, this collection is only an introduction, an attempt by a particular group of theologians and biblical scholars who are active in mission to work out what missional ethics might signify in their situations.

In order to structure our exploration the following essays are presented in two sections: foundations and issues. Naturally, this is an artificial device, since treatment of particular topics sheds important light upon theoretical considerations, and vice versa. Nevertheless, it is logical to examine how theologically important ideas such as Trinity, creation and hope can inform our understanding of missional ethics before considering more specific themes, and readers are encouraged to start at the beginning even if they then decide to dip into the later articles in another order.

The relationship of the Trinity to missional ethics is the theme of Christopher Wright's essay, in which we are offered a biblical theology of the

---

23. Vinoth Ramachandra, 'A Brief Reflection on Edinburgh 2010 by Vinoth Ramachandra', p. 2. Available at http://edinburgh2010.oikoumene.org/en/resources/papersdocuments.html, accessed 21 June 2011.

calling of the people of the triune God, Father, Son and Holy Spirit. Wright explains how each person of the Godhead is involved in the election, redemption and sanctification of the church. The location of the people of God is not as important as its role: the church is 'sent into the world' by God even if this sending is not cross-cultural. Wright examines the missional ethical role of each person of the Godhead. God the Father has a name, YHWH. He is unique and universal: Creator, Ruler, Judge and Saviour. He is also the Father of his people, the giver of his Son. And he is the one whom we observe, trust and imitate in mission and ethics. The Son's identity derives from his Father's and Wright teases out the missiological implications of the 'Great Commission'. Turning to the Holy Spirit, he highlights the role of the Spirit in creation, the mission of Jesus and the life of the church, as they impinge upon missional ethics. God the Trinity, of course, is not only Three, but One, and Wright concludes his essay with discussion of unity in diversity, not only in the Godhead but also in the church, in particular, drawing out the missio-ethical import of Jesus' prayer in John 17.

We live in God's creation and Brian Brock explores the implications of this for missional ethics using the metaphor of gardening. He argues that because human beings cannot give life our mission must – can only – follow and serve God's giving of life. God's first gift of life occurred in a garden, a particular place, and was accompanied with a particular charge: to garden in the garden. Mission, therefore, does not originate as a rejoinder to the need for salvation, but in a response to God's presence in and care of what he has formed. Brock states that 'mission construed in these terms is distinguishable from mission as militancy in that its aim is not first to change people, but to reveal the life-giving God'. Although we garden in a fallen world, subsequent to the expulsion from Eden, thinking of our missio-ethical responsibilities as a response frees us from 'making history', that is, creating our own world, for it is God's Word that has already made history as the precondition for everything that we might do or be.

It is faith in *this* God – both who he is and what he does, although they are indivisible, two sides of the same coin – that differentiates Christian hope from false hopes or mundane optimism. Grant Macaskill's chapter explores how the Christian understanding is distinctive in a thorough examination of biblical hope. Starting with creation and fall, Macaskill sketches how hope features in covenant and prophecy, the roles of the Messiah and Spirit, and future hope. His conclusion explains why missional ethics is a central feature of the church's calling. This is not simply a matter of ensuring coherence between message and life. Instead, and much more profoundly, because the church is the realization of hope, 'we are called to embody the gospel as those who have been brought from death to life'. Thus, claims Macaskill, '[t]o fail to embody transformation is to live in contradiction to the nature of the church's existence'.

Matt Jenson continues the discussion of how the church is the agent of God's mission 'between the times', using as a test case the experience of homosexuality. He focuses upon Christian identity 'in Christ' and the implications for believers' relations, which are reconstrued as familial ones: brothers and sisters with the same heavenly Father, and Jesus as their elder sibling. Jenson relates the experience of Sandy, a bipolar lesbian, concluding that 'the church is right to tell gay people the good news and call them to a life of discipleship *if and only if* it is willing to live as their family. If the church is unwilling to be family to gay people, it has no business giving them the gospel.' Because cultural literacy concerning Christian things is lacking, the article turns to issues of formation, arguing that all Christians – straight and gay – need to learn who they are in the light of Christ. This discovery, avers Jenson, will be that their sexuality is indeed part of who they are but not without remainder, and that sexual desires are *only* that, not the sum of people's identity 'in Christ'. Turning to Augustine, Jenson challenges us to consider how desire may be formed in community and offers a challenge to churches to be loyal to other believers so that we might learn to struggle well – including with (homo)sexual desire – in the presence of God.

In the last of the 'foundational' essays, Andy Draycott explores preaching. He understands preaching as 'the church's free public speech', something that shapes reflection on missional ethics and so is ethically formative. Draycott seeks to ground his account of preaching in the 'prophethood of believers' and so contends with an objection against the very notion that the 'prophetic' could be rhetorically appropriate in public. He then challenges the idea that preaching can be either prophetic or pastoral, missional or ethical. Having answered these objections, Draycott explicates how preaching is free public speech. It is free because it is authorized and empowered by God. It is public because it opens up the Word of God to the church for the world. And it is speech not in a banal sense, but because it leads to 'godly conference', a serious weighing of its import for the life of the church, including its mission and ethics.

Turning to specific issues, Sarah Ruble considers how the story-shaped nature of missional ethics both enables and obscures ethical reflection. She does this via a history of the presentation of mission in *Christianity Today*, one of North America's most popular Christian magazines. Her fascinating essay unpacks the presentation of the relationship between evangelism and social action, highlighting how the construction of stories is intimately involved with questions of power, including interpretative power relating to gender. Ruble's discoveries have important implications for how we tell the gospel story, including the story of missional ethics, for power 'deeply shapes the stories we tell'. Those with interpretative power want to hold onto it in order to protect the message, in other words, to safeguard 'orthodoxy'. Naturally, this means great discernment is required to sift real orthodoxy from the experiences of the powerful. Ruble's challenge is apposite: 'When trying to discern if we are acting as story-shaped people, we must ask what has shaped the stories we are evaluating.'

One of the most important social contexts for mission is the family. 'Families', of course, can take many forms, and particular configurations can sometimes become highly politicized. Joshua Hordern argues that in the church's witness regarding family ethics it should be attentive to both the Scriptures and particular context. His chapter creatively juxtaposes ancient Israelite family modalities, contemporary philosophies of justice and the experiences of extended family in non-Western societies – throughout his chapter he refers to the Insider Movement in Muslim societies. He considers the nature of the good news for families using the categories of endogamy and exogamy, highlighting how the former can be reconceived as marriage between those 'in Christ'. Yet this wonderful new reality is not straightforward from a missional perspective. Hordern discusses the practical difficulties of familial exogamy in societies where cousin marriage is considered desirable, contending that the good of Christian liberty must be held in tension with the missional benefits of cultural appropriateness. Hordern's analysis also enables him to pose important questions to contemporary political theory, which has often failed to recognize the created givenness of familial life. He highlights how, far from being independent individuals, we are interdependent people, something that has significant implications for how our commitment to justice is to be worked out.

Guido de Graaff considers the dynamic of friendship and mission, and how both relate to ethics. While friendship has been seen as a means of mission, de Graaff highlights how practitioners of mission have come to see the process as less of a one-way street and more a matter of reciprocity. Reciprocity has been a key facet of the theorization of friendship since antiquity, and de Graaff surveys how it was conceived by Plato, Aristotle and Seneca, before turning to Christian understandings of friendship. Interestingly, while mission has come to view reciprocity as key, within Christian friendship there is a desire 'to ensure that this dynamic is somehow firmly rooted in, or tempered by, the non-reciprocal dynamic of *agapē*'. De Graaff addresses this puzzle by distinguishing between the moral and epistemic. In the context of mission, he contends, reciprocity is primarily epistemic. So although the proclamation of the gospel is fundamentally non-reciprocal, the process of mission allows preconceptions to be challenged. De Graaff also maintains that reciprocity is necessary at the moral level, for friendship is with others: 'Love that is truly responsive seeks reciprocation, since it is focused on a unique and living being, a *person*.'

Turning to the issue of political speech, Jonathan Chaplin considers the theme of Christian political reasoning, that is, 'reasoning about the responsibility of government for promoting the public good, from the standpoint of Christian political convictions'. After explicating this definition, he asks how Christian public reasoning can be missional, proposing that part of the church's missionary task is to offer 'winsome public wisdom'. There is, of course, a chorus of voices that would exclude Christian wisdom from public discourse on the basis that it is sectarian or irrational. Chaplin carefully refutes such assertions, demonstrating that Christian reasoning, whether explicit or implicit, is intelligible to many people, both in Western democracies with a Christian heritage and elsewhere. He argues that it is not necessary for Christians to explicate the whole process of theological reflection in the public realm. However, although much of this can remain at the level of presupposition, in order for Christian political reasoning to be authentically 'winsome', practitioners must return frequently to the biblical and theological sources of wisdom that underpin their proposals. Chaplin is clear that political engagement by Christians should not be considered 'pre-evangelism'; nor should its success be measured in terms of converts. Instead, Christian speech should be assessed according to gospel criteria. Chaplin offers two such standards for Christian political reasoning: fidelity to biblical truth, and discernment of the spirits of the age.

The character of the people of God is an important part of their witness. Nathan Moser examines how Isaiah's servant figure can inform the church's character, grounding his reflections by attending to the insights of Latin American theologians. Moser addresses four important issues in his chapter. First, how the Scriptures extend an invitation to us to be the servant of the Lord. Second, how the will of God to be revealed in the nations is the reason we are to engage in the mission of the servant. Third, how the Spirit of God liberates us for service and authenticates our character and mission in the world. And, finally, how the Son of God is our paradigm for servanthood. In sum, Moser suggests that we are to be gentle and non-imposing leaders who participate fully in the humanity of those within our missional horizon.

Money, it is said, makes the world go round. And that, according to Sean Doherty, is a problem. In contradistinction to much economic ethics, Doherty argues that a 'missional ethic of money will resist the impulse to begin with constructive dialogue with economic science. This may come later. But the opening moves will be to proclaim the good news, to call people to repentance and costly discipleship, and to draw on the transforming power of the gospel.' His start point is a defence of the idea that money is good and poverty not good. Doherty proceeds to explain why money makes a very poor master. The fundamental question concerns faith, for how we handle possessions is closely linked to whether we trust God and Doherty, following Luther, argues that greed with respect to money indicates a profound lack of faith. After a discussion about the ethics of various ways of earning money, Doherty considers the spiritual as well as practical benefits of giving. He concludes with an explanation of how the call to bring money matters under the lordship of Christ is truly missional.

In the final essay Daniel Carroll looks at the challenges of immigration through a missional lens. Like all of this volume's authors, Carroll has chosen an important theme: over 200 million people are currently on the move to other lands, a figure that excludes internal migrations. He starts at the beginning, with Genesis 1, affirming that immigrants, like all people, are made in the image of God. Carroll then surveys migration in the context of God's mission in the book of Genesis, highlighting how immigrants are called to be a blessing to the people in their new lands, before turning his attention to the New Testament. He then considers how strangers are to be welcomed into the missional community according to Old Testament law, with particular emphasis upon the motivation for this openness, namely, God's prior rescue of his people from oppression. Carroll also examines eschatological hope and migration. He points out that contemporary migration is a foretaste of the future, saying that then, 'diversity will not be feared as a threat, burden or curse; it will be the fulfilment of God's goal for redemption of humanity'. The implications for the church are clear: do we think about and engage with immigrants and/or our hosts in the light of our eschatological hope?

This volume has been penned with the conviction that ethics is central to the church's missional task. We aim not to pronounce the last word on the matters that we have addressed, but to encourage others to join the conversation and to stimulate reflection that will feed the life of the body of Christ. For the answer to the question 'What is missional ethics?' is that it is all the ways in which Christian ethical practice flows out of, supports and advances the wider mission of the church to proclaim the gospel – in other words, the church's living witness.

© Jonathan Rowe, 2012

PART 1: FOUNDATIONS

2. TRINITY

PRELIMINARY EXPLORATIONS OF A BIBLICAL TRIANGLE

Christopher J. H. Wright

Introduction

The first thing that struck me as I began to work on the title of this chapter in the context of this book is that it seems somewhat odd to be doing a biblical survey of three words – Trinity, missional, ethics – none of which as a term in itself is actually in the Bible, although all three, of course, are profoundly biblical in terms of the realities of which they speak.

There has been something of a recovery of the relevance of the doctrine of the Trinity to mission, but it is far from novel. Some fifty years ago Lesslie Newbigin wrote a short book that was at one level a child of its era, and at another somewhat prophetic of the recovery that I mention. Newbigin says that when

> the Church began to take the message of salvation through Jesus Christ out into the pagan world, it very soon found itself compelled to articulate a fully trinitarian doctrine of the God whom it proclaimed. It is indeed a significant fact that the great doctrinal struggles about the nature of the Trinity, especially about the mutual relations of the Son and the Father, developed right in the midst of the struggle between the Church and the pagan world. These trinitarian struggles were indeed an essential part of the battle to master the pagan world view at the height of its power and self-confidence . . . During the period in which the intellectual struggle took place

to state the Gospel in terms of the Graeco-Roman culture without thereby compromising its central affirmation, it was the doctrine of the Trinity which was the key to the whole theological debate.[1]

Newbigin goes on to point out that in our contemporary world one can only preach Christ in contexts that have never yet heard of him in terms of his biblical identity as the Son of God, which necessarily implies the revelation of God as his Father, and trusts in the work of the Spirit to convince and convict of the truth of the message. He continues by affirming that

> even in its most elementary form the preaching of the Gospel must presuppose an understanding of the triune nature of God. It is not, as we have sometimes seemed to say, a kind of intellectual cap-stone which can be put on to the top of the arch at the very end; it is, on the contrary, what Athanasius called it, the *arche*, the presupposition without which the preaching of the Gospel in a pagan world cannot begin.[2]

This chapter is no more than its subtitle claims – a preliminary exploration. I am uncomfortably conscious of my own lack of expertise in systematic theology (ancient or modern), and particularly in the rich field of trinitarian doctrine. Some of the sections below function only as 'placeholders' inviting the reader or others to fill them in with further research and reflection.[3]

Missional ethics and the people of the triune God

What is meant by 'missional ethics'?

The term 'missional ethics' speaks to me of the conviction that how we behave as believers should be governed by the purpose of our existence as the people

---

1. Lesslie Newbigin, *Trinitarian Doctrine for Today's Mission* (first published, Edinburgh, 1963; Carlisle: Paternoster, 1998), p. 34.
2. Ibid., p. 36.
3. A book that is very relevant to our theme unfortunately came to my attention too late to be included in the interaction of this chapter, but seems certain to advance theological engagement with the topic considerably: John G. Flett, *Mission, Trinity, and Church: The Witness of God: The Trinity, Missio Dei, Karl Barth, and the Nature of Christian Community* (Grand Rapids: Eerdmans, 2010). A summary insight into Flett's argument can be read in his '*Missio Dei*: A Trinitarian Envisaging of a Non-Trinitarian Theme', *Missiology* 37.1 (2009), pp. 5–18.

of God as revealed in the Bible, which is to respond to God's saving grace by glorifying God for eternity, and by serving the mission of God within history. In that sense, biblical ethics is intrinsically missional, for all our life is shaped by being called by God to belong to his people and fulfil the mission for which that people were created.

If we go back to the origins of God's people in the Old Testament at the call of Abraham, then the ethical dimension of their *raison d'être* is clear. They are called into a way of living that is distinct from the rest of the nations. Their mission is shaped by what they are to be and do, long before we hear about what they are to say or preach.[4] Israel's mission was (among other things) to be a model for the nations of what a people redeemed and governed by God should look like. Three texts can be cited as core evidence for this perspective on Old Testament missional ethics: Genesis 18:19; Exodus 19:4–6 and Deuteronomy 4:6–8.[5]

God's call of Abraham was explicitly for the ultimate purpose of blessing the nations (Gen. 12:1–3). This fundamentally missionary intention of the election of Israel echoes through the Old Testament at almost every level. There was a universal goal to the very existence of Israel. What God did in, for and through Israel was understood to be ultimately for the benefit of the nations. Furthermore, what God ethically required of Israel served the same universal, missionary purpose. Genesis 18:19 makes this connection very explicitly. Having repeated the divine agenda in verse 18, 'all the nations of the earth shall be blessed in him', God goes on,

> For I have chosen him, that he may charge his children and his household after him to keep the way of the LORD by doing righteousness and justice; so that the LORD may bring about for Abraham what he has promised him.

---

4. Without deliberately setting out to achieve this, it turned out that when I wrote my book *The Mission of God's People: A Biblical Theology of the Church's Mission* (Grand Rapids: Zondervan, 2010), simply by following the flow of key biblical texts on that subject some 50% of the book focused on the life, behaviour and ethical distinctiveness of God's people, before the rest of the book began to focus on the witnessing, speaking and proclamational dimensions of our mission.
5. The following three paragraphs are drawn from Christopher J. H. Wright, *Deuteronomy*, New International Biblical Commentary on the Old Testament (Grand Rapids: Hendrikson; Carlisle: Paternoster, 1996), pp. 11–13.

Syntactically and theologically, the verse binds together election, ethics and mission, with ethics as the middle term. It will be the moral nature of the people of Abraham, who keep the way of Yahweh in righteousness and justice and bless the nations, that will enable God to fulfil the point of choosing Abraham. The text has a programmatic nature, all the more powerful by being in the form of direct divine speech. The very election of Israel in all its particularity not only has a universal 'missionary' goal but also leads to a clear and distinctive ethical agenda for God's people in the world as part of the condition of that goal being accomplished. Exodus 19:4–6 is a similarly definitive text that links Israel's obedience to the covenant law to their identity and role as God's priesthood in the midst of the nations. The idea of Israel as 'a light to the nations' is another way of expressing the idea (cf. Isa. 42:6; 49:6b), and it is clear that the imagery of 'light' is strongly moral (not just religious) in content (cf. Isa. 58:6–8; 60:3).

The most significant of these texts for the case being made here is Deuteronomy 4:6–8. Its point is that if Israel would be shaped and characterized by the laws and institutions of the Sinai covenant, then they would be a highly visible exemplar to the nations both as to the nature of the God they worshipped and as to the quality of social justice embodied in their community. This seems to be a deliberate linking of Israel's role among the nations to the socio-ethical structure of their corporate life: mission and ethics combined. The mission of Israel was to be a model to the nations. Mission was not a matter of going but of being; to be what they were, to live as the people of the God Yahweh in the sight of the nations.

Who are the people of God?

So who, then, are the 'people of God'? There is a continuity between Old and New Testaments that we must keep in mind, as does *The Cape Town Commitment*, which seeks to combine the narrative, ethical and missional dimensions of being God's people.

> The people of God are those from all ages and all nations whom God in Christ has loved, chosen, called, saved and sanctified as a people for his own possession, to share in the glory of Christ as citizens of the new creation. As those, then, whom God has loved from eternity to eternity and throughout all our turbulent and rebellious history, we are commanded to love one another. For 'since God so loved us, we also ought to love one another,' and thereby 'be imitators of God ... and live a life of love, just as Christ loved us and gave himself up for us.' Love for one another in the family of God is not merely a desirable option but an inescapable command. Such love is the first evidence of obedience to the gospel,

the necessary expression of our submission to Christ's Lordship, and a potent engine of world mission.[6]

God calls his people to share his mission. The Church from all nations stands in continuity through the Messiah Jesus with God's people in the Old Testament. With them we have been called through Abraham and commissioned to be a blessing and a light to the nations. With them, we are to be shaped and taught through the law and the prophets to be a community of holiness, compassion and justice in a world of sin and suffering. We have been redeemed through the cross and resurrection of Jesus Christ, and empowered by the Holy Spirit to bear witness to what God has done in Christ. The Church exists to worship and glorify God for all eternity and to participate in the transforming mission of God within history. Our mission is wholly derived from God's mission, addresses the whole of God's creation, and is grounded at its centre in the redeeming victory of the cross. This is the people to whom we belong, whose faith we confess and whose mission we share.[7]

The 'missio-ethical' dimensions of election, redemption and sanctification

All three Persons of the Trinity are active together in our salvation, of course, but a number of New Testament texts give particular emphasis to electing by the Father, redeeming by the Son and sanctifying by the Holy Spirit. Two texts in particular connect all three together:

- Ephesians 1:3–14, where we are chosen by the Father, to be adopted as sons through Christ, and are sealed with the Holy Spirit.
- 1 Peter 1:1–2, where we are chosen by the Father, sanctified by the Spirit, for obedience to Jesus Christ and sprinkling by his blood.

In both contexts, these dimensions of our salvation are linked both to our ethics and to our mission. We are to be holy and blameless and live to the praise of God's glory in the context of God's great mission to bring the whole cosmos

---

6. See 2 Thess. 2:13–14; 1 John 4:11; Eph. 5:2; 1 Thess. 1:3; 4:9–10; John 13:35, references that formed part of the original document. *The Cape Town Commitment*, © The Lausanne Movement, I.9, without original emphases. I take the liberty of quoting at length from this document in what follows, since I was very much involved with its production, as Chair of the Statement Working Group at the Third Lausanne Congress, Cape Town, October 2010. It was certainly seeking to be missional, ethical and trinitarian.
7. *Cape Town Commitment*, I.10.a.

into unity under Christ (Eph. 1:4, 10, 12). We are called to be holy as he is holy, and to live in such a way that the nations come to acknowledge God (1 Pet. 1:15; 2:12).

These New Testament teachings are comparable to the Old Testament where, for Israel, their *election* in Abraham meant walking in the way of the Lord in righteousness and justice (e.g. Gen. 18:19), their *redemption* from Egypt meant living with responsive compassion towards the poor and needy in their own society (e.g. Deut. 15:7–15), and their *consecration* (being 'made holy') through the covenant at Sinai was to be lived out in the sight of the nations (e.g. Deut. 4:6–8).

Thus, at a basic level, the trinitarian complementarity in salvation is integrated with the purpose of our calling (our mission) and the way we are to live worthy of it (ethics).

Missional ethics and the 'sending' of the Trinity

The sending God

The original use of the term *Missio Dei* signified the classical doctrine of the Father sending the Son and the Father and Son sending the Spirit. Within the developing missiology of the early World Council of Churches, however, it was expanded by Karl Hartenstein and George Vicedom to include the sending *by* God of the church in mission. This was crystallized in the statement of the International Missionary Council of 1952 in Willingen that, 'The missionary obligation of which we are a part has its source in the Triune God himself.'[8]

Sending is the act of all three Persons. There is a missional dynamic within God's own being which flows over with continuity into the way in which the church also sends and is sent by God.[9]

---

8. Quoted by L. Pachau, '*Missio Dei*', in John Corrie (ed.), *Dictionary of Mission Theology: Evangelical Foundations* (Nottingham: Inter-Varsity Press, 2007), p. 233. It is often said that this development was influenced by Karl Barth who, in the 1930s, insisted on deriving Christian mission from the nature of God, not merely from human activism in response to Christ's command. But a direct link between Barth and the later ecumenical use of *Missio Dei* is questioned by Flett, *Mission, Trinity, and Church*.
9. Much of the following three sections is drawn from my *Mission of God's People*, pp. 210–211.

The Father as sender: of the Son and the Spirit
Jesus did not just arrive. He was sent. It is one of the most noticeable dimensions of his self-consciousness – the driving awareness that he had been sent by his Father to do his will. It is certainly one of the dominant motifs in John's presentation of Jesus. Approximately forty times in John's Gospel we read about Jesus being sent – whether from the evangelist or from Jesus' own lips (e.g. John 3:17, 34; 4:34; 5 – 8 passim; 11:42; 17:18; cf. also 1 John. 4:9, 14). Indeed, coming to believe that Jesus was the one whom God had sent is part of John's express purpose for his readers, for in believing that, they will come to salvation and eternal life.

Since God sends his Spirit in the Old Testament, it is not surprising that God the Father is said to do the same in the New (John 14:16, 26; 15:26), or that Jesus will do it according to the Father's promise (Luke 24:49).

The Son as sender: of the Spirit and the apostles
Jesus sends the Spirit with specific missional tasks related to salvation and revelation (John 15:26; 16:7–15; 20:22–23).

Jesus also, of course, sends his disciples. He sent them twice on missions during his earthly lifetime, and then after his resurrection, in the various forms of the Great Commission. Noticeably, it is John who records that Jesus models his sending of the disciples on his own sending by the Father – something he has emphasized so repeatedly throughout the Gospel (John 20:21).

The Holy Spirit as sender: of Jesus and the apostles
The Holy Spirit is involved in the sending of Jesus. It is never quite expressed in the form that the Spirit 'sent' Jesus, but certainly Jesus is sent with, or in the power of, the Spirit. His mission is precisely one that is laid on him by the anointing of the Spirit (Luke 4:18–19), and Luke stresses at several points that all Jesus did was by the filling or leading of the Spirit. He further records Peter telling the same thing to Cornelius (Acts 10:38). Paul sees the instrumentality of the Spirit in the resurrection of Jesus (Rom. 1:4), while Hebrews connects 'the eternal Spirit' with Christ's self-offering in sacrificial death (Heb. 9:14).

The Holy Spirit, along with Jesus, is also the sender of the apostles. It was the Holy Spirit who expressly chose and named the first missionaries from Antioch and sent them on their way (Acts 13:1–4). And it was the Holy Spirit who guided their journeys, sometimes by prevention as much as direction (Acts 16:6–7).

So then, there is a marvellous interlocking network of sending in the New Testament presentation of God's involvement in the mission of Jesus and the church. God the Son is sent by God the Father and God the Spirit. God the Spirit is sent by God the Son and God the Father. The apostles are sent by God the Son and God the Spirit. Only God the Father is the unsent sender. He sends the Son and the Spirit, but he himself is never 'sent'.

The mission of God's people, then, is not some external structure built by the church itself – a programme or a strategy devised by an institution. Sending in mission is a participation in the life of God. The mission of God's people, in this dimension of sending and being sent, is to be caught up within the dynamic sending and being sent that God the Holy Trinity has done and continues to do for the salvation of the world and the revelation of his truth.

We might simply add to the point made in this section that all the *ethical* dimensions of our mission are likewise driven by the fact that our mission is a participation in the action of God and must therefore be done in a way that is consistent with God's will and character. Missional ethics thus draws its dynamic from the ethical character of the God whose intrinsic trinitarian sending lies behind any sending and being sent that we are involved in.

People God sent (Old and New Testaments): why and how

'Sending' is a prominent concept in both Testaments. God sends many people to accomplish many things. An analysis of these[10] shows up two particular reasons for God's sending that are relevant to mission. There are *those whom God sent to save* – or rather to be the agents of God's saving action – such as Joseph (Gen. 45:4–8), Moses (Exod. 3:10–15) and the judges – and even the eschatological 'saviour' whom God would send in response to the cries of the Egyptians, in a re-run of the exodus (Isa. 19:20–21). And there are *those whom God sent to speak* – or to be the agents of God's Word – such as Moses again, Isaiah (Isa. 6:1–7), or Jeremiah (Jer. 1:7–9). God's sending is thus a prominent dimension of both God's saving and revealing activity.

The missio-ethical dimensions of such divine sending are fairly prominent in the texts. Being sent by God requires submission to the sovereignty of God, and accepting even adverse circumstances as ordained by God. This applied not only at a personal level (as many a prophet found), but even to the whole people of Israel whom God 'sent' into exile and commanded to continue their mission of being a blessing to the nations even there among their enemies (Jer. 29:4–7). Being sent by God required faithfulness, trustworthiness and the courage to suffer for speaking the truth. And for those very reasons, being sent by God often began with an acute sense of personal inadequacy and sinfulness, and thus required the cardinal virtue of humility.

---

10. See Wright, *Mission of God's People*, pp. 202–210.

'As the Father has sent me, so I send you'

The clearest expression of the continuity between God's trinitarian sending and the missional sending of the church is in Christ's classic statement, both in his so-called high-priestly prayer and then to his disciples after the resurrection, where it is specifically connected to the gift of the Holy Spirit.

> As you [Father] have sent me into the world, so I have sent them into the world. (John 17:18)

> As [*kathōs*] the Father has sent me, so I send you [disciples]. (John 20:21)

Much has been written on what may be said to be implied by the word 'as', but it surely cannot just be a neutral or sequential term. It has ethical and missional tones.

For Jesus, being sent by the Father into the world involved incarnation – entering into the reality of a fallen human world with all its brokenness, suffering and frustration. Being sent by Christ into the world must mean something analogous for us. For Jesus, it meant the self-emptying humility that Paul ascribes to Jesus in Philippians 2:6–15 – *and applies* to Christian relationships, with missional results (Phil. 2:2–4, 14–16). And for Jesus, the prime purpose of being sent into the world was 'that the world might be saved through him' (John 3:16–17), so Christ's sending of his disciples has the same salvific intent (Luke 24:45–47).

So then, this great biblical flow of sending – Father, Son, church (in the power of the Spirit) – is missional and ethical, redemptive and relational, evangelistic and exemplary.

Missional ethics and the Persons of the Trinity

Missional ethics and God the Father

YHWH, the sovereign LORD God
In terms of a fully biblical theology we understand, of course, that the God who acts and speaks in the Old Testament is none other than the God revealed in trinitarian fullness in the New Testament. In that sense, all that YHWH is and does is the work of the whole Trinity, even though we certainly meet the Spirit of YHWH frequently, and possibly have glimpses of the pre-incarnate Son of God in some of the Old Testament's theophanies. Nevertheless, it seems to me that when we read of YHWH in the Old Testament it is

predominantly God the Father whom we are encountering. One indication of this is the nature of the pre-eminent and universal roles that YHWH performs as Creator, Ruler, Judge and Saviour. But another is the way the identity of YHWH as God of Israel and as personal Father must have 'coalesced' in the consciousness of Jesus.

Jesus was fully human. He grew up in a devout and believing Jewish home, and was without doubt a worshipping, praying child, young man and adult. The daily habit of prayer that we read of in the Gospels must have been ingrained in him from childhood. So when Jesus worshipped and prayed, in his home or in the synagogue in Nazareth, to whom was his worship directed? Who was the God whose name he read in all the Scriptures he recited and all the songs he sang? To whom did Jesus pray at the knees of Mary and then through all his life? The answer is, of course, to the LORD, Yahweh (though he would have said *Adonai*). Jesus would have recited the *shema'* daily with his fellow Jews, and he knew the 'LORD our God' of that text to be the God of his people, the God of his human parents and the God whom, as a man, he worshipped. So Jesus' whole perception of God was entirely shaped by the Scriptures we call the Old Testament. When Jesus thought of God, spoke of God, reflected on the words and will of God, set out to obey God – it was *this* God, Yahweh God, who was in his mind. 'God' for Jesus was the named, biographied, character-rich, self-revealed God Yahweh, the Holy One of Israel. When Jesus and his disciples talked together of God, this is the name they would have used (or would have known but piously avoided pronouncing).

But of course, Jesus also knew this God of his Scriptures in the depth of his self-consciousness as *Abba*, as his own intimate personal Father. Luke tells us that this awareness was developing even in his childhood, and it was sealed at his baptism, when he heard the voice of his Father, accompanied by the Holy Spirit, confirming his identity as God's beloved Son. So in the consciousness of Jesus the *scriptural* identity of God as Yahweh and his *personal* intimacy with God as his Father must have blended together. The God he knew from his Bible as Yahweh was the God he knew in prayer as his Father. When Jesus took the psalms on his lips on the cross, the God he was calling out to in the agony of abandonment was the God addressed in Psalm 22:1 as Elohim, but throughout the psalm as Yahweh. The psalmist was calling out to Yahweh. Jesus uses the psalmist's words to call out to his Father.

Now since all our understanding of God as Father must start out from knowing Jesus, it makes sense for us also to think of Yahweh, the God of Old Testament Israel and the God of the one true faithful Israelite Jesus, as

God the Father, for that is who Yahweh primarily was in the consciousness of Jesus himself.[11]

YHWH, Father of Israel

God called Israel into existence as his people for the sake of his mission to bring blessing to all nations. His relationship with them is portrayed as parental from very early on. 'Israel is my firstborn son,' he declared to Pharaoh (Exod. 4:22), and the language of both fatherhood and motherhood is poetically deployed in Deuteronomy 32:6, 18. This generated a conception of the relationship between God and Israel which, like the covenantal metaphor, spoke of protective care with authority and discipline on God's side, and love, respect and obedience on Israel's. In other words, God's mission for Israel included an ethical dimension that could be portrayed in father–son ways.

With its efforts to present a whole-Bible approach to missional theology, *The Cape Town Commitment* includes this aspect of the fatherhood of God in paragraphs that are worth quoting in this and following sections.

> We love God as the Father of his people. Old Testament Israel knew God as Father, as the one who brought them into existence, carried them and disciplined them, called for their obedience, longed for their love, and exercised compassionate forgiveness and patient enduring love.[12] All these remain true for us as God's people in Christ in our relationship with our Father God.[13]

The Father who gave the Son

> We love God as the Father, who so loved the world that he gave his only Son for our salvation. How great the Father's love for us that we should be called the children of God. How immeasurable the love of the Father who did not spare his only Son, but gave him up for us all. This love of the Father in giving the Son was mirrored by the self-giving love of the Son. There was complete harmony of will in the work of atonement that the Father and the Son accomplished at the cross, through the eternal Spirit. The Father loved the world and gave his Son; 'the Son of God loved me and gave himself for me.' This unity of Father and Son, affirmed by Jesus himself, is

---

11. For the previous three paragraphs see Christopher J. H. Wright, *Knowing God the Father through the Old Testament* (Oxford: Monarch, 2007), pp. 18–20.
12. Deut. 32:6, 18; 1:31; 8:5; Isa. 1:2; Mal. 1:6; Jer. 3:4, 19; 31:9; Hos. 11:2; Ps. 103:13; Isa. 63:16; 64:8–9. References part of the original text.
13. *Cape Town Commitment*, Part I.3.a.

echoed in Paul's most repeated greeting of 'grace and peace from God our Father and the Lord Jesus Christ, who gave himself for our sins . . . according to the will of our God and Father, to whom be glory for ever and ever. Amen.'[14]

This ultimate self-giving act of Father and Son together is presented in the New Testament both as the model for our mission (John 20:21) and as the model and motivation for our ethics (1 John 4:9–11).

The Father whom we observe, trust, and imitate – in mission and ethics

We love God as the Father whose character we reflect and whose care we trust. In the Sermon on the Mount Jesus repeatedly points to our heavenly Father as the model or focus for our action. We are to be peacemakers, as sons of God. We are to do good deeds, so that our Father receives the praise. We are to love our enemies in reflection of God's Fatherly love. We are to practise our giving, praying and fasting for our Father's eyes only. We are to forgive others as our Father forgives us. We are to have no anxiety but trust in our Father's provision. With such behaviour flowing from Christian character, we do the will of our Father in heaven, within the kingdom of God.[15]

This is the kind of living that draws people to God – in other words, it is ethical and missional together. So then, our understanding of God as Father is not just a doctrine in our systematics, but a key to how we should live in relation to God, to one another, and to the world.

Missional ethics and God the Son

Jesus and the identity of God

The uniqueness and universality of Jesus Christ is central to all Christian mission that is rooted in the Bible. It is because of who Jesus is that we engage in mission – or rather, participate in the mission of God that centres on Christ. And it is because of who Jesus is that we are called to live in ways that reflect his character, teaching and example. Once again, *The Cape Town Commitment* seeks to capture this combination of the biblical identity and significance of

---

14. *Cape Town Commitment*, Part I.3.b. See also the references that formed part of the original text: John 3:16; 1 John 3:1; Rom. 8:32; Heb. 9:14; Gal. 1:4–5; 2:20.
15. *Cape Town Commitment*, Part I.3.c. See also the references that formed part of the original text: Matt. 5:9, 16, 43–48; 6:4, 6, 14–15, 18, 25–32; 7:21–23.

Jesus with the missio-ethical implications of such claims, set within their proper trinitarian framework.

> God commanded Israel to love the LORD God with exclusive loyalty. Likewise for us, loving the Lord Jesus Christ means that we steadfastly affirm that he alone is Saviour, Lord and God. The Bible teaches that Jesus performs the same sovereign actions as God alone. Christ is Creator of the universe, Ruler of history, Judge of all nations and Saviour of all who turn to God.[16] He shares the identity of God in the divine equality and unity of Father, Son and Holy Spirit. Just as God called Israel to love him in covenantal faith, obedience and servant-witness, we affirm our love for Jesus Christ by trusting in him, obeying him, and making him known.[17]

The cross of Christ and the mission of God[18]
'It is finished!' cried Jesus at the climax of his suffering on the cross, meaning, 'It is accomplished.' What had been accomplished? Nothing less than the fullness of the mission of God. And out of the multidimensional fullness flows not only our salvation, but the length and breadth of our mission and ethics as well.

It was the purpose or mission of God:

- *to deal with the guilt of human sin*, which had to be punished for God's own justice to be vindicated. And at the cross God accomplished this. God took that guilt and punishment upon himself in self-substitution through the person of his own Son. For 'the LORD has laid on him the iniquity of us all' (Isa. 53:6), and '[Christ] himself bore our sins in his body on the cross' (1 Pet. 2:24).
- *to defeat the powers of evil*, and all the forces (angelic, spiritual, 'seen or unseen') that oppress, crush, invade, spoil and destroy human life, whether directly or by human agency. And at the cross God accomplished this: 'He disarmed the rulers and authorities . . . triumphing over them in it' (Col. 2:15).

---

16. See also the references that formed part of the original text: John 1:3; 1 Cor. 8:4–6; Heb. 1:2; Col. 1:15–17; Ps. 110:1; Mark 14:61–64; Eph. 1:20–23; Rev. 1:5; 3:14; 5:9–10; Rom. 2:16; 2 Thess. 1:5–10; 2 Cor. 5:10; Rom. 14:9–12; Matt. 1:21; Luke 2:30; Acts 4:12; 15:11; Rom. 10:9; Titus 2:13; Heb. 2:10; 5:9; 7:25; Rev. 7:10.
17. *Cape Town Commitment*, Part I.4.
18. Most of the paragraphs in this section are drawn from Christopher J. H. Wright, *The Mission of God, Unlocking the Bible's Grand Narrative* (Downers Grove: InterVarsity Press; Nottingham: Inter-Varsity Press, 2006), pp. 312–316.

- *to destroy death*, the great invader and enemy of human life in God's world. And at the cross God did so, when through Christ's death he destroyed 'the one who has the power of death, that is, the devil' (Heb. 2:14).
- *to remove the barrier of enmity and alienation between Jew and Gentile*, and by implication ultimately all forms of enmity and alienation. And at the cross God did so, 'For he is our peace; in his flesh he has made both groups into one and has broken down the dividing wall . . . so that he might create in himself one new humanity in place of the two, thus making peace, and might reconcile both groups to God in one body through the cross, thus putting to death that hostility through it' (Eph. 2:14–16).
- *to heal and reconcile his whole creation*, the cosmic mission of God. And at the cross God made this ultimately possible, for it is God's final will 'through [Christ] . . . to reconcile to himself all things, whether on earth or in heaven, by making peace through the blood of his cross' (Col. 1:20) – the 'all things' here must clearly mean the whole created cosmos, since that is what Paul says has been created by Christ and for Christ (vv. 15–16) and has now been reconciled by Christ (v. 20).

So then, all these huge dimensions of God's redemptive mission are set before us in the Bible. God's mission was that:

- sin should be punished and sinners forgiven;
- evil should be defeated and humanity liberated;
- death should be destroyed and life and immortality brought to light;
- enemies should be reconciled, to one another and to God;
- creation itself should be restored and reconciled to its Creator.

All of these together constitute the mission of God. *And all of these led to the cross of Christ.* The cross was the unavoidable cost of God's total mission – as Jesus himself accepted, in his agony in Gethsemane: 'not my will, but yours, be done.'

It is equally true, and biblical, to say that *the cross is the unavoidable centre of our mission*. All Christian mission flows from the cross – as its source, its power and as that which defines its scope.

It is vital that we see the cross as central to every aspect of holistic, biblical mission – that is, of all we do in the name of the crucified and risen Jesus. It is a mistake, in my view, to think that, while our evangelism must be centred on the cross (as of course it has to be), our social engagement and other forms of practical mission work have some other theological foundation or justification. Why is the cross just as important across the whole field of mission? Because in all forms of Christian mission in the name of Christ we are confronting the powers of evil and the kingdom of Satan – with all their dismal effects on human life and the wider creation. If we are to proclaim and demonstrate the reality of the reign of God in Christ – that is, if we are to proclaim that Jesus is King, in a world which likes still to chant 'we have no king but Caesar' and his many successors, including Mammon – then we will be in direct conflict with the usurped reign of the evil one, in all its legion manifestations. This – the battle against the powers of evil – is the unanimous testimony of those who struggle for justice, for the needs of the poor and oppressed, the sick and the ignorant, and even those who seek to care for and protect God's creation against exploiters and polluters, just as much as it is the experience of those (frequently the same people) who struggle evangelistically to bring people to faith in Christ as Saviour and Lord and plant churches. In all such work we confront the reality of sin and Satan. In all such work we are challenging the darkness of the world with the light and good news of Jesus Christ and the reign of God through him.

By what authority can we do so? With what power are we competent to engage the powers of evil? On what basis dare we challenge the chains of Satan, in word and deed, in people's spiritual, moral, physical and social lives? Only the cross. Only in the cross is there forgiveness, justification and cleansing for guilty sinners. Only in the cross stands the defeat of evil powers. Only in the cross is there release from the fear of death and its ultimate destruction altogether. Only in the cross are even the most intractable of enemies reconciled. Only in the cross will we finally witness the healing of all creation.

The fact is that sin and evil constitute bad news in every area of life on this planet. The redemptive work of God through the cross of Christ is good news for every area of life on earth that has been touched by sin – which means every area of life. Bluntly, we need a holistic gospel because the world is in a holistic mess. And by God's incredible grace we have a gospel big enough to redeem all that sin and evil have touched. Every dimension of that good news is good news utterly and only because of the blood of Christ on the cross.

Ultimately all that *will* be there in the new, redeemed creation will be there because of the cross. And conversely, all that will *not* be there (suffering, tears, sin, Satan, sickness, oppression, corruption, decay and death) will not be there because they will have been defeated and destroyed by the cross. That is the length, breadth, height and depth of God's idea of redemption. It is exceedingly good news. It is the fount of all our mission.

So it is my passionate conviction that holistic mission must have a holistic theology of the cross. That includes the conviction that the cross must be as central to our social engagement as it is to our evangelism. There is no other power, no other resource, no other name, through which we can offer the whole gospel to the whole person and the whole world, than Jesus Christ crucified and risen.

The missio-ethical implications of 'the Great Commission'
The so-called 'Great Commission' in Matthew 28:18–30 is viewed by many as the key biblical text that mandates the global mission of the church. Unfortunately, it has been interpreted in some quarters as exclusively an evangelistic mandate, as if all that Jesus had said was, 'Go and preach the gospel.' There is no doubt whatsoever that preaching the gospel is an utterly essential task in biblical mission, but it is clearly not all that the Great Commission contains.

The Great Commission actually includes all of the 'five marks of mission' that have been identified in some traditions:[19] evangelism, teaching, works of compassion, seeking justice, and care for creation.

The care for creation is there, not only because it was in fact the very first mandate given to humanity at our creation, but because Jesus affirms his sovereignty over heaven *and earth*. Jesus' Lordship over the earth reminds us that the earth belongs to God and creation care is simple obedience to the first commandment, to love the Lord our God, by caring for his property.

> The earth is created, sustained and redeemed by Christ.[20] We cannot claim to love God while abusing what belongs to Christ by right of creation, redemption and inheritance. We care for the earth and responsibly use its abundant resources, not according to the rationale of the secular world, but for the Lord's sake. If Jesus is Lord of all the earth, we cannot separate our relationship to Christ from how we act in relation to the earth. For to proclaim the gospel that says 'Jesus is Lord' is to proclaim the gospel that includes the earth, since Christ's Lordship is over all creation. Creation care is thus a gospel issue within the Lordship of Christ.[21]

Evangelism and teaching are there as the essential elements in obeying the command to 'make disciples of all nations'. Jesus immediately adds two methodological lines to that instruction: 'baptizing them in the name of the

---

19. The term seems to have been first used within the Anglican Communion in its report 'Bonds of Affection' (1984) and again in 'Mission in a Broken World' (1990).
20. See references in the original text: Col. 1:15–20; Heb. 1:2–3.
21. *Cape Town Commitment*, Part 1.7.a.

Father and of the Son and of the Holy Spirit, and teaching them . . . ' Baptizing presupposes the evangelistic preaching of the gospel, and teaching is what must necessarily follow in order for converts to become disciples.

Compassion and justice are there in the necessary implications of what Jesus told his apostles to teach those who were being discipled: 'teaching them to obey *everything that I have commanded you*.' Even if we look no further than what Jesus had taught his disciples in Matthew's Gospel so far, it includes very explicit instructions about showing compassion and mercy to the needy, and seeking the justice that is at the heart of God's kingdom (as the Old Testament had made abundantly clear in multiple texts). Jesus had spent three years teaching his disciples what it meant to *be* disciples. Now he tells them to go and replicate themselves by leading people in all nations to that same measure of humble submission to Jesus as Lord which Paul calls simply 'the obedience of faith among all the Gentiles' (Rom. 1:5; 16:26).

The Great Commission is thus integrally and comprehensively trinitarian, missional and ethical. Perhaps the whole of this chapter could have been better spent simply expounding it! It is *missional* in its echo of the Abrahamic promise now transposed into a command, so that all nations may indeed come into the blessing of becoming disciples of the Lord of heaven and earth. It is *trinitarian*, for that task involves bringing people into knowledge of, and into baptized relationship with, the one true living God in three Persons. And it is *ethical*, for it explicitly includes obedience to the commands of Jesus which surely lies at the heart of all Christian ethics and in this text lies also at the heart of Christian mission.

Missional ethics and God the Holy Spirit

The role of the Holy Spirit in mission may seem to many, most obviously, to begin at Pentecost and reverberate through the book of Acts. But that would be to ignore the strength of the Old Testament's witness to the work of God's Spirit in relation to God's mission, beginning in the second verse of the whole Bible and continuing to almost its last (Rev. 22:17). Obviously, a trinitarian understanding of missional ethics cannot be complete without the work of the Holy Spirit. This is a major issue that needs far more emphasis than can be given here. However, the *Cape Town Commitment* at least tries to ensure that such a trinitarian emphasis is preserved and kept in strong relationship to mission and ethics.

> We love the Holy Spirit within the unity of the Trinity, along with God the Father and God the Son. He is the missionary Spirit sent by the missionary Father and the missionary Son, breathing life and power into God's missionary Church. We love and

pray for the presence of the Holy Spirit because without the witness of the Spirit to Christ, our own witness is futile. Without the convicting work of the Spirit, our preaching is in vain. Without the gifts, guidance and power of the Spirit, our mission is mere human effort. And without the fruit of the Spirit, our unattractive lives cannot reflect the beauty of the gospel.[22]

The Spirit of God in the Old Testament
I have sought to expound the variety of ways in which God's Spirit is portrayed in the Old Testament in my book *Knowing the Holy Spirit through the Old Testament*.[23] The chapter headings speak of the creating Spirit, the empowering Spirit, the prophetic Spirit, the anointing Spirit and the coming (eschatological) Spirit. Briefly summarized:

> In the Old Testament we see the Spirit of God active in creation, in works of liberation and justice, and in filling and empowering people for every kind of service. Spirit-filled prophets looked forward to the coming King and Servant, whose Person and work would be endowed with God's Spirit. Prophets also looked to the coming age that would be marked by the outpouring of God's Spirit, bringing new life, fresh obedience, and prophetic gifting to all the people of God, young and old, men and women.[24]

Even from such a short and inadequate survey one can see the missional and ethical dimensions of the Spirit's work.

The Spirit in the mission of Jesus and of the church
We have already noted the connection and continuity between the inner sending at work within the Trinity and the sending of the church into the world for God's continuing mission. Another very strong dimension of that continuity is the way the Spirit of God is active within the ministry of Jesus, and then is given by Jesus to empower the church for ministry in his name. Luke is particularly emphatic on the role of the Spirit in the life of Jesus, and records

---

22. *Cape Town Commitment*, Part 1.5.
23. Christopher J. H. Wright, *Knowing the Holy Spirit through the Old Testament* (Oxford: Monarch; Downers Grove: InterVarsity Press, 2006).
24. *Cape Town Commitment*, Part I.5.a. See also the references in the original text: Gen. 1:1–2; Ps. 104:27–30; Job 33:4; Exod. 35:30 – 36:1; Judg. 3:10; 6:34; 13:25; Num. 11:16–17, 29; Isa. 63:11–14; 2 Pet. 1:20–21; Mic. 3:8; Neh. 9:20, 30; Zech. 7:7–12; Isa. 11:1–5; 42:1–7; 61:1–3; 32:15–18; Ezek. 36:25–27; 37:1–14; Joel 2:28–32.

particularly the anointing of the Spirit that Jesus himself claimed as the fulfilment of one of the great eschatological prophecies (Luke 4:14–21; cf. Isa. 61:1–2). Mark even speaks of the Spirit *driving* Jesus out into the desert, in his temptation narrative (Mark 1:12). Jesus then emphasizes the role that the Spirit will play in the ongoing life and mission of the disciples, after Jesus had 'left' them. In the classic discourses of John 14 – 16, the Spirit will bear witness to Jesus, will teach the disciples all that Jesus had not been able to in his earthly lifetime, will convict the world, and will bring comfort and strength to the disciples in times of struggle and persecution.

> At Pentecost God poured out his Holy Spirit as promised by the prophets and by Jesus. The sanctifying Spirit produces his fruit in the lives of believers, and the first fruit is always love. The Spirit fills the Church with his gifts, which we 'eagerly desire' as the indispensable equipment for Christian service. The Spirit gives us power for mission and for the great variety of works of service. The Spirit enables us to proclaim and demonstrate the gospel, to discern the truth, to pray effectively and to prevail over the forces of darkness. The Spirit inspires and accompanies our worship. The Spirit strengthens and comforts disciples who are persecuted or on trial for their witness to Christ.[25]

> Our engagement in mission, then, is pointless and fruitless without the presence, guidance and power of the Holy Spirit. This is true of mission in all its dimensions: evangelism, bearing witness to the truth, discipling, peace-making, social engagement, ethical transformation, caring for creation, overcoming evil powers, casting out demonic spirits, healing the sick, suffering and enduring under persecution. All we do in the name of Christ must be led and empowered by the Holy Spirit. The New Testament makes this clear in the life of the early Church and the teaching of the apostles. It is being demonstrated today in the fruitfulness and growth of Churches where Jesus' followers act confidently in the power of the Holy Spirit, with dependence and expectation.[26]

---

25. See references in original text: Acts 2; Gal. 5:22–23; 1 Pet. 1:2; Eph. 4:3–6, 11–12; Rom. 12:3–8; 1 Cor. 12:4–11; 14:1; John 20:21–22; 14:16–17, 25–26; 16:12–15; Rom. 8:26–27; Eph. 6:10–18; John 4:23–24; 1 Cor. 12:3; 14:13–17; Matt. 10:17–20; Luke 21:15.
26. *Cape Town Commitment*, Part 1.5.b and c.

Missional ethics and the unity of the Trinity

The missio-ethical implications of the 'social Trinity'
Systematic theologians would, I believe, use the phrase 'economic Trinity' for what we have considered so far – the role of each Person of the Trinity within the economy of God's saving work and the mission that flows from it. Increasing interest, however, is directed to the importance of the 'social Trinity', in the recovery (within Western scholarship) of the theology of the Cappadocian Fathers and their understanding of the perichoretic, inter-relational nature of the divine Being-in-three-Persons. Such interest is seen in the work of, for example, Miroslav Volf, Stanley Grenz and Colin Gunton.[27] Such trinitarian theology, however, is not only profoundly helpful in our understanding of the being of God, but also has rich implications for the nature of humanity, made in the image of God, and even more so for the nature and mission of the church, as the community created to represent and reflect God in the world.

If the people of God have been created to embody within human community that quality of unity and love that exists from all eternity within the Trinity, and to give expression to that unity and love in our life together in the world, then our very existence is *missional* (because such reality confronts the broken and rebellious world, challenges its sin and calls it back to God) and *ethical* (because such identity and mission call for a corresponding *way of life* that can be seen to be consistent with the unity and love of God).

The missio-ethical thrust of Jesus' prayer in John 17:20–26
This throws into stark prominence the missional urgency of the final prayer and command of Jesus in John's Gospel, and we can do no better than conclude this biblical survey with a brief exposition of John 17:20–26. The request that Jesus made of his Father is doubly emphatic. There are three elements in verses 21–23, each one repeated twice:

---

27. See, as a tiny selection, Colin E. Gunton, *The One, the Three and the Many: God, Creation and the Cultures of Modernity*, The Bampton Lectures 1992 (Cambridge: Cambridge University Press, 1993); Colin E. Gunton, *A Brief Theology of Revelation: The 1993 Warfield Lectures* (Edinburgh: T. & T. Clark, 1995); Stanley J. Grenz, *Created for Community: Connecting Christian Belief with Christian Living* (Grand Rapids: Baker, 1996); Miroslav Volf, *After Our Likeness: The Church as the Image of the Trinity* (Grand Rapids: Eerdmans, 1998). See, however, Flett, '*Missio Dei*', for critique of an exaggerated dichotomy between the 'economic' and 'social' Trinity, and its misuse in some missiological formulations of the *Missio Dei*.

- the Son's prayer – 'that they may be one';
- the trinitarian model – 'as you and I are one';
- the missional outcome – 'that the world may believe'.

Here is missional ethics (the unity of the church for the sake of the world) grounded in trinitarian reality. Three aspects of this prayer for unity and the preceding command to love one another can be observed here.

Unity that reflects God's being
What would John have understood from the words 'as we are one'? What kind of unity was that in the Gospel record so far?

- The Father and Son share one life (John 5:26; 6:57), and yet they are not identical as Persons. In the same way believers share in the family life of God as those born again by God's Spirit, yet with all the variety of background, ethnicity and gifting.
- The Father and Son share one purpose (John 4:34). There is a strong emphasis in John's Gospel on the unity of will between Father and Son, right up to and including the cross itself. Similarly, believers have a common mission and goal, while having multiple tasks and ministries in pursuit of it.
- The Father and Son share one agenda (John 5:19). What Jesus did, the Father did in and through him, such that 'he who has seen me has seen the Father'. Similarly, Christian unity does not mean that we all do the same thing, but that all the things we do as believers have the coherence of a single agenda – to serve God, glorify Christ and bring blessing to the world.

That is the quality of Christian love and unity Christ prays for. Being one – with all its demanding practical implications – reflects the trinitarian Being of God.

Unity that reveals God's glory (v. 22)
Jesus speaks about revealing his glory to and through his disciples. But how can anybody see the glory of God? The Old Testament inculcates the strong negative affirmation that God cannot be seen. The invisibility of YHWH seems to have been something of an embarrassment (e.g. Ps. 115:2). So how has God solved the problem of his own invisibility? John answers that question by twice using the same phrase, 'No-one has ever seen God', but following it with the only two means by which the invisible God has made himself visible.

First, he has made himself visible through the incarnation of Jesus (John 1:18). That is why Jesus can make the climactic statement that to have seen him was to have seen the Father. But that was all very well for that generation of disciples who actually did see the incarnate Jesus. How can the rest of the world and subsequent generations 'see' God?

Second, he has made himself visible through the love of Christians for one another (1 John 4:12). The impact of this verse is that genuine Christian love is revelatory. God's glory is seen in the unity of his people in the midst of a divided world, in the love of his people in the midst of a hate-filled world.

Unity that serves God's mission (vv. 21–23)
This takes us right back to the origins of God's people. For what purpose did God call into existence this people, this community of believers, for whom Jesus now prays that they should be 'one' in love for one another? Since God's promise to Abraham we have known that the mission of God's people is that the nations of the world should be blessed. And we now know through John that such blessing comes through knowing Jesus and believing in him. God's mission is to be known by all nations and indeed throughout all creation. This vision has deep Old Testament roots and John may well be drawing on the imagery of Ezekiel 37:15–28, where the prophesied unification of God's people is for the very purpose that the nations will come to know who the living God is.

Three times in John's Gospel (13:34; 15:13, 17) and five times in 1 John (3:11, 23; 4:7, 11, 12), we hear this urgent missional and ethical command of Christ that those who claim to be his disciples should love one another. Immense realities are at stake in whether we obey him or not.

Conclusion

We began by pointing out that biblical ethics are intrinsically missional (since the life of God's people is governed by the purpose of their existence), and that biblical mission is intrinsically ethical (since we cannot fulfil the purpose of our calling without living as God requires). What I trust this biblical journey has made clear is that biblical mission and biblical ethics are simultaneously also trinitarian, for they originate in and are shaped by the living God who, in the totality and unity of his being and doing, is God the Father, Son and Holy Spirit.

© Christopher J. H. Wright, 2012

3. CREATION

MISSION AS GARDENING

Brian Brock

'*Go* ye into all the world.' Going is inescapably part of the church's mission. But after Christians have 'gone', they will always discover that, once again, they 'are' somewhere. Christians come into existence in a place, and whether they move from that place or stay in it they do not escape the claim and task of being part of the church's mission. This means it is crucial to be as clear as we can about how we understand the 'hereness' of mission. I want to suggest that the doctrine of creation and the text of the primeval history of Genesis have something to tell us in this regard. They teach us that the Christian missionary who 'goes' and the Christian who 'stays' are *both* being drawn by the gospel to care for specific people whom they discover God has concretely loved long before they arrived on the scene.

Beginning with a theological question about how the mission to which every Christian is committed might be understood in the light of the doctrine of creation, I will end by asking what it means that mission flows from 'soft hearts'. My overall aim is to display how ethical perception is inextricably tied up with the softness or hardness of the heart. How can we, like the Good Samaritan, come to embrace those we are taught to overlook, look down upon and protect ourselves from? A crucial task of Christian ethics and mission today is to give a thoroughly theological account of how the trinitarian God frees us from the self-delusions that blind us to the neighbour as we wrap ourselves in the flags of nation, church, race, class, gender and, yes, the mantle of orthodox theology.

I will further suggest that the role of the doctrine of creation in defining mission is not linked to the so-called culture-making mandate to 'subdue' and 'have dominion', but to the more primal scriptural claim that humans were made to care for and tend a garden. My core contention is that human care cannot *give* life, and so Christian mission can only follow and serve *God's* giving of life. Doing so appropriately begins as humans subdue their self-chosen designs for dominion. In sum, the doctrine of creation teaches Christians to be more attentive to the material conditions of creation as it exists, and as God is already involved with it, rather than stemming from any type of world-remaking project. The church more accurately images God the more it is stripped of its pretensions to control and mastery, not as it imposes its designs on creation. Any violent subduing associated with mission is only properly understood as directed towards that in us which wishes to make our own human definitions of missional success the focus of missional activity rather than God's healing love.

On beginning in a garden

The relationship of the heart, perception and the remaking of human action I have just indicated is implied by a prominent aspect of the creation account: the planting of humans in a *garden*. 'The LORD God planted a garden in Eden, in the east; and there he put the man whom he had formed' (Gen. 2:8). Why a garden rather than a farm, the seaside, a mountaintop or wilderness? Notice that God *planted* and put Adam *in* the garden. That the first humans are so planted tells us at least that humans were meant to be enclosed, to have horizons, that is, to belong to a fixed and definite place rather than to be exposed and vulnerable in an amorphous and open-ended cosmos.[1] Nor did the first humans

---

1. Robert Harrison comments, 'A garden is literally defined by its boundaries ... they keep the garden intrinsically related to the world that they keep at a certain remove ... the stillness is relative, dynamic, and unabstracted from the environment. Indeed, one could say that the stillness *draws its energy* from the whirl around its edges. For stillness is a form of energy.' *Gardens: An Essay on the Human Condition* (Chicago: University of Chicago Press, 2008), pp. 57–58. This porous boundedness is constitutive of the relation of Israel's temple to the rest of creation. '[O]ne may be able to perceive an increasing gradation of holiness from outside the garden proceeding inward: The region outside the garden is related to God and is "very good" (Gen. 1:31) in that it is God's creation (= the outer court); the garden itself

bear the burden of being great civilizers, perceiving themselves as carrying the 'first man's burden' to civilize the untamed wild. The first couple was placed neither in an untended and unbounded wilderness, nor on a bounded but untended seaside. They were placed in a garden, a tended place with boundaries. But far from being constricted by these limits, this was to be the blessed scene of work that was not toil and did not need to make the world good.

What matters to the authors of Genesis is that God has created a space of peace in creation in which to appear and speak with creatures. In this defined place humans are faced for the first and definitive time with the command of God. God's appearing in this way is evidence of his desire to be present in and rule a kingdom of peace. Four is an ancient signal for universality, making the enigmatic mention of the 'four rivers' of Genesis 2:10–14 a literary clue that this bounded place in principle, if not in fact, was intended to embrace the whole world. These rivers flow out to the corners of the earth, indicating the divine desire to extend this rule of grace and peace outward into all of creation.[2]

This theological reading of the four rivers is an attempt to discern how the biblical writers already wove the mission of Israel (and so the church) into the primeval history. If it is fair to find it there, Christian mission cannot be simply a response to the post-lapsarian need for redemption, because its content would not always have included a call for repentance. Mission in an unfallen world was tied up with divine presence and the flourishing of creation, and so, the writers of the Old Testament teach us, with the temple. The dominant historical-critical consensus was once that what is being pictured here is a royal garden, a place cared for and tended by the Lord, depicted as an Ancient Near Eastern king, but this consensus has recently been immensely broadened in a manner that invites theological comparisons with all sorts of modern gardening.[3]

---

is a sacred space separate from the outer world (= the holy place), where God's priestly servant worships God by obeying him, by cultivating and guarding; Eden is where God dwells (= the holy of holies) as the source of both physical and spiritual life (symbolized by the waters).' G. K. Beale, *The Temple and the Church's Mission: A Biblical Theology of the Dwelling Place of God* (Nottingham: Inter-Varsity Press, 2004), p. 75.

2. Henri Blocher, *In the Beginning: The Opening Chapters of Genesis* (Nottingham: Inter-Varsity Press, 1984), p. 114; Karl Barth, *Church Dogmatics* III/1 (Edinburgh: T. & T. Clark, 1958), p. 255.

3. Terje Stordalen, *Echoes of Eden: Genesis 2 – 3 and Symbolism of the Eden Garden in Biblical Hebrew Literature* (Leuven: Peters, 2000).

The effect of these new historical and canon-critical readings is to re-emphasize the canonical point that Adam and Eve are put[4] in this garden solely to direct their care to what God has already cared for, the soil and so the garden and its inhabitants.[5] This is their proper lot as creatures, to be wholly absorbed in care for (to literally 'serve'[6]) this cared-for place, and as they reproduce, to follow its life-giving streams and eventually extend its boundaries – the original benign 'mission creep'. While this organic form of mission was interrupted by the fall and expulsion from the garden, the life-giving rivers continue to flow from it.[7] Biblical scholars have helpfully noted that the temple was constructed in a manner that clearly signalled the resumption of this mission of care, and following the divine river of solicitude towards creation, Jesus embraces this mission by calling himself the new temple.[8]

---

4. '[T]he word used for God "putting" Adam "into the garden" in Gen. 2:15 is not the usual Hebrew word for "put" (*śûm*) but is the word typically translated "to rest" (*nûaḥ*) ... Adam would achieve a consummate "rest" after he had faithfully performed his task of "taking care of and guarding" the garden. This is in line with the "rest" that God promises later to Israel if they live faithfully in the Promised Land.' Beale, *The Temple and the Church's Mission*, pp. 69–70.

5. 'Not to be identified with the more general term "earth" (*'ereṣ*) [in v. 5] the *'ădāmâ* denotes the specifically arable land. The ground is what the man is to cultivate, literally "work" or "serve" (*'bd*, Gen. 2:5; 3:23).' William P. Brown, *The Ethos of the Cosmos: The Genesis of Moral Imagination in the Bible* (Grand Rapids: Eerdmans, 1999), p. 137.

6. 'In Hebrew "to till" is literally "to serve". Even in his relationship with the soil, mankind must maintain his humility. The use of the verb paves the way for the condemnation of the "destroyers of the earth" (Rev. 11:18), those guilty of ecological depredation. Not only will man rule over nature by obeying its laws (F. Bacon), but he will do so for the good of creation itself, so that it may fulfil its "vocation" to glorify the Creator. The cultivated garden will be like a song of praise to the God of order and of life, the God of peace.' Blocher, *In the Beginning*, p. 120.

7. 'While God might have driven Adam and Eve out of the Garden of Paradise, God still ensured that the living waters issuing from the garden continue to irrigate the whole earth and cleanse its polluted streams and lakes.' Vigen Guroian, *Inheriting Paradise: Meditations on Gardening* (Grand Rapids: Eerdmans, 1999), p. 9.

8. See Crispin Fletcher-Louis, 'God's Image, His Cosmic Temple and the High Priest: Towards an Historical and Theological Account of the Incarnation', in T. D. Alexander and S. Gathercole (eds.), *Heaven on Earth: The Temple in Biblical Theology* (Carlisle: Paternoster, 2004); Beale, *The Temple and the Church's Mission*.

The biblical links on which this traditional reading of creation, temple and divine sustenance are based are nicely encapsulated in Jean Vanier's theological account of mission:

> The prophet Ezekiel had a vision (Ezek. 47:1–12) of waters flowing from the Temple. It began as a small stream, but then it grew into a deep river impossible to cross. On each bank of the river there was an immense number of trees constantly bearing fruit; their leaves were medicinal and brought healing. The waters too were healing waters; wherever they flowed, life was abundant and fish were plentiful. John the Evangelist had a similar vision (Rev. 22:1) of crystal clear water, the river of life, flowing from the throne of God and of the Lamb, giving life, bearing fruit.[9]

The church in this vision is not the initial source of mission, 'it is a sign and a revelation and the fruit of the source of life called to flow over humanity, cleansing, healing, giving life and freedom, bearing much fruit'.[10] God's fidelity and tenderness, his *ḥesed* love, gives all creation and humans form and stability, making them flourish. This love does not manipulate, does not overwhelm, but gives itself as the condition of true freedom which must be received by giving up our desires to flourish on our own terms.[11] The church's mission is thus determined not by the concepts of human activity and choice, but by human recognition of and consent to God's action. The crucial theological point is not that we keep the logical univocity of the biblical metaphor of water

---

9. Jean Vanier, *Community and Growth* (London: Darton, Longman & Todd, 1979), p. 101. Vanier's language clearly also echoes patristic readings. 'A fountain sprang up out of paradise, sending forth not only visible streams but also spiritual streams arising as a fountain from this high tableland. Alongside this fountain there have grown, not willows without fruit but abundant trees reaching to heaven itself, with fruit every in season and remaining still incorrupt. If someone is intensely hot, let him come to this fountain and cool down this feverish heat . . . not only those literally inflamed by the sun's heat but also those set on fire by sin's burning arrows. It does so because it takes its beginning from above and has its source from there, from there it is fed. Many are the streams of this fountain, streams that the Paraclete sends forth; and the Son becomes its custodian, not keeping its channel open with a mattock but by making our hearts receptive.' John Chrysostom, Homily on John 46:4, in Andrew Louth (ed.), *Genesis I – II: Ancient Christian Commentary on Scripture* (Downers Grove: InterVarsity Press, 2001), p. 59.
10. Vanier, *Community and Growth*, p. 102.
11. Ibid., pp. 63, 81.

and watering straight, but that we preserve the all-important relation between divine and human action: 'So neither the one who plants nor the one who waters is anything,' says Paul, 'but only God who gives the growth' (1 Cor. 3:7–9). It is on these grounds that I have understood the question of the relation of creation to mission not as 'Where should we *go* to spread the good news?' but as 'How is the good news *actually spread*, wherever we are?'

Vanier suggests that mission construed in these terms is distinguishable from mission as militancy in that its aim is not first to change people, but to reveal the life-giving God. Serving God's life-giving love and renewal does subdue evil and make converts, but through their displacement by God's upbuilding love. This means Christians also do not properly think of themselves as an 'elite core of experts'. God's mission takes believers into strange and unfamiliar cultural worlds and material localities in which they are decisively not experts. In such unfamiliar contexts the work of mission is to discover what divine forgiveness and care mean within the rich texture of specific contexts.[12] Vanier has learned this by observing that God cares for those who cannot speak, cannot care for themselves, and so cannot be 'civilized' or 'converted' in the ways we typically picture these activities. They can only be loved as an expression of God's love, and this love, Vanier observes, does indeed change things, but not because it sets out with 'expertise' to 'change the world'.

What the creation account commits Christians to affirming is that God made the first humans out of earth, appeared to them, spoke to them and in so doing invited them to live in worship and communion, to be those whose living embodied grateful receipt of divine speech and care. And it was in a garden that this offer was rejected in a way it could not have been by any other creature. But reject that offer they did, and so Adam and Eve, and with them all of us, were cast out 'east of Eden' (Gen. 4:16). Had they not been, the suggestion seems to be that the boundaries of this garden could have expanded outwards without undermining its appropriately local nature, and its fragrance would have drawn and perfumed the whole of creation as imagined in the Song of Songs: 'Awake, O north wind, and come, O south wind! Blow upon my garden that its fragrance may be wafted abroad' (Song 4:16). There would have been no going to 'strange lands', nor would there ever have been 'displaced peoples' – human life would have been characterized by seamless and appreciative embedding in local contexts.

---

12. Ibid., pp. 86–87, 99–100, 102.

Gardening in a fallen world

This unproblematic relation to one's local context in creation was broken up and the atomization of humans began with their being cast out of the garden, a process only further accelerated by the dispersal of Babel. Now humanity begins its slide into abstraction and distraction, sometimes acutely feeling and at other times becoming insensate to its distance from God. To be cast out is to have to 'remember' and so to be less securely in touch with God's Word, and so to have to wonder if we are hearing rightly or at all. The garden is thus the heart of the matter – in it humanity was truly present with both God and creation, but outside it finds it difficult to become truly present in any meaningful way to *either* God *or* creaturely reality.

Insecurity about God's presence is directly linked to insecurity about our rooting in place. As we lose the sense that God walks with us and begin to think of him in general terms, as a being 'over there' to be *thought about* rather than *spoken to* (Gen. 3:1), we likewise lose our ties to concrete locale. As the Babel and Exodus narratives so forcibly remind us, human nomadism is an artefact of faith's existing within societies driven and organized by humans who believe in their own power. This nomadism can be internalized in each of us. Without the sense that God is meeting us in the people before us, rooting us in relationships and so places, we easily drift into thinking of ourselves as located only within general coordinates of space and time.

Willie Jennings has recently shown how the colonial moment in Christendom can be considered crucial in this regard in that during it Christian theology sacralized, and was thus co-opted by, this atomization. Christian missionaries of the seventeenth century adjusted the gospel to a rapidly expanding Western world by denying the theological relevance of the rooting of human cultures in places. In reinventing Christianity as a placeless and so creationless religion, the means for a theologically robust resistance to the depredations of our globalized world was lost. Only now could the slave ship become possible in Christendom, which could justify systematically tearing people from family, place and clan because they would be converted in the process. To do this Christians had to thin out how they understood salvation and divine love, and only once this theological dilution was accomplished could they proceed as if it was normal to tear people out of their 'places' to be 'converted' and dropped down as good Christians in any productive unit of the developed world.[13]

---

13. Willie James Jennings, *The Christian Imagination: Theology and the Origins of Race* (New Haven: Yale University Press, 2010), chs. 1, 4.

Modern humanity with its outspoken yet extremely narrow desire for individual freedom as the supreme human good can be seen as at the end point of the trajectory begun with the expulsion from the garden.

I am developing Vanier's ideas of mission as following the life-giving Spirit in order to re-narrate the extension of divine presence and rule in a manner that does not deny the import of creaturely reality in this way. Christian denials of creation have typically been defended by specific readings of the primeval history. A dominant modern Christian way to do this has been to make the fall and the image of God the only themes in the primeval history that are taken to be relevant for defining Christian mission. I want to suggest that the church's mission must be more roundly doctrinally described than the single emphasis on Christians as icons of God's sovereign kingly rule or as purveyors of salvation as eternal life typically admit. The way we understand Adam's and Eve's role in extending the garden is thus one way to broaden out our account of the church's mission.

G. K. Beale begins with this same desire to give a more theologically rounded account of mission and suggests that Adam's and Eve's missional work must be read through Christ's priestly activity. 'Believers express their identification with Christ's Adamic kingship when they spread the presence of God by living for Christ and speaking his word and unbelievers accept it, and Satan's victorious hold on their heart is broken.'[14] While Beale notes that the tending of the garden to which Adam and Eve were created was not simply a secular activity, but was their materially enacted receipt of God's Word, he nevertheless focuses his account of mission solely on the doctrine of redemption. It is telling then that he can offer nothing more than a negative account of the pre-lapsarian activity depicted in the garden of Eden: 'Our continual priestly tasks are what the first Adam's were to be: to keep the order and peace of the spiritual sanctuary by learning and teaching God's word, by praying always, and by being vigilant in keeping out unclean moral and spiritual things.'[15] Vanier has already indicated why the biblical creation account and the doctrine of creation demand we say more. The fullness of life bestowed by God's love consists of more than preaching and keeping one's self morally pure, but in living as those who receive and reciprocate God's life-giving gifts, both physical and spiritual.

Neither is this activity of missional extension to be construed simply as secular culture shaping, as in classic Reformed accounts of the extension of God's presence in creation. J. Richard Middleton's account of the God whom

---

14. Beale, *The Temple and the Church's Mission*, pp. 396–397.
15. Ibid., p. 398.

humans are to image draws heavily on 'imaging' as the reflection of the work of a political king primarily interested in culture formation. Middleton suggests that 'the *imago Dei* refers to human rule, that is, the exercise of power on God's behalf in creation', and therefore that 'God has ... started the process of forming and filling, which humans as God's earthly delegates, are to continue'.[16] The ethical conclusion is fairly straightforward: 'the human calling as *imago Dei* is itself developmental and transformative and may be helpfully understood as equivalent to the labor or work of forming culture or developing civilization.'[17] In distinction from Beale, it is only as an afterthought that Middleton links this kingly work with a priestly work: 'the *imago Dei* also includes a priestly or cultic dimension ... humans have pride of place and supreme responsibility, not just as royal stewards and cultural shapers of the environment, but ... as priests of creation, actively mediating divine blessing to the nonhuman world – and – in a post-fall situation – interceding on behalf of a groaning creation until that day when heaven and earth are redemptively transformed.'[18]

In Middleton's *imago Dei*-focused account of mission humans are one-way conduits passing divine blessings down to the rest of creation.[19] Rather than learning to follow the already extensive rivers of the life-giving Spirit, Middleton's formulation suggests that without human vanguards, this life-giving Spirit will be dammed up. The not-so-subtle and ineradicable subtext of these treatments is the assumption that mission is about 'going' and 'sorting out' something which is almost inevitably imagined as 'over there' and 'disordered'. Such formulations have had no little influence on the focus of modern evangelism

---

16. J. Richard Middleton, *The Liberating Image: The Imago Dei in Genesis 1* (Grand Rapids: Brazos, 2005), pp. 88, 90.
17. Ibid., p. 89.
18. Ibid., pp. 89–90.
19. In a similar vein, James Davidson Hunter has recently drawn applause for interpreting the task of tilling and keeping as the creation mandate to be 'worldmakers': 'The passion to change the world, to shape it and finally change it for the better, would seem to be an enduring mark of Christians on the world in which they live.' James Davidson Hunter, *To Change the World: The Irony, Tragedy and Possibility of Christianity in the Late Modern World* (New York: Oxford University Press, 2010), p. 4. Guroian succinctly states the problem here: 'Modern Christians have spoken a lot about 'stewardship' of the earth. But I think we are overly practiced at the kind of management that this word easily connotes. We need another perspective, another metaphor. Scripture gives us the symbol of the Garden.' Guroian, *Inheriting Paradise*, p. 13.

on 'going' to the exclusion of sustained thought about the 'staying' that is intrinsic to the biblical traditions of mission. The critical theological question is whether humanity as the representative of the eternal king or as the high priest of creation appropriately refers to us, or to Jesus Christ. Any response to Beale and Middleton demands that we return to the question of how we are to understand the work of the *one* high priest who redeems creation and so offers it back to God, who acts as the *one* king who conquers the rebellious peoples and makes them into a kingdom of peace.

This is why it is worthwhile returning to meditate on gardening. We were created to garden, and some of us remain gardeners today. We, like the authors of Genesis, live after the expulsion from Eden. They too had to reach back to imagine life before the fall, and depicting Adam and Eve as gardeners seemed the most theologically fitting vocation for the humans meant to walk with God. And so, however torn this world of thorns and thistles might be, it will illumine our reading of Genesis to pause for a moment to dwell on what it means to be a gardener. This is another way of asking, 'How are we to live Christian mission as an expression of God's care for people in particular places?'

There is a circularity, of course, about a faith that starts with an authoritative Scripture and finds in that Scripture a tale about a garden in which God speaks a command that is itself the origin of Scripture. The effect of such an opening of the narrative of Scripture is to set us before God and to press us with the choice to harden ourselves or actively explore the divine claim on us. To embrace God as Creator who must be heard and responded to is something we *do*, a matter of actions that must take place in our daily local context, and is not just an embrace of a set of conceptual affirmations. That the first humans are depicted as doing this in a *garden* is intended to cause us to think about the concrete implications for our action of recognizing, of embracing the speaking of God into the places in which we are set. We too can be remade in the image of the one who cared for the world. That Genesis depicts humans in such a place as the garden is a profound reminder that all materiality is a place shaped and tended, before we existed, and to which we must re-learn to attend. This set of connections suggests that what we have in the image and reality of the garden is a *physical* concomitant of the *temporal* space called Sabbath. Sabbath was the *time* and the garden the *place* of God's chosen resting with humans. 'God brings [Adam] to this part of the earth to fulfil his determination for the whole earth and therefore really to live,'[20] as Barth nicely puts it. But even east of Eden,

---

20. Barth, *Church Dogmatics* III/1, p. 251.

this same God continues to speak, to claim us, to make us real, solid and so free in the places in which we too are set.

Such a casting of the matter again reminds us that the one decision about whether to hearken to God's word or not that happens at conversion must be continually reaffirmed in very mundane contexts. Being 'set in a garden' shaped the lives of the first couple so thoroughly that they could not possibly have realized all the ways it did so. Their world was not to be *built* but to be *maintained in attentiveness* and it was this attentiveness to *creatures* that constituted their obedience to God's command. The theological import of the Genesis depiction of the first humans being set in a garden is not that it causes us to ponder *gardens*, but that it raises the question, 'What does it take to be a good *gardener*?'

The new heart and perception gardening requires

The philosopher David Cooper has beautifully reflected on what the practice of gardening reveals about our modern condition in which we are taught to think of ourselves as freedom seekers who feel compelled to cash that freedom out by 'making a difference' or 'making history' (or at least 'being there' for historically momentous occasions).

> We are prone to think of our achievements as ones of our own making and doing. At an obvious level, we are right to think this: It was I who wrote this book, my friend who built that greenhouse, Cézanne who painted that landscape. But we are also prone, thereby, to ignore the pre-conditions – not at all of our own making and doing – of these achievements. For anyone to do anything, there must already be, one might say, a space of possibilities. And for there to be this space, there must already be some general understanding of the world and ourselves; already a sense of what matters, of what would be worth doing; already available 'moods' and 'attunements' that enable aspects of our world to assume a certain tone, attractive, repellent, or whatever; already be a light in which things show up for us in the ways they do and invite us to treat them in this or that manner.[21]

All our action and thought arises in a creation thoroughly formed by material and social structure. Absolutely everything we do can therefore be understood primarily as a *response* to created reality, and this is a more theologically accurate

---

21. David E. Cooper, *A Philosophy of Gardens* (Oxford: Clarendon Press, 2006), pp. 145–146.

way of thinking than to believe we are co-creators or must 'make things good'. Scripture makes bold to name this antecedent reality as first God, and secondly creation, that space opened up by God's creative Word. As Luther puts it, the divine speech alone has the power to bring things immediately into existence, all creation being therefore 'nothing but nouns in the divine rule of language'.[22] All human speech and action can therefore at best only be joyfully receptive to this original speech. To confess that we are creatures, then, is to affirm that we are set within a grammatical structure that precedes us. What the philosopher must call the preconditions of the 'space of possibilities' we inhabit, Scripture trains believers to call creation.

How might we come to rightly hear God's speaking, having been trained in a myriad of ways that our daily lives can proceed perfectly well without it, where it is our habit to proceed without perceiving? Here Christians may continue to learn from secular philosophers of gardening, who are also concerned with the deadening of human powers of perception. Any such deadening 'is bad news for gardeners', writes Robert Harrison,

> for nothing is less cultivated these days in Western societies than the art of seeing. It is fair to say that there exists in our era a tragic discrepancy between the staggering richness of the visible world and the extreme poverty of our capacity to perceive it. Thus even though there are plenty of gardens in the world, we live in an essentially gardenless era. I don't know how to phrase this without sounding curmudgeonly, so I will simply assert as a matter of fact that among the young people I encounter on a daily basis – and I encounter quite a few, given my profession [professor] – most are much more at home in their computers, or in the fictions and skits that reach them on a screen, than they are in the three-dimensional world. In fact I have the impression that a great many of them no longer see the visible world at all, except peripherally and crudely ... It is not that the world is any less visible than it was in the past; rather its plenitude registers with us less and less. It is *in us* that the transmutation takes place.[23]

We need, then, to revisit the details of how material beings make claims on us.

Cooper suggests that gardening attunes the gardener to three fundamental aspects of creation.[24] First, gardening fosters a fine-grained respect for *life*. The good gardener takes the givenness of the life before him or her as having its

---

22. Martin Luther, *Luther's Works, Vol. 1, Lectures on Genesis, Chapters 1 – 5*, ed. J. Pelikan (Saint Louis: Concordia Publishing House, 1958), p. 49.
23. Harrison, *Gardens*, pp. 114–115.
24. Cooper, *A Philosophy of Gardens*, pp. 95–96.

own shape, structure and flourishing. We do not tell the strawberry plant when to bloom: it tells us. To garden well, we must learn to give up the modern habit of desiring to impose our own designs on everything. Even industrial agriculture, which tries hard to tell the strawberry when to bloom, is still forced to concede its givenness by making expensive concessions to its demands.

Second, caring for life restructures *time*. This submission demands arranging our time and priorities in a way that conforms to their object. We moderns think of time as a flow of indistinguishable abstract and interchangeable units. That we do so shapes our experience of ourselves and our activities. Abstract time is modern in being a deductively and conceptually articulated conception grounding a global and simultaneous grid encompassing all human action. Time patterned by care is related to but structurally different from the clock time (which the New Testament refers to with the language of *chronos*), in that humans in fact experience time as the working out of one care after another. The sequential and dynamic nature of care is nicely encapsulated by Robert Harrison: 'like a story, a garden has its own developing plot, as it were, whose intrigues keep the caretaker under more or less constant pressure. The true gardener is always "the constant gardener".'[25] Drawn up into this never-ending movement, we are literally conformed to that for which we care.

As we are drawn into activities of caring our awareness of general conceptions of time, which make us feel as if we must figure out how to 'spend' it, fades, displaced by our engagement in filled-out, concrete and sequential activities. 'Time goes so fast' when we are caring for things. 'They grow up so quickly,' we say. To understand ourselves as coming to have a shape through being claimed for care by other lives stands in sharp contrast with the modern self-image in which we 'manage' our 'resources' for maximum 'efficiency' so that we can 'shape ourselves' into an image that we find attractive. Care is a faithfulness that is content to act as creatures, to be responsive rather than aspire to construct *ex nihilo*. Only the one Creator can create from nothing, and thus it is of the essence of faithful creatureliness not to aspire to rise above care. It is not accidental that Jesus inaugurates a new age characterized by care for others and divinely given new life. The New Testament authors use a new word to denote the time of the kingdom, *kairos*.

Another example of time structured by care is this: a baby wakes up, is fed, changed and plays in regular patterns, to which parents are well advised to attend before they are compelled to by the sonic cattle prod of the infant's

---

25. Harrison, *Gardens*, p. 7. Later he writes, 'Time in its subjective and objective correlates is the invisible element in which gardens come to bloom.' p. 117.

crying. If this small life is to grow, the literal womb must be replaced by a womb-like human attentiveness keyed to her particular needs, anticipating and freely meeting them. Children exist in a social womb of attention and love that becomes visible only when it is withdrawn or torn by anger or violence. That children demand this of us disciplines us to become those capable of love. Such love cannot be sustained without a wider 'womb' of supportive relationships sustaining and upholding these proximal carers. Social support networks for carers are, in fact, integral to the care of children, the aged, or those with permanent severe handicaps.

This caring is asymmetrical. We are born into it and can only withhold it or pass it on. What we are incapable of doing is repaying those who have cared for us. It is a mark of appreciating our having been cared for to invest in the type of social networks that can sustain the most vulnerable among us. These webs of care exist even among non-Christians, and Christian mission becomes demonic when it does not recognize that through them God is already providing people's daily bread – and so tramples over them. Whether Christian or not, we fallen creatures are limited and control limited resources, and so we find it difficult to care. We feel our finitude, it ignites our fear and so we walk away, preaching the righteousness of walking away. True care is only possible out of a fundamental abundance, and the provision of this abundance is the work of the Spirit, that river beside which believers must be planted if they are to bear the fruit of witness to divine love (Ps. 1). Put negatively, our self-protectiveness marks a withered faith in Jesus' promise to send his sustaining Spirit.

This reference to the Spirit brings us to Cooper's third observation about gardening: caring is fundamentally an action of *hope*. Our labour can never guarantee success. A garden requires us to think ahead several years to the fruit, and to reckon with a million variables beyond our control, weather, pests, the health of the soil, and so on. That the ethos of gardening is grounded in hope distinguishes it from pursuits like painting, sculpture and architecture. The gardener's entire attention is on what the Platonist and idealist finds abhorrent – the changing and ephemeral nature of beings. Painters, for instance, may paint a landscape and evoke the crashing of waves, a fierce wind or sunlight moving across a vista. But in doing so they take great pains to ensure that the natural materials that make up the painting do *not* change.

> By contrast, gardens not only depend on nature but exemplify – 'refer to', 'body forth' – this very dependence ... 'states of the atmosphere, and circumstances that we cannot always detect, affect all landscapes'. Moreover, The Garden, more palpably subject to 'misadventure and mischance' than The Building, more effectively explodes

'the myth of manageability' that infects our comportment toward the world – better exemplifies, that is, the precarious reliance on contingencies beyond 'the enforced will of human ingenuity'.[26]

The garden also differs from the farm, which is primarily organized by the very practical interest in producing sufficient food. The garden is a more holistic affair, one in which human endeavour turns towards drawing out what is most often hidden in life, the subtle, the fragile, from what is invisible but all important – the soil. The farmer must fill the silo with grain, but the gardener's prize is the rare and tender, displayed in the flourishing of organisms like the butterfly or orchid, or even that most ephemeral of bodily creatures, the wind. '[T]here are aspects of familiar natural phenomena which ordinary experience, without quite distorting the phenomena, nevertheless typically fails to expose, to make available to thought,' Cooper writes.

> [T]he point is important, and so, therefore, is the fact that gardeners often facilitate, through devices that impinge on the senses, the exposure or 'expression' of these aspects . . . 'The Japanese garden designer', wrote Ezra Pound, 'creates a theatre for the wind to speak.' The poet's point could be put by saying that the Japanese garden, through its bamboos and wind-chimes, expands the range of meanings that the wind may have for us. Blowing through the garden, it is not the enemy we encounter in our face on the way to the office, nor the friend that cools us on a baking beach: rather, we experience it as animator. In 'speaking' through the chimes and bamboos, it animates certain qualities of these: those qualities, as it were, themselves come to speak – the resonance of the wood from which the chimes are made as they knock against each other, the delicate but sturdy flexibility of the bamboos as the wind rustles and bends them.[27]

The Japanese gardener can organize her garden in order to help us 'see' the wind only because, at some point, she became aware that the wind is there to be seen, by the swirls it has left on a quiet pond, or as a surprising and playful mover of fallen leaves.

Put in the technical terms of epistemology, such an account inverts the Enlightenment-trained preference for perceiving all beings through taxonomies of eternal features or recurrent structures. Here I know I have a dog because he has four legs, a tail, a muzzle, and so on. I can name this being

---

26. Cooper, quoting Gertrude Jeckyll, *A Philosophy of Gardens*, pp. 137–138.
27. Ibid., p. 141.

because it has *traits*, *faculties* that characterize every member of the class. He is thus essentially a representative of a larger class, and a better or worse one at that.

But are Christians right to think of human beings as better or worse representatives of a class? Jennings has traced how Christian mission has often been deeply shaped by presumptions that the colour of a human skin or the state of a culture's technological advancement is an accurate indicator of how good a Christian we can expect people to become.[28] It is only good stewardship not to spend too much effort on those groups who have no 'leadership potential'. In our age of efficiency and industrialization, therefore, it becomes ever more apparent how it must be a work of the Spirit to attune us to perceive the reality not of 'essence', which can be described in general terms, but of 'accident', the actual creatures lying or standing before us *with* the networks of family, agriculture, governance and local flora and fauna that make them who they are.

The setting of the first humans in a garden now appears as an invitation to think again about the grammar of the incarnation, itself not an 'eternal truth of reason' but an 'accidental truth of history'.[29] This Christological claim must directly shape our missiology, Jennings suggests.

> A Christian doctrine of creation should not be articulated as though it is first an academic dissertation about divine power and ownership or human stewardship of the earth or about theoretical possibilities of the exact nature of human origins or about the precise relationship between biblical accounts of creation and the actual cosmic order of material existence. A Christian doctrine of creation is first a doctrine of place and people, of divine love and divine touch, of human presence and embrace, and of divine and human interaction. It is first a way of seeing place in its fullest sense. Christianity is in need of place to be fully Christian . . . The moment the land is removed as a signifier of identity, it is also removed as a site of transformation through relationship . . . At heart, there was an important aspect of the connection between creation and redemption that . . . never seemed to take hold in the Christian imagination.[30]

---

28. Jennings, *The Christian Imagination*, ch. 2.
29. 'There is nothing in the opinion of Lessing that God's Word is an "eternal truth of reason," and not an "accidental truth of history." God's history is indeed an accidental truth of history, like this petty commandment.' Karl Barth, *Dogmatics in Outline*, trans. G. T. Thomson (London: SCM, 1949), p. 109.
30. Jennings, *The Christian Imagination*, p. 248.

Christian thought begins from and constantly returns to the coming of God into and through a specific people in a specific place and time, with the expectation that he will continue to do so. 'Just as you did it to one of the least of these . . . you did it to me' (Matt. 25:40). Such a gospel not only brings an eternal truth, but brings it to beings who are time and place saturated, who live in locations with specifically configured climates, who eat a cuisine linked to that place and climate and whose dialects of speech and thought are not swept away by the gospel, but are appreciatively attended to and learned from as reservoirs of knowledge about the one Creator's world. It is in this sense that faith in the good news of Jesus Christ makes Christian mission perceptive, as care makes a gardener: 'Looking is as creative as making, provided it is possessed of the art of seeing.'[31] There is no care which is not shaped both by the object of care and by the one who gives the care. This affirmation liberates Christian mission in allowing us to affirm that each gardener sees and attempts to draw out different aspects of the lives she encounters. Just as there is no generic recipient of missional care, so there are no factory-produced identical missionaries.

In the churches of our modern developed world, we have been trained to praise the winners, admire the strong, to seek out the 'up-and-comers' for our evangelistic outreaches, mainly because of our recent love affair with the business-derived idol of 'growth strategy'. We have become comfortable with slash-and-burn missional styles that desire to wipe away the old unruly diversity of the given and refuse to attend and pick through the thicket of life as it actually is. We prefer the much quicker project of bulldozing this diversity in the pursuit of what promises to be a more controllable set of beings who will conform to our expectations, even if a loss of diversity occurs in this saving of labour.

Instead, the biblical traditions imagine the Christian life as characterized by giving more than one takes away, of passing on rather than hoarding. All creatures, says Luther, participate in a great cosmic web of reciprocal relations. The sun does not shine for itself, water does not flow for itself, plants do not give fruits for themselves; every creature lives by the law of love, sharing freely of itself with its neighbours. Or rather, God intends the creation to be reciprocal in this way, an intention which only the devil and humanity resist. The refusal to hand on transforms plants as receivers of God's goodness who share it as fruit with others into thorn bushes and choking vines. In Luther's account, at the centre of the renewal of creation we find the problem of the passions of the human heart in which the collapse of mutuality and reciprocity

---

31. Harrison, *Gardens*, p. 122.

enters the world. Only transplantation into the caring heart of Christ that is fed by the streams of the Spirit can uproot the selfishness which destroys reciprocity.[32]

To even *see* the least of these, to speak Christ to people as they are, demands being granted a divinely renewed ability to perceive and respond to reality. Anglican Morning Prayer begins with a psalm that has been used prominently in daily worship in the Western church for well over a thousand years, the *Venite*, Psalm 95. At the climax of that psalm the hearing of God's Word is linked with the softening of the human heart. The rather free 1662 translation succeeds in getting the theological emphasis right for modern ears: 'Today, if ye will hear his voice, harden not your hearts: as in the provocation, and as in the day of temptation in the wilderness' (vv. 7b–8).[33] As Scripture warns us with multiple examples, the most difficult problem the hardening of our heart presents is that it hides itself from us. This is one of its primary effects, this failing of our senses. As a result, Christian theology must learn how to refuse the hardening of our hearts by seeking what it might mean for our hearts to be softened. The penetration of the gospel into our sinful lives exposes our sin; the deeper the encroachment of the gospel, the more plainly our sin appears before us. Somehow if we would hear God, and note that the psalm says 'today', our hearts must be softened. If this softening is constitutive of missionary activity taking the form displayed by Christ, it cannot be militant or elitist.

Consider for a moment how activities like driving or playing music depend on immediate and reflexive perceptions of the relevant aspects of our context. Playing a guitar well, as the Germans put it, is a matter of developing *Fingergefühl* – feeling in the fingers. Here 'knowing' is bodily and sensate. In such contexts perception and our ability to act at all are inexplicably and wholly intertwined. It is this complex to which the biblical metaphor of the awakening of the senses points, suggests Bernd Wannenwetsch. Because God's working is not on the surface of things, God must create in us the ability to *perceive more*. The creation of new sensitivities to the world around us is the means of our learning to hear and follow God. There are many who have eyes but do not see, ears but do not hear (Ps. 115:1–7), but the work of Christ is the opening of the senses (Mark 7:31–37), so answering the prayer of the psalmist that God might 'open

---

32. Martin Luther, 'Psalms 1 and 2 from Works on the First Twenty-two Psalms, 1519 to 1521: A Composite Translation', in *Luther's Works, Vol. 14, Selected Psalms III*, ed. J. Pelikan (Saint Louis: Concordia Publishing House, 1958), p. 300.

33. The more literal NRSV has it, 'O that today you would listen to his voice! Do not harden your hearts, as at Meribah, as on the day at Massah in the wilderness.'

my eyes, so that I may behold wondrous things out of your law' (Ps. 119:18, cf. vv. 70, 103). The prayer for the renewal of the senses, the softening of the heart, is thus central to Christian living because to come again into God's presence is the condition of becoming present and sensate to the world of creatures. 'God's greatest work is to open all my senses' by giving a new heart, as Luther puts it. This new heart does not 'tune in' to God on some higher metaphysical or spiritual frequency, but is enlivened to Christ's rule in and through the normal bodily senses. Faith is the horizon of hope in the heart that orients and so stimulates the senses to perceive.[34]

Let us be clear: though the wind becomes perceptible in a new way when we see its effects on water, to see it is not to have seen *through* the world to some numinous essence. In the same way, to perceive the Spirit's work is to see the world as it *is* and as it *engages* our activity. To be a gardener means to have a certain form of attentiveness in which the 'real' emerges before our perception, the 'sound of the wood as a chime' becomes audible and perceivable only as the Spirit animates. As Cooper observes about gardening,

> The wood one chops, the squash one waters, the aubretia one secures to the stone wall – each is there vividly and saliently before one 'just as it is'. But this is not at all the sense ... which the detached scientist or botanist might have when subjecting the same things to objective inspection and analysis. On the contrary, it is at the same time a sense of intimacy with them, an engaged experience of them: of the squash as something that needs to be watered, of the aubretia as gracing the wall that protects the cottage garden. To such a sensibility, then, things are present 'just as they are', not *despite* the place they have in relation to our lives, but *through* this. *This* squash, *this* aubretia – these are not simply bits of matter with certain shapes and botanical properties, but they are what they are through the particular ways they engage the gardener.[35]

Christian blessedness is found in letting the creation that is the object of God's concern appear and in *serving* this living concern to provide for beings who already exist, beings whom we have not made and with whom God already is intimately involved. The task of mission is not reducible to the single-faceted language of the social gospel, which constantly looks to see 'where the Spirit

---

34. Bernd Wannenwetsch, 'Plurale Sinnlichkeit: Glaubenswahrnehmung im Zeitalter virtueller Realität', in *Neue Zeitschrift für Systematische Theologie und Religionsphilosphie*, 42 (2000), pp. 299–315.
35. Cooper, *A Philosophy of Gardens*, p. 148.

is at work' in movements for social liberation and justice. God is *already* feeding and clothing humanity, the psalmist tells us (Ps. 104), and we need to let ourselves be pushed into caring for those God loves, learning to receive God's gifts which God is *already* offering, apportioning and appointing by the Spirit (1 Cor. 12).

Jesus Christ embodies this life of the renewed heart and opened eyes. And because the Holy Spirit is the Spirit of *this* Christ, through the Spirit this Christ binds humans to the concerns and needs of concrete neighbours. Activity harnessed to this listening for God's Word reveals the beings before us, their claim on us and thus our common source and sustainer. In the neighbour the confronting Word of Christ is specific and concrete. As a result, Christian life is nothing other than practical experimentation in attentiveness to God's love for concrete neighbours. Jean Vanier's is one such experimental life, and he is rightly upset when people mischaracterize his life in moralistic terms.

> I get upset when people tell me, 'You're doing a good job.' I'm not interested in doing a good job. I'm interested in an ecclesial vision for community and in living in a gospel-based community with people with disabilities. We are brothers and sisters together, and Jesus is calling us from a pyramidal society to become a body.[36]

In binding us to concrete others, the living Word exposes as self-justificatory the church's moral rationalizations (based on visions of numerical growth and increasing cultural influence) which configure our societies and justify remaining aloof from human need. But in this confrontation of our self-absorption by the *verbum externum*, the Word that comes from outside us and reveals creation as that for which God cares, new ways of living out care for others are perceptible beyond what the world imagines possible. This trinitarian account of responsibility ties moral growth to processes of coming to embody a history with others, in all their sin and blindness.

Such a binding together recasts the fundamental orientation of our moral vision. We no longer ask with the rich young ruler, 'What should I do?' (see Matt. 19:16), but begin to ask, 'How do I love my neighbour?' With the latter question one's own personal vocation is emphasized, as well as the drama of living with concrete neighbours. The focus of ethical enquiry turns towards discerning the specific *acts* of justice that open up new ways of living together in our particular context. What it means for *us* to image God always lies beyond

---

36. Jean Vanier, *Living Gently in a Violent World: The Prophetic Witness of Weakness*, ed. J. Swinton (Downers Grove: InterVarsity Press, 2008), pp. 34–35.

ourselves, is only perceivable piecemeal, but is actualized in us by means of the Spirit's tying our care to concrete neighbours.[37] The same wind that hovered over creation, that was blown into the mouth of Adam and that founded the Christian church at Pentecost appears among us in special association with the 'least of these', in binding us to the ones from whom our societies teach us to expect the very least.

We draw to a conclusion by ending where we began: with the problem of our self-assertion as the main barrier to the trinitarian God's mission in the world. Here there must be a proper violence in striving after the kingdom, as Jesus himself reminds us when speaking of John the Baptist: 'From the days of John the Baptist until now the kingdom of heaven has been coming violently, and the violent take it by force' (Matt. 11:12). There is a breaking, a wrenching away from inherited cultural certainties that can only be perceived by family and friends as violence to accepted communal norms (Matt. 10:37). Embedded within love for others must be a proper hatred expressing an active rejection of evil outside and inside ourselves. To love the neighbour we must learn to hate the ease with which we habitually excuse ourselves from concern for others. Such righteous self-hatred violates our self-defined integrity, committing us to a painful process of being given a *new* and *public, outward-centred* self. This death of our false selves is a real death, as we are taught in baptism. At the same time, it is the locus of new birth. Out of the fetid compost of our discarded idolatrous selves comes new life, out of the humus of decaying self-identifications comes the humility of repentance that springs from lives taken into Christ.

The composting image indicates how the processes of sanctification take time, death and severance. But this is not a passive process, nor a private one. It demands the ongoing investment of our energies and that of the church. This was the insight that animated medieval penitential practices, and one way to appreciate the life of Jean Vanier is to see it as a prophetic penance done for a modern church in love with growth and cultural relevance and so severed from the intellectually disabled. In so doing he serves the exposure of the guilt and complacency of the church and calls it back to the gospel of its Christ. The same is true of those Christians who, instead of retreating into home schooling, become teachers in 'failing schools', live with the shunned on the 'bad' side of town, or devote their lives to caring for the homeless, the abused, the abandoned and the prisoner. Such a binding to the outsider, because of the

---

37. Hans Ulrich, *Wie Geschöpfe Leben: Konturen Evangelischer Ethik* (Münster: Lit Verlag, 2005), pp. 96–98, 126–129.

sins of society and church, is painful, but it is the church's salvation, as the church, often against its will, is reminded that Christ did not die so that we would not have to interact with the unwashed heathens, but so that we would learn to love them as our brethren.

May God grant each of us to become a gardener, for ourselves and for the sake of all creation.

© Brian Brock, 2012

4. HOPE

Grant Macaskill

It is a concept at once profound and profane, magnificent and mundane; a word that we can whisper with excitement or throw thoughtlessly into a sentence: hope. From a biblical and theological point of view, it is a word that requires to be used in terms of the shape of God's redemptive work in Christ and to be differentiated from the empty hopes that are not founded upon God. Properly so used, 'hope' expresses the identity of the church as a community of fulfilment and expectation and has deep moral significance, describing the essential relationship between God's people and the world that he is redeeming. Severed from such a theology, though, 'hope' can become, at best, a vague descriptor of optimism and, at worst, a vehicle for false expectations and for a skewed social mandate, taking on the character of the false (or worldly) hopes from which it ought to be differentiated. The latter is a perennial problem for the church, one against which we must be on constant guard. What follows, then, is intended to clarify the points of distinction between 'worldly' and Christian concepts of hope. Most of our space will be given over to a study of hope in the New Testament, but such a study requires to be contextualized in the canon as a whole. Consequently, we begin with some reflection upon the Old Testament.

Hope in the Old Testament

Creation and fall

Canonically, our reflection upon the concept of hope in the Bible must begin with the accounts of creation and fall in Genesis 1 – 3. However we understand these chapters, they describe the world in its two states: 'very good' (Gen. 1:31) and 'cursed' (Gen. 3:17). The former, of course, is the state of blessing in which the creation exists according to the design and intent of its Creator, untainted by sin. As such, a reflection upon it provides some of the key materials for a theology of hope, as we anticipate the ultimate redemption of our world from sin's curse. Our anticipatory hope thus properly has a retrospective element, by which we look back upon the account of creation for insight into what it means to exist in accordance with God's will. The uptake of 'new creation' or 'new earth' language at certain key points in the biblical texts (Rev. 21:1; 2 Pet. 3:13, both drawing upon Isa. 65 – 66) reflects such a truth.

What is particularly striking about the description of the creation, in the paired accounts of Genesis 1 and 2, is the kind of relationality that is portrayed. While, broadly, Genesis 1 is given over to describing the differentiation of the cosmos into different zones and species, there is also a profound sense that the things that fill the different realms of the cosmos are derived from them:

> Then God said, 'Let the earth put forth vegetation: plants yielding seed, and fruit trees of every kind on earth that bear fruit with the seed in it.' And it was so. (Gen. 1:11)

> And God said, 'Let the waters bring forth swarms of living creatures, and let birds fly above the earth across the dome of the sky.' (Gen. 1:20; cf. 1:24).

Even more striking is the kind of language, and particularly the Hebrew wordplay, found in Genesis 2:7 and 2:22–23. Man (*'ādām*) is made from the soil (*'ădāmâ*) while the woman (*'iššâ*) is made from the man (*'îš*): 'bone of my bones and flesh of my flesh'. We, as readers, are left with the impression of a web of blessed relationships, with God's own life the vitality at its heart (Gen. 2:7). The fall account of Genesis 3 involves the thoroughgoing disintegration of those relationships. The relationship between humanity and God is, of course, fundamentally shattered, fellowship replaced by fear (Gen. 3:8, 10). But so, too, is the relationship between humanity and the earth; sweat-covered brows, thorns and thistles are now the standard experience. The communion between man and the dust now has a morbid undertone:

> By the sweat of your face
> > you shall eat bread
> until you return to the ground,
> > for out of it you were taken;
> you are dust,
> > and to dust you shall return.
>
> (Gen. 3:19)

This provides a helpful background to the biblical themes of redemption and informs a biblical theology of hope. The problem of sin entails the disintegration of relationality at personal and cosmic levels, and that which we hope for is the restoration of our personal, cosmic and Godward relationships.[1] At the same time, the effects of sin are not simply in the realms of human experience, but are cosmic and creational; our hope, correspondingly, is not simply a personal one (though it is not less than this), but is also a hope for the transformation and redemption of the entire cosmos.[2]

Reflection on the creation accounts therefore informs the notions of hope in the Old Testament and these frame the broad outlines of the narratives of redemption therein. We will unpack some of the key aspects of these below, but it is important to bear in mind that these national and cosmic redemptive expectations frame more local and personal ones. To note this is to stress the other side of the point that has just been made. Individuals may be aware of the predicament that sin brings upon the world and, within it, upon God's people and they may hope for a reversal of such a state of affairs, but within this they will also have a sense of their own predicament, in terms of their own experience both of sin and of a sin-cursed world. Hope, then, is never just a non-specific expectation of a better global future, but also more immediately of the possibility that God's grace will address particular experiences of the curse. The fall account of Genesis 3 itself suggests such possibilities: God's immediate response to the sin of the first couple includes clothing them and providing for the needs generated by the curse, even as the work of global redemption is begun. As we will see below, the concept

---

1. For the treatment of these themes in Genesis 1 – 2 and also the trajectories of restoration through Scripture, see W. P. Brown, *The Ethos of the Cosmos: The Genesis of Moral Imagination in the Bible* (Grand Rapids: Eerdmans, 1999).
2. This point is developed in ethical directions by Oliver O'Donovan, *Resurrection and Moral Order: An Outline for Evangelical Ethics*, 2nd ed. (Leicester: Inter-Varsity Press, 1994).

of 'covenant' is at the heart of this combination of the universal and the particular.

From creation to covenant
As we move towards this important concept, it is important to note that the vocabulary of hope in the Old Testament covers not only notions of optimism and the expectation of a good future, but also the ideas of endurance and waiting. Alongside *tiqwâ/tôḥelet* and their Greek equivalent *elpis*, both of which indicate an optimism for the future, there occur also *miqweh/hypomonē* and *qāwâ/yāḥal/hypomeinō*, nouns and verbs, respectively, that denote endurance and the activity of waiting. The point is significant for two reasons. First, it emphasizes that the context for hope is often that of a difficult present, a time in which believers must endure unpleasant circumstances. Such circumstances are an inevitable part of living in a world afflicted by the presence of sin, however directly or indirectly one may have participated in or encountered such sin. Second, and proceeding from this, hope is not a passive state or a set of expectations that one possesses; it is a virtue[3] that must be exercised, as one actively maintains trust in God and fidelity to his law in the face of difficulty.

This latter point reminds us also of the fact that the believer's hope proceeds from trust in the character and sovereignty of God. While this is a rather basic observation, it is also profoundly important as the key point of differentiation between the sure hope of the believer and the empty hope of the wicked: the believer 'waits' upon the Lord or upon his Word. Such an expectation will be vindicated by time (a point I will qualify below), while hopes not founded upon God will be proved hollow. Thus, in Proverbs 10:28, we read:

> The hope (*tôḥelet*) of the righteous ends in gladness,
> but the expectation (*tiqwâ*) of the wicked comes to nothing.

The hope of the believer, then, proceeds from faith in an external agent. Importantly, this faith is itself shaped and informed by the covenant. There is a foundational awareness that Israel is the people of God – that it will be through this people that the Abrahamic promise of global blessing (Gen. 12:3)

---

3. I use the word 'virtue' here in the sense that it is widely used in biblical studies at present, recognizing that the activities of the moral life are connected to the character that has been formed in the individual. See, for example, the collection of studies in W. P. Brown, *Character and Scripture: Moral Formation, Community and Biblical Interpretation* (Grand Rapids: Eerdmans, 2002).

will be fulfilled – and that the relationship between those parties is expressed in terms of commitment in the covenant: 'I am the LORD your God, who brought you out of the land of Egypt' (Exod. 20:2). Characteristically, the language of 'hoping in' or 'waiting upon' is used in connection with the divine name YHWH, with all its covenant associations, and not simply with the epithet 'God' (Pss 37:34; 38:15; Isa. 38:15).[4] All of this provides the relational basis for the hope of the believer, which relies upon the fact that the LORD will 'remember' his people and his covenant with them (e.g., Lev. 26:45), with all the promises that go with it. In the context of the Old Testament, those promises particularly concern the ownership of the land and God's blessing of it, and the presence of God with his people. The exodus, understood as the liberation of the descendants of the patriarchs, is the fundamental paradigm, and exile its dark shadow.

The mention of exile reminds us that the covenant also informs the believer's hope in a negative sense, which is vital for us to grasp if we are to make sense of the treatment of hope in the New Testament. There are two interwoven problems: the predicament of sin, of Israel's inability to maintain fidelity to the covenant, and the consequent experience of disaster or of exile. Taken together, these constitute the problematic of Israel, as the people at the heart of the divine purposes for the world, as the heirs of the Abrahamic promise. These concerns emerge most obviously in books such as Lamentations, Jeremiah and Ezekiel, to which we will return below, but they actually run through and structure much of the Old Testament. The concerns are given particular prominence in Deuteronomy 28 – 30, where the future of Israel is neatly anticipated and the need for an internal circumcision stressed:

> Moreover, the LORD your God will circumcise your heart and the heart of your descendants, so that you will love the LORD your God with all your heart and with all your soul, in order that you may live. (Deut. 30:6)

In both Ezekiel and Jeremiah, the need for such an internalization of the covenant is clear. Disaster befalls Jerusalem on account of the sins of God's people and the glory of the LORD deserts the temple. The people are seen to be incapable of maintaining fidelity to the terms of the covenant and experience the consequences of their failures. It is clear that their hearts remain uncircumcised, that they do not – cannot – love the LORD with all their heart

---

4. Where the title 'God' is used in connection with the idea of waiting (e.g. Ps. 25:5) it is flanked by uses of YHWH.

and so live. Their hope, their only hope, lies in the possibility that God will transform them, writing his law upon their hearts (Jer. 31:33), washing them of their sins (Ezek. 36) and vivifying them by his Spirit (Ezek. 37).

The anticipation of such a time of transformation aggregates other hopes to itself: the days in which God's people will be renewed will also be the time when the world will flock to Zion and when justice will be established. Isaiah 40 – 66 articulates this hope, the fulfilment of the covenant made with Abraham, that in him all nations would be blessed. It is little wonder that these chapters of Isaiah were so influential for New Testament writers, for the themes of global, even cosmic, salvation are so strong there. In Isaiah 40 – 66 the themes of hope become clustered around a particular figure, the Servant. In recent years it has been fashionable to diminish the significance of the Servant as a Christological or messianic figure and also to suggest that the Servant passages, especially Isaiah 53, were less influential for the theology of the New Testament writers than historically assumed.[5] While this may be a valid reflection on the specifically Christian use of Isaiah, which has given particular gravity to that book and has distinctively appropriated some of its texts as prefiguring Jesus, a case can be made that such scepticism has gone too far. Other texts likely to be from the Second Temple era, such as the *Similitudes of Enoch*, attest a messianic reading of Isaiah and of the Servant, whereby the Servant is understood to be a royal Davidic figure, bringing salvation and equity to the world.[6] The anticipation of transformation and renewal, the expectation of salvation, come thus to be focused on a singular figure, an anointed one, in whom the nations will place their hope (Isa. 42:4).

In time, the people will return from exile and will rebuild Jerusalem and the temple. But the events narrated in Ezra and Nehemiah hardly fulfil the hopes expressed in the prophecies discussed above. If anything, those books emphasize the sobering fact that sin still blights God's people; there is a disturbing sense of *plus ça change, plus c'est la même chose*. The people still need to be transformed and, while there is repentance among the people, there is still no true upholding of the covenant (see, for example, Ezra 9 – 10). Such a sense that the problem of the exile is not yet truly dealt with emerges in other texts,

---

5. Classically, Morna Hooker, *Jesus and the Servant: The Influence of the Servant Concept of Deutero-Isaiah in the New Testament* (London: SPCK, 1959; repr. Eugene: Wipf and Stock, 2010).

6. See my study, 'Parables, Thrones and Justice: Matthew and the *Similitudes of Enoch*', in *The Similitudes of Enoch and the New Testament*, ed. J. H. Charlesworth and D. Bock (New York: T. & T. Clark, forthcoming).

particularly in the Minor Prophets. In Malachi, for example, there is an abiding sense that God still has to purify his people of their sins, visiting them as a refiner's fire to ready them for their renewal.

All of this provides a background to the development of a theology of hope in the New Testament. Before we turn to that, however, some brief cautionary comments on hope in the Old Testament are in order. The presence in Scripture of what is sometimes described as 'counter-order wisdom', books such as Job and Ecclesiastes that challenge simplistic construals of the act-consequence system, warns us of our finitude and the limits of our perspective. The experience of suffering may be a result of covenant failure, and it may be part of the testing and refining of faith, so that in certain senses the experience of suffering or evil is explicable. Yet it may also be inexplicable or senseless from an earthly perspective. The imperative of hope here is not to maintain an expectation of a better future that is imminent, but to sustain a trust in God's goodness and sovereignty in the face of the 'evidence' that confronts our senses and to be prepared to configure hope eschatologically.

In a sense, this eschatological dimension to hope has been developing through the trajectory outlined above and becomes connected in the prophetic writings to the idea of the Day of the Lord or the last days. In apocalyptic literature – both that found in Scripture in books such as Ezekiel, Daniel and Zechariah and also that found in Second Temple literature – eschatology is much more clearly developed with theodicial concerns. It is probably a mistake to see the genre of apocalypse as primarily one of theodicy, as some have, but nevertheless there is a clear engagement with the problem of evil, specifically focused on the fortunes of God's people, and how that problem relates to the goodness and sovereignty of God. At least in part the problem is resolved by the bringing of a longer perspective to bear on the present time.

Hope in the New Testament

The New Testament writings, for all their diversity, are unified by a sense that the present time is one of fulfilment, itself an eschatological time, yet a fulfilment that is, as yet, only partial. The various writers develop their fulfilment motifs using a number of strategies: Matthew's Gospel opens with a genealogy structured into groups of fourteen in order to emphasize the place of the present time within the divine plan and its early chapters are densely populated with the word 'fulfilled'. Mark opens with a quotation from Isaiah 40, positioning the story in relation to the account of Deutero-Isaiah. Luke's Gospel opens with a statement that it is about fulfilment (Luke 1:1) and follows this with a description of various figures whose words describe present events as constituting, at least in part, the redemption of Israel (Luke 1:67–79). John is more subtle, weaving a range of allusions through his text (perhaps most impressively a strong allusion to Ezek. 36 and 37 in John 3, with the conjunction of water and Spirit), but for all the subtlety there is no doubt that this is a fulfilment story. Paul is replete with the language of fulfilment, that the coming of the Christ was 'when the fullness of time had come' (*hote de ēlthen to plērōma tou chronou*), a point that we will consider further below. Peter describes the present time in terms of the hopes of the prophets (1 Pet. 1:10–12). James, similarly, speaks of the new birth through the implanted Word being a matter of fulfilment. For the time being, we will say nothing of Revelation, but the use of prior biblical texts in that book is clearly indicative of fulfilment.

All of this points to a clear consciousness among the writers of the New Testament that the advent of Christ represents a fulfilment of the Old Testament writings. Two particular symbols arise in the midst of the diversity: the Messiah and the temple, with the latter inextricably linked to the Spirit.

There has been a drift in biblical scholarship towards minimizing the significance of the Messiah as a figure of expectation for Jews of the Second Temple period: Jews of this period, we are reminded, expected a range of divine mediators or figures of deliverance, not just one.[7] This is overly simplistic and has been challenged in recent years in a number of works that have re-established the place of messianic expectation in Second Temple Judaism.[8] It remains the case, though, that the language of the Messiah/Christ is particularly conspicuous in the New Testament and in the Christian tradition that has drawn upon it. It is important that we acknowledge this density: for the New Testament writers, Jesus is the singular figure upon whom all hopes are devolved and texts in the Old Testament that may have been read differently by other contemporaries are now interpreted as being about him as Messiah. Christology, shaped by the experience and the narrative of the incarnation, becomes a hermeneutical framework or interpretative lens that develops fresh readings of Old Testament texts through the wisdom revealed to God's people. The Christian reading of Isaiah 53 is a magnificent example of this.

Messiah language is bound up with that of 'kingdom'. The Messiah is the anointed king and the use of the terms 'Christ' and 'kingdom' is mutually

---

7. Indicative of such an approach is George Nickelsburg, *Ancient Judaism and Christian Origins: Diversity, Continuity and Transformation* (Minneapolis: Fortress, 2003).
8. See Markus Bockmuehl, *This Jesus: Martyr, Lord, Messiah* (Edinburgh: T. & T. Clark, 1994).

reinforcing. This inevitably gives a somewhat national dimension to the notion of fulfilment found in the New Testament: in some sense it is understood to be the climax of the story of Israel, as its king takes his throne and brings renewal and deliverance to his people, now expanded to incorporate the Gentiles. These latter terms will, as we will see presently, lead us into the question of the Spirit and the temple as part of the experience of salvation. It is worth raising at this point, however, an issue that will continue to run through the rest of this chapter: the question of how, or whether, the Messiah is understood to fulfil Israel's story or to represent a *novum*. This question is a prominent one in New Testament studies at present, with the rise of 'apocalyptic' readings of Paul that see the revelation of Jesus as representing a fundamentally new reality, initiated by grace and not emerging from the story of Israel.[9] Such readings emphasize the discontinuity of the gospel from the antecedent narrative and are often openly set against those readings that understand the gospel in terms of fulfilment. The debate is a significant one and we can hardly expect to resolve it here, but it does bring into sharper focus the fact that the coming of the Messiah in no way emerges as a natural outworking of Israel's service of God. The gospel may be the fulfilment of Old Testament hopes, but those hopes themselves are shaped by the incapacities of humanity, including Israel, by the need for God to act on behalf of his people. The advent of the Messiah is a radical act of deliverance by God, unmerited by his people, and it is vital to our understanding of the identity of the church that we maintain such a conviction.

The advent of the Messiah is bound up also with the fate of the temple. As we have already noted, the problem of sin in the Old Testament results in the loss of the divine presence: the temple is left empty and is then destroyed. Even after the work of Ezra and Nehemiah, there is a sense that the glory is absent from the temple. Part of the messianic hope, particularly as it is developed in Zechariah, is that the Davidic heir will rebuild the temple and ensure the restoration of God's glory or the divine presence to it. Again, there is a quite striking emphasis in the New Testament on the church as temple (e.g., in 2 Cor. 6:16; 1 Pet. 2:5), a theme intertwined with the image of the church as the body of Christ. The church, then, becomes seen as the dwelling place for the divine

---

9. J. Louis Martyn, *Theological Issues in the Letters of Paul* (Edinburgh: T. & T. Clark, 1997); Douglas Harinck, *Paul Among the Postliberals: Pauline Theology Beyond Christendom and Modernity* (Grand Rapids: Brazos, 2003); Douglas Campbell, *The Deliverance of God: An Apocalyptic Re-Reading of Justification in Paul* (Grand Rapids: Eerdmans, 2009).

glory, and this itself is seen as the consequence of the death and resurrection of Jesus: sin has been dealt with, the old reality crucified and new one established, the temple torn down and rebuilt in three days (John 2:20–22).

Clearly, the death and resurrection of Jesus is pivotal to this renewal and this has a radical impact upon the understanding of the suffering of believers. Those sufferings are depicted as a participation in the suffering of the Christ and are potentially reconfigured as redemptive for the world. Even as the Messiah gives himself for the church, so the church gives itself for the world, overcoming evil by sacrifice. Most strikingly, this is taken up in the book of Revelation, with the church's resistance to Babylon, to the beasts and to their master, the dragon, a matter of following in the footsteps of the Lamb: believers are witnesses (martyrs), whose own martyrdom is effective in the war against evil because it is a participation in the work of Jesus, the great Witness.[10] Again, then, hope becomes redefined by Christology, a concept now capable of taking the suffering of God's people into a new redemptive framework. While most vividly depicted, perhaps, in Revelation, such ideas are more widely found in the New Testament (e.g., in 2 Cor. 1:5–6; 4:10; Phil. 3:10; Col. 1:24; 1 Pet. 4:13).

Temple imagery relates, however, to a further key concept of New Testament hope: the presence of the Spirit in the church. The centrality of the Spirit to the gospel can be seen in texts such as Galatians 3:2, 5, 14 and in the thrust of 2 Corinthians 1 – 5, where the new covenant is specifically the covenant of the Spirit (2 Cor. 3:6). It is impossible to resist the impression that the relatively small number of texts in the Old Testament that speak of the Spirit as an eschatological reality have taken on disproportionate significance in the early church, particularly the Ezekiel texts. The importance of this is that the presence of the divine glory with, or within, the temple-church represents the fulfilment of the prophetic expectation of a transformed, renewed people, cleansed and divinely constituted to live in proper communion with God and to function properly in his service. The vivifying role of the Spirit, his function as *paraclete* (John 14:16–17, 25–26; 15:26–27; 16:7–11) and his moral leadership of the church all connect to this theme in the New Testament writings. In fact, this complex of church and Spirit is also key to the narrative of Acts, where the astonishing fact that the Spirit is being received by Gentiles leads to the discussion and decision of the Jerusalem council that the Gentiles, too, are being brought into the rebuilt tent of David (Acts 15:16). Arguably, the narrative of Acts is dominated by the account of the Spirit's reception, from Pentecost to

---

10. See Richard Bauckham, *Theology of the Book of Revelation* (Cambridge: Cambridge University Press, 1993), pp. 66–108.

the Jerusalem council, and the consequent shift of attention to the Gentile mission.

The reason I stress this point so heavily is twofold. First, the complex of Christ-Spirit-temple is basic to, and is developed by, the broad New Testament theme of 'new creation'. The theme is most extensively worked out by Paul in 2 Corinthians 3 – 5, where the apostle's description of the New Covenant as the covenant of the Spirit (2 Cor. 3:6, see above) leads eventually to the statement that if anyone is in Christ they are 'new creation' (2 Cor. 5:17). Paul's grammar here is interesting: the statement is made without any verbs, so that it is literally: 'If anyone in Christ – new creation.' As such, it resists the traditional rendering that represents the individual believer as a distinct new creation, whereby the significance of the second half of the statement is limited by the first. Rather, the grammar suggests the individual in Christ to be part of a bigger cosmic reality of new creation, a reading that makes better sense of the following statement that 'the old things have passed away, the new things have come'.[11]

Such an emphasis also emerges, of course, in Romans 8, especially verses 22–23, where the regenerative work taking place in believers is understood to represent their relocation from the flesh-governed world to the Spirit-governed world: 'you are not in the flesh; you are in the Spirit' (Rom. 8:9). When we consider the starting point for our reflections on hope – the creation account and the fall from properly shaped relationality into conflict – the significance of this theme of new creation may be recognized. The believer, in Christ and in the Spirit, participates in a new reality in which the legacy of the fall is reversed for ever. The use of temple imagery for the church is important to this: that building was always at the heart of the covenant and constituted a space within which the relationship between God and his creatures would be maintained, where the Glory would dwell within his rebellious world, and around which the plans for salvation to come to the world through Israel would revolve. The great texts of hope in the Old Testament, particularly those with creational themes, centre on this place: nations will flock to Zion (the mountain on which the temple is built) even as God institutes the new creation (Isa. 65), from the altar of the temple a river will flow that will revivify the earth (Ezek. 47).[12] Imagery from these texts is explicitly drawn upon at points in the New

---

11. This is my own translation, stressing the neuter and plural forms of the substantives, 'old' and 'new'.
12. See T. Desmond Alexander and Simon Gathercole (eds.), *Heaven on Earth: The Temple in Biblical Theology* (Carlisle: Paternoster, 2004).

Testament, notably in Revelation 21 – 22, with the description of the Bride. The fact that the eschatological temple is explicitly associated with the church, though, is important. The new creation is not yet a universal reality; it is a reality only for those in Christ (2 Cor. 5:17). The cosmos groans, waiting for the liberation that will be realized only when the children of God are revealed, when their adoption is complete (Rom. 8:19–23). It is in, from and through the church, then, as the community of people in Christ that the blessings of new creation flow to the world. In the church, the basic relationship that was broken, between God and humanity, has been restored and from this healing, other healings take place, with all the ethical significance of that truth. As we are led by the Spirit, we are led into an outward-looking Christ-likeness, manifest in 'love, joy, peace, patience, kindness, generosity, faithfulness, gentleness, and self-control' (Gal. 5:22–23).

This, though, leads us to the second key reason for stressing the centrality of the Spirit to our hope. In addition to its obvious missional dimension, the sealing of believers with the Spirit also represents the expectation of the church, the 'not yet' aspect of her eschatology. Paul's description of the seal as an 'instalment' (*arrabōn*) in 2 Corinthians 1:22 highlights this and reveals the essence of Christian hope: a full and thoroughgoing Spirituality – the capitalization is deliberate – when God will truly be all in all. Such an existence is described in 1 Corinthians 15, which is not an account of a bodiless resurrection, but rather of a Spiritual one. The cosmic expectations of Pauline theology, no less than the personal, also represent the transformation of physical reality into Spiritual, and the great sweep of Romans 8 reflects this. We must, of course, stress the conquest of death as an enemy and the hope of immortality, but that aspect of our hope is given its force by the kind of existence that will be experienced by the church at the resurrection.

What needs to be stressed is that this, too, represents a radical transformation, resulting from the parousia (1 Cor. 15:51–52) and not from the development or ascent of the church. The return of Christ thus cuts across any progressivist reading of church history: the church exists between two advents and must see itself as a community of hope shaped by those two realities, incapable of achieving the perfection that awaits prior to its Saviour's return.[13] Hope, as Paul notes in 1 Corinthians 13, remains.

---

13. See Richard Bauckham, 'The Future of Jesus Christ', in *The Cambridge Companion to Jesus*, ed. M. Bockmuehl (Cambridge: Cambridge University Press, 2001), pp. 265–280.

From the Bible to the church's mission

Clearly we have only scratched the surface of the biblical themes of hope so far, and have done so with limited concern to differentiate the distinctive contours of each writer, but what we have noted allows us to reflect on the mission of the church and the ethics of that mission. Essentially, of course, the mission of the church is the outworking of this hope. The church participates in God's work of reconciling to himself those who have 'no hope and [are] without God in the world' (Eph. 2:12) and exists as the community so redeemed. This does not limit the church's mission to what is classically described as evangelism, since, as the temple of God's Spirit, the church lives in anticipation of the full renewal of the cosmos, with lives, conduct and community shaped by that anticipation and functioning as its firstfruits.

From this, of course, it follows that the hope of the church, of transformation and renewal, must be lived out. The church cannot proclaim the hope of transformation if it does not evidence that in its own life, *for it is itself the realization of hope*. This observation is not just a matter of ensuring consistency between message and life, but, more profoundly, a recognition that we are called to embody the gospel as those who have been brought from death to life. To fail to embody transformation is to live in contradiction to the nature of the church's existence. Two points are worth stressing here. First, as we have noted above, particularly in the context of our reading of Revelation, the church's embodiment of the gospel hope involves martyrdom. This is the core image in Revelation of the church's relationship to the world, and it indicates more than just sacrifice: it represents the sacrifice that is required in the resistance of evil. The saints in Revelation refuse to participate in the idolatries of Babylon, with all the systemic violence that those idolatries generate (see, for example, Rev. 17 – 18), and their resistance is depicted as a participation in the victory of the Lamb over its enemies. Such an emphasis on martyrdom is not unique to Revelation, however distinctively developed it is there: the image of believers putting to death the world or the flesh (Rom. 8:13; Col. 3:5) represents the same underlying concept, as does the requirement that we take up our cross (Matt. 16:24 and par.). As members of the church we are not simply to witness: we are to be witnesses. What must be stressed is that this defiance of the world is given meaning by a proper Christian theology of hope, which sets life in this world in a broader temporal and eternal context, and is informed definitively by the death and resurrection of Jesus. Second, the embodiment of the gospel is fundamentally social and relational. The misery of sin that has been defeated by the gospel, from which we have an exodus, is the misery of a life curved in on itself, away from God and away from others. Our hope involves the uncurving of ourselves and that is something that can only be achieved in relationship, first with God, by means of the Spirit, and beyond that with the cosmos. The church, as temple, is the place in which such relationships are restored, renewed and maintained, an observation that can be fruitfully developed through reflection on the role of the temple in Jewish and biblical theology. The place of the church, then, is emphasized by a properly configured theology of hope over against individualistic construals of the Christian life. It may be a cliché, but it bears repeating that such individualism, as a feature of our society, is a constant creeping threat to the life of the church. It is from this observation, too, that the commitment of the church to social justice proceeds. Themes of justice and equity resound throughout the Old Testament, but particularly in the texts of hope in Isaiah (see, for example, Isa. 42:1–3). As participants in the new creation, members of the church are fundamentally committed to the new world of equity that the Messiah rules and the presence of the church in different localities ought to be marked by some realization of such equity.

The final point that must be stressed is that, as a community of expectation, the church must resist the temptation to view itself and its work as part of a progression, or process, rather than in terms of partial fulfilment and anticipation. In late modernity, this is more of a risk than ever, particularly as we grow further removed from the devastation of the Great Wars and their shattering effect on the early modern myths of progress. Recessions apart, we live in a context in the late modern West in which we are surrounded by symbols of progress, carried along in the technological slipstream of Moore's Law. All of this, along with the growth of the middle classes and the acquisition of power by those outwith the elites, can lure the church into seeing itself through the lens of a new myth of progress, seduced by notions of power and effectiveness. Such notions may inevitably affect our understanding of how the church functions in relation to the political or social spheres and they can pull us away from the daily acts of martyrdom that must mark us as the people of the Lamb. For our hope to be true, it must begin and end with God.

© Grant Macaskill, 2012

5. CHURCH

Matt Jenson

Several years ago, I stepped in as the interim pastor of our little urban Nazarene church in Kansas City.[1] The church was a strange mix of seminarians and addicts in recovery, one where theological reflection was sharpened by our life together. Sandy had seen our church sign reading 'All welcome' and thought, 'That's me.' When she told Brian, our pastor, that she did not have anything to give, he wisely replied, 'That's OK, we'll give to you for a while.'

I should mention that Sandy was bipolar. She had done drugs, too, and dealt them. She had been homeless. I believe she had been a prostitute at one point. Her life had been hard, and her hope remained tenuous. I kept her gun at my place; another pastor kept her bullets. And Sandy was a lesbian. Not long after taking over for Brian, I began to get together with her for coffee and conversation. Often enough, she would want to talk about the Bible, and usually about whether homosexuality was right or wrong. She was not combative; if anything, she wanted to take Scripture seriously and face up to its demands. She was a dear member of our community, and we loved her.

I got a call later from Sandy. 'Matt,' she said, 'I just wanted to call and let you know that I'm going to leave Trinity. I've been talking with some

---

1. Thanks to Uche Anizor, Danny Carroll, Andy Draycott and Darian Lockett for helpful comments on an earlier draft of this chapter.

friends, and I want to be at a church that accepts me entirely for who I am.'

I was sad and a little surprised, having watched Sandy begin to flourish as our church embraced her. 'Sandy, have you ever felt not welcomed by us?' I asked.

'Never,' she answered.

There was little to do at that point beyond telling her that we loved her and letting her know that we would leave the light on should she want to come back home.

The mission and its church

To speak of missional ethics is to enter the realm of the church. If it is also to enter other realms – the world on the one hand and the kingdom of God on the other – the church's existence between the times witnesses to the passing character of the former and the outstanding character of the latter. The world reminds the church of the way things used to be and demonstrates the need for mission, while the kingdom spurs the mission on and is its hope.

Many discussions of church and mission in the last fifty years have come down to the question of whether and to what extent the church exists for the sake of mission, or mission for the church. These amount to debates about the relative importance of the church *vis-à-vis* the kingdom. The church certainly does not exist for its own sake, but as an agent of the kingdom, we are rightly reminded. Some, however, take this to imply a merely instrumental role for the church, or even suggest the church's expendability. We can sharpen the dilemma by asking a question: Does the church's mission of witnessing to the kingdom involve the church in a programme of planned obsolescence?

This is an attractive proposal for many who are sceptical of institutions. A more sophisticated – though, I suspect, constitutionally similar – account so foregrounds the category of apocalyptic, with its disruptive dynamic and its insistence that the coming of the kingdom can in no way be anticipated, that it appears reluctant to traffic in ecclesial continuities. An iconoclastic reminder that the church must never treat itself as an end in itself, this reminder nevertheless makes too little of the peculiar presence and power of the Spirit and the kingdom in the church.

The missional church is a witness to the kingdom. It uses a 'rhetoric of indication' to point away from itself to the triune God and his kingdom.[2] It

---

2. John Webster, *Word and Church: Essays in Church Dogmatics* (New York: T. & T. Clark, 2006), p. 124.

gives testimony to Jesus rather than drawing attention to itself. But in addition to being a witness, the missional church is the way in to the kingdom. It is the entrance to the kingdom; even more, it is where the kingdom is present on earth. We need to take care here. God has established his reign in Christ and with ease can bring it to bear outside the church, can even do so as a witness *against* a disobedient church. Still, Jesus' reign is acknowledged and celebrated in the church; the church is where the King dwells among his people. '[T]he messianic community constitutes part of the messianic rule – there must be an Israel in which God rules.'[3] The mission of the church cannot, then, abandon the church.

In what follows I will consider the nature of the church, its mission and the ethics implied in and demanded by this mission. In particular, I will consider homosexuality as a test case through which to understand the church's place in our consideration of the ethics of mission and the mission of ethics. I am convinced that homosexuality is an ecclesiological question as much as, if not more than, it is a question of biblical interpretation or ethics. It is also a context in which many are tempted to abandon the church precisely for the sake of its mission, despairing, perhaps, of the church's capacity to live out the mission of God among homosexuals.

Let me be clear on what I will *not* do. First, I will not argue the morality of homosexuality *per se*. Scripture, it seems to me, speaks clearly, if only occasionally, to this and insists that homosexuality runs against the grain of God's good creation. Nor do arguments that punt to eschatology evade such a conclusion, as whatever else new creation means it means divine vindication of creation.[4]

---

3. William J. Abraham, *The Logic of Evangelism* (Grand Rapids: Eerdmans, 1989), p. 93. This is the backbone of Oliver O'Donovan's argument that Christendom is a result, albeit at times ambivalent, of Christian mission in *The Desire of the Nations: Rediscovering the Roots of Political Theology* (Cambridge: Cambridge University Press, 1999).

4. Much can, has been and should be said about the Bible's understanding, evaluation and response to homosexuality. Most helpful for their clarity and nuance are Richard B. Hays, *The Moral Vision of the New Testament: Community, Cross, New Creation: A Contemporary Introduction to New Testament Ethics* (San Francisco: HarperSanFrancisco, 1996), pp. 379–406; Oliver O'Donovan, *Church in Crisis: The Gay Controversy and the Anglican Communion* (Eugene: Cascade Books, 2008); and Wesley Hill, *Washed and Waiting: Reflections on Christian Faithfulness and Homosexuality* (Grand Rapids: Zondervan, 2010). Hill's is certainly the most thoughtful, honest and hopeful account of the faithful struggle of gay Christians I have read. I follow

In saying too little on this point, I acknowledge the partiality and provisionality of all theological speech. One simply cannot say everything. At the same time, I suspect that the hubbub over the rightness or wrongness of homosexual activity, along with its polarizing energy, has distracted the church from the more difficult questions surrounding the character of its mission amongst gay people. These questions will occupy us in what follows.

Second, in considering the character of the church's mission, I will be less concerned with decisional ethics than with wisdom and the cultivation of Christian character in community. If by 'ethics' we mean the establishment and application of moral norms, I worry that we limit ourselves prematurely to affirmations and denials rather than lengthier descriptions of how the gospel of our Lord Jesus Christ shapes our life together. We have itchy trigger fingers when it comes to sexual ethics, when what we need is patience and careful pastoral discernment. The most pressing problems of discernment with regard to homosexuality do not concern *whether* it is right or wrong but *how* we are to live together as God's people in hospitable holiness.

The church is your family

The family is in crisis, they tell us. It is under attack from novel elements in society, or perhaps older marginal elements recently emerged into the light of day. Maybe it is because of the rise in divorce rates, the absence of fathers in urban centres, a *laissez-faire* approach to sexuality and the moral meandering that accompanies it. Children are introduced to sex at an alarmingly early age, long before they have attained the maturity in which they might engage in responsible moral deliberation, long before they have begun to consider consequence at all. Perhaps, too, we ought to lay the blame at the feet of our technologies and the hyperactive, overconnected, yet alienated lives we now lead.

Whatever the reason, they are right. The family *is* in crisis, though that is nothing new. What they seldom notice, however, is the deepest source of the crisis – the incarnation of the Son of God. The one in whom God and humanity

---

his preference to limit 'gay' and 'homosexual' to adjectival rather than nominative roles, insisting that the noun, that grammar of identification, be reserved for depictions of our being in Christ. O'Donovan makes the point about creation's vindication frequently in his writing, most systematically in *Resurrection and Moral Order: An Outline for Evangelical Ethics*, 2nd ed. (Grand Rapids: Eerdmans, 1994).

are united, divides; the great Shepherd of the sheep gathers, yes, but he also scatters. Consider this stout clarification of mission:

> Do not think that I have come to bring peace to the earth; I have not come to bring peace, but a sword.
>
> > For I have come to set a man against his father,
> > and a daughter against her mother,
> > and a daughter-in-law against her mother-in-law;
> > and one's foes will be members of one's own household.
>
> Whoever loves father or mother more than me is not worthy of me; and whoever loves son or daughter more than me is not worthy of me; and whoever does not take up the cross and follow me is not worthy of me. Those who find their life will lose it, and those who lose their life for my sake will find it. (Matt. 10:34–39)

We do not often attend to the context of that final gnomic remark. The life I am called to lose as I walk the way of Jesus is my family life. Nor does Jesus reserve such words for others. On learning that his family has come to visit him, he tartly replies, '"Who are my mother and my brothers?" And looking at those who sat around him, he said, "Here are my mother and my brothers! Whoever does the will of God is my brother and sister and mother"' (Mark 3:33–35). Jesus puts the family in crisis.

When Peter, understandably, asks, 'Look, we have left everything and followed you. What then will we have?' Jesus reassures him that 'everyone who has left houses or brothers or sisters or father or mother or children or fields, for my name's sake, will receive a hundredfold, and will inherit eternal life' (Matt. 19:27, 29). Jesus himself begins to fulfil this promise as he invites the disciples into his filial relationship with the Father. They may have left family for Jesus' name's sake, but they have received a Father in heaven and brothers and sisters who do the Father's will. The church, then, is a family; indeed, it is *your* family. As one recent writer puts it, 'Water is thicker than blood.'[5]

Let us look briefly at our new Father, his Son and the new siblings that make up this new family. J. I. Packer aptly writes:

> [Y]ou sum up the whole of New Testament religion if you describe it as the knowledge of God as one's holy Father. If you want to judge how well a person understands Christianity, find out how much he makes of the thought of being

---

5. Jana Marguerite Bennett, *Water is Thicker than Blood: An Augustinian Theology of Marriage and Singleness* (New York and Oxford: Oxford University Press, 2008).

God's child, and having God as his Father. If this is not the thought that prompts and controls his worship and prayers and his whole outlook on life, it means that he does not understand Christianity very well at all. For everything that Christ taught, everything that makes the New Testament new, and better than the Old, everything that is distinctively Christian as opposed to merely Jewish, is summed up in the knowledge of the Fatherhood of God. 'Father' is the Christian name for God . . . Our understanding of Christianity cannot be better than our grasp of adoption.[6]

Note well the link in these last two sentences. To call God 'Father', as Jesus invites us to do, is the privilege of those who have been sealed with the Spirit of adoption (Rom. 8:15).[7] The nineteenth-century infatuation with 'the fatherhood of God and the brotherhood of man' is mere sentiment as long as it remains disconnected from our adoption in Christ. I know God as my Father and those in the church as my sisters and brothers because Jesus has called me brother (Heb. 2:11–12) and because the Spirit enables me to call God 'Father' (Rom. 8:15). The love of the Father who adopts us in his Son is the basis of the church, the content of its teaching and the context of its mission (see Eph. 1:4–5).

How, though, ought the church to speak of the fatherhood of God, especially in a day when the very idea of a father carries such baggage? Here Barth is helpful:

Faith in God the Father must be proclaimed in such a way that implicitly at once, and unconfused by recollection of other fatherhoods, faith in the only-begotten Son may be impressed upon the hearers.[8]

Theologians who propose going *beyond* God the Father protest too much. Theirs is a well-worn and a short path, one that stops far short of the Father, having been distracted, confused and waylaid by 'other fatherhoods'. Nor will it do to manage our industriously idolatrous minds by downgrading the language of paternity to metaphor. 'Father' is more a name than a title for God in Scripture; more specifically, it is a word in and by which we may address the God of Israel and Jesus Christ. In praying the Lord's Prayer, we do not speak

---

6. J. I. Packer, *Knowing God* (Downers Grove: InterVarsity Press, 1993), pp. 201–202.
7. In the Old Testament, Israel corporately called God 'Father', but only the king could claim that relationship as an individual (see 2 Sam. 7:14; Ps. 2:7). My thanks to Danny Carroll for this observation.
8. Karl Barth, *Church Dogmatics* I/1, p. 392.

to one who is something like a father, but to the very particular, holy God and Father of our Lord Jesus Christ, and the Father 'from whom every family in heaven and on earth takes its name' (Eph. 3:14). Packer is right: 'Father' is God's name. God *is* Father, the Father of the Son. He is not merely *like* a father. In fact, he is very unlike most fathers, in the glorious perfection of his fatherhood. And Jesus really is the Son of this Father, such that 'sonship' is the pattern of discipleship. To follow Jesus is to walk in the way of the Son as a son or daughter of God. To speak of the 'sonship' of believers is not to capitulate to patriarchy but to foreground the Son in whom we are made children of God. Thus, while we deploy a metaphor in speaking of the church as 'family', this metaphor conveys significant ontological depth and reflects the realism intrinsic to the language of kinship in the New Testament. The church is God's family in a much more robust sense than it is, say, the ark of salvation.

Calvin instructs us well. For while he recognizes as acutely as any – and long before Feuerbach and Freud – the labyrinthine character of the human mind, he does not shrink from confidently speaking of, and to, the Father. He excoriates speculation, but it does not occur to him that his only remaining option is the cynicism of endless deferral. He insists that the only fit witness to God is God himself, a claim that even *requires* such deferral if a witness is absent. But it is not. It is present in Scripture and the Spirit's inner testimony in believers, and so we may and must address the Father with confidence.

The Father is first father of the Son, Jesus. Only by virtue of Jesus' invitation to his adopted brothers and sisters may we join him in praying to 'our Father'. Hence Barth's insistence that faith in the Father entails faith in the Son. And this Son, this one who is the 'exact imprint of God's very being' (Heb. 1:3), extends the invitation to join his family at the table to the most unlikely and unlikeable. That notorious fellowship he carries on with sinners is what makes Jesus' new family so shocking. Not only does it relativize our biological and ethnic allegiances, but it redirects our allegiance to a group of – let's be honest – people with whom we would rather not fraternize. God loves sinners, and Jesus forgives his enemies, reconciling irreconcilable parties in his one body through the cross (Eph. 2:16). *This* Father and his Son invite people into a family where people who do not belong together, belong together. The church has an inherently desegregating orientation. The person sitting in the chair next to me could be *anyone* – young or poor or married. It is a place where people whom we would not pick for friends become our brothers and sisters.

For this reason, affinity-based churches – and affinity-based missions – distort the logic of the gospel. The church does not, and therefore cannot, promise to be a place for people to meet people just like them. If there is any place for homogeneous units in a church, it is only a peripheral and penultimate place, one that fills a gap and looks to groups of people who are nothing like one another.

After all, we believe in the holy *catholic* church, the church founded on difference. The church includes within itself a number of 'natural' divisions, and its catholicity is the pudding that proves the words of Paul: 'There is no longer Jew or Greek, there is no longer slave or free, there is no longer male and female; for all of you are one in Christ Jesus' (Gal. 3:28). In her catholicity, the church points to the future, to a day when every tongue and tribe and nation will be worshipping before the throne of God and of the Lamb.

Lovely words, these. If they are true, though, they are not easily enfleshed. The church may witness to the kingdom, but in so doing it occupies a painfully distended space between the kingdom's arrival in Jesus and its completion in the eschaton. It rejoices in the presence of the kingdom in the Spirit (Rom. 14:17), even as it yearns and prays for the kingdom to come (Matt. 6:10; Luke 11:2).

Andrew Walls identifies two principles in tension with one another, though both are derived from the gospel of Jesus Christ.[9] The indigenizing principle describes the way in which the gospel makes its home in the world. Never without a cultural form, the good news of Jesus encounters a new sphere and takes on the dress, speech and customs of that culture. The gospel is culturally relative, in the sense that it is not more or less at home in any culture. On the other hand, the pilgrim principle describes the way in which the gospel cannot make its home in the world. Instead it evokes in the church a desire for a better city.

The church as family serves as promise and threat. It is the promise that the gospel really does make its home in the world, that the Father sets up a household of children adopted in the Son and sealed by the Spirit, that it establishes us in the church among a people with whom we may go on pilgrimage to the eternal city. The church, we might say, is our home away from home. It is threat, too, though. Consider the havoc Jesus' words about what makes for family might wreak on the nuclear family, living in 'the indolent peace of a clannish warmth in relation to these persons, with its necessary implication of cold war against all others'.[10] Jesus calls such homebodies to go on pilgrimage to the heavenly city in the company of his larger family.

---

9. Andrew Walls, 'The Gospel as Prisoner and Liberator of Culture', in *The Missionary Movement in Christian History: Studies in the Transmission of Faith* (Maryknoll: Orbis Books, 1996), pp. 3–15.
10. Barth, *Church Dogmatics* IV/2, p. 551.

If the church as family is bad news for cosy nuclear families, it is decidedly good news for single people, including those who are gay. (Of course, it is not *only* bad news to families, as we have already seen. Nor is it simply good news for singles. I suspect, though, that we are sufficiently aware of these things to leave them without comment.) To those who may never have biological children, the church issues a call to spiritual paternity and maternity. To those who see no prospect for the joy, intimacy and mutual help of marriage, the church offers itself. Consider just one example: Joe Hellerman argues that the closest and most important relationships in antiquity were between siblings, with the expectation being that one's emotional needs would be met first by one's brothers and sisters.[11] Paul's incessantly fraternal language, then, far from being the tepid greeting many Anglo-Americans suspect it is, calls Christian brothers and sisters to see one another as intimates. Indeed, it suggests that those who look to their spouses exclusively to have their needs met are settling, missing out on the richest fellowship of joy, intimacy and mutual help imaginable – the household of God. All of which, again, is good news for gay people. But news has to be heard, and to be heard it has to be understood. We will turn now to consider the intelligibility of the gospel as the church seeks to proclaim the Word among gay people.

Making sense of the gospel among gay people

We have a tendency to consider homosexuality abstractly, abstracting from the life of the gay person as well as the life of the church in which the proclamation of the gospel and the calling forth of faith's obedience makes sense. The injunction to repent and believe often stands alone, a withering scrap of moralism dislodged from the evangelical context of encounter between the holy, loving God and his sinful, wayward creature. But obedience requires that sense be made of a command, and sense demands context.

> Commands are events that occur within a relationship. They are given *by* somebody *to* somebody at a particular juncture. The order barked out at the new recruits by the

---

11. See Hellerman's extensive work on the church as family in *When the Church Was a Family: Recapturing Jesus' Vision for Authentic Christian Community* (Nashville: B. & H. Academic, 2009); *The Ancient Church as Family* (Minneapolis: Fortress Press, 2001); and *Jesus and the People of God: Reconfiguring Ethnic Identity* (Sheffield: Sheffield Phoenix Press, 2007), pp. 265–287.

sergeant major needs a parade ground for its context. There must be an understood relation between barker and barked-at. Otherwise what is barked can have no reference, and if it has no reference, it cannot be obeyed ... Even Abraham had to reckon that this was YHWH speaking to him [and commanding him to sacrifice his son], the same YHWH whose promise had led him out of Mesopotamia to the land his descendants had to occupy, who could bring his purposes to bear in the teeth of seeming contradiction.[12]

Even radical divine commands like God's to Abraham make *some* sense. For all its merits in putting before us a bracing account of obedience to the God whose ways are not our ways, Kierkegaard's evocation of God's command and Abraham's response nearly empties it of any sense. The church's mission requires a careful unfolding of the gospel's intelligibility in the lives of its hearers. This need not – and indeed must not – suggest that the gospel will be anything less than a scandal, but it does suggest that we ought to help people understand the nature of the scandal. The cross is foolishness, but too often the sinful folly of the church obscures the world's vantage on Calvary. In its mission, the church articulates the gospel's sense; it does not accommodate the gospel to its listeners.

The Spirit authenticates the good news about Jesus in the witnessing community. It is the community's truthfulness that demonstrates the gospel's truth. Jesus asks the Father to 'sanctify [his disciples] in the truth' and prays that all who believe in him might 'become completely one, so that the world may know that you have sent me and have loved them even as you have loved me' (John 17:17, 23). That is, the church witnesses to Jesus; like John the Baptist, it gives testimony to him rather than drawing attention to itself (John 1:8). But it is precisely this testimony which the Spirit motivates, animates and appropriates as Jesus draws all people to himself (John 12:32). The church gives sense to the gospel in two ways – through articulate speech and in a fitting way of life.

Contextualization, then, just is the church's truthfulness at a certain place, in a certain time. It is the way the church speaks and lives gospel truth truthfully. Contextualization does not derive from the church's mission, nor does it crown it. It *is* the church's mission. Here is where we have failed, tragically and persistently, in offering and making sense of the gospel among people with gay desires. We have failed to elucidate Jesus' promise of a new family

---

12. O'Donovan, *Church in Crisis*, pp. 70–71.

to those we have called to say 'no' to such desires.[13] And as long as we fail to illustrate Jesus' identification of those who do the will of the Father as his family, we have nothing to say to gays and lesbians. It may be that some will hear the Word of God despite our having garbled it, but that will be a case of salvation *despite* the church's witness, a case when we not only are not the light of the world but are – at best – a lampshade.

Failing to tell the truth to gay people

A year or so after Sandy called to say she was leaving Trinity, she committed suicide. I cannot help but wonder whether she would have been alive today had she remained among us, a frail and fractured family, sure, but one in which she would have been taught the ways of repentance, forgiveness and reconciliation.

She had been lied to, had been told that a church that would call her to repent could not be a church in which she would find a home. Yet, along with my anger at those who would so mislead her comes a sense that it is our fault, too. We have failed to tell the truth to gay people for so long.

Churches keen to adhere to Scripture's teaching on homosexuality typically fail in two ways. First, they compromise the doctrine of justification by grace alone through faith alone. The Reformation's great gift to the church lies in its insistence that God loves sinners, and only sinners. This austere confession evinces a certain anthropological pessimism, yes, but it does so in the service of evangelical confidence. God may only love sinners, but he *does love sinners*. My failure to qualify for the gospel on the basis of a spiritual résumé ought, in good Lutheran fashion, to drive me to rejoice in the freedom of the gospel. But we are curiously inconsistent in announcing the gospel to gay people. The nervous addendums that we tack onto presentations of the gospel, postscripts that come in the conditional form of 'but you had better stop being gay!', are

---

13. Philip Turner is right: 'Sexual relations themselves are not necessary as a cure for loneliness. What is necessary is the fellowship of men and women in Christ. This is the word beyond "no" the church has to speak to single people. If it dares to speak, it will find not only that its common life is transformed beyond all recognition, but also that its teachings begin to appear to single and married people alike as a treasure to be shared rather than as a burden to be inflicted.' See Philip Turner, 'Sex and the Single Life', *First Things* (May 1993).

evangelically insipid; more, they are treacherous. They reflect a diseased hesitancy to embody the radical hospitality of God in Christ.

A second failure stems from an over-realized eschatology. If we succeed in consistently articulating and embodying the gospel of grace, we still often enough fail to take seriously the intransigence of sin. This is a failure of what Richard Hays calls 'the art of eschatological moral discernment', which 'lies in working out how to live lives free from bondage to sin without presuming to be translated prematurely into a condition that is free from "the sufferings of the present time" (Rom. 8:18)'.[14] What would it have looked like, I wonder, to anticipate, with Sandy, 'the freedom of the glory of the children of God', even while we 'groan inwardly while we await for adoption, the redemption of our bodies' (Rom. 8:21–23)? Here is a litmus test: What would you do if you knew that a gay Christian man in your church would always be attracted to other men?

Staging an evangelical literacy campaign

These days, it will take time to make sense of the gospel, whether among gay or straight people. We occupy a strange moment, where evangelical literacy – an intellectual 'competence' in the things of the gospel – is disastrously low, even as we are saturated in the vocabulary of salvation. We hold to the outward linguistic form of godliness but deny its power (2 Tim. 3:5). Or, rather, we inhabit a form of whose content we are ignorant. Having long ago denied its power, now we forget it. Still, as Aristotle insisted, forms inhere in things; and so, if we have evacuated the form of godliness of its substance, something has taken its place – and in so doing distorted the form.

Anglo-American society is both over- and under-saturated with Christianity. Its patterns and forms of thinking are everywhere, but they have been hollowed out, the husk robbed of its kernel. Many missional efforts fail precisely in that they assume that familiarity with the husk yields knowledge of the kernel. We call people to repent and believe the gospel, not realizing the impoverished state of our language. What is repentance? What constitutes belief? And does the gospel have anything to do with life, or is it something about how to go to heaven when I die?

What we need is a literacy campaign. As a church we need to think of our missional efforts as teaching the world to (in Stanley Hauerwas's words) speak Christian. The strategic challenge, and it is also an ethical one, comes in

---

14. Hays, *The Moral Vision of the New Testament*, p. 394.

determining what to do when people think they are already literate. The church has long turned to some form of catechumenate to instruct people in the faith, though rarely has it had to consider how one might catechize people who have never been catechized but who think they have been.

Here, in contrast to countless programmes and proposals, we do well to take our time. Many deride an evangelism mill that churns out decisions without ever making disciples. We may be zealous to see people converted to Christ, but we are so impatient. William Abraham suggests we think of and practise evangelism as initiation into the kingdom of God. He reminds us that 'becoming a Christian is a complex and radical affair', being 'at once corporate, cognitive, moral, experiential, operational, and disciplinary'. It includes conversion, baptism, an introduction to the twofold love command, the creed and the Spirit's gifts, as well as the disciplines of the spiritual life.[15] Such a layered account of initiation into the kingdom of God corresponds to the comprehensive character of Jesus' call. And, of course, 'the higher the initial demands [say, taking up one's cross and following Jesus as one struggles with homosexuality], the greater the need for communal support'.[16] To put it bluntly: the church is right to tell gay people the good news and call them to a life of discipleship *if and only if* it is willing to live as their family. If the church is unwilling to be family to gay people, it has no business giving them the gospel.

Perhaps, though, this is another case of a self-important church clogging the process of discipleship. After all, the early church eagerly and quickly baptized new believers, often immediately after they had heard the news about Jesus and responded in repentance and belief. Why put added burdens on people? Might this involve a compromise of the gospel, a smuggling in of works through the back door of grace? Gerhard Lohfink explains the rapid belief and baptism of the first Christians: they had already been catechized in the life of Israel. Even the prominent Gentiles were 'God-fearers', receiving extensive instruction from Jewish teachers; the Ethiopian eunuch may not have been able to understand the Isaiah scroll, but he carried it with him and took the long journey to Jerusalem to worship (Acts 8:26–39). 'Judaism was the catechumenate of the primitive Church.'[17] Instruction in the faith is non-negotiable, then, and was present as part of Christian initiation from the beginning.

---

15. Abraham, *The Logic of Evangelism*, pp. 82, 103, 142.
16. Ibid., p. 129.
17. See Gerhard Lohfink, *Does God Need the Church? Toward a Theology of the People of God* (Collegeville: The Liturgical Press, 1999), p. 268. Without original emphasis.

Evangelism is initiation into the kingdom of God. But it is *only* initiation. It is merely a whetting of the appetite, in which the new believer tastes for the first time and sees that God is good. Through catechesis, we learn that those who follow in the way of Jesus are those who seek first the kingdom of God and his righteousness (Matt. 6:33). To be a Christian is to desire the kingdom into which we have been initiated. In so doing, we join God's pilgrim people:

> They confessed that they were strangers and foreigners on the earth, for people who speak in this way make it clear that they are seeking a homeland. If they had been thinking of the land that they had left behind, they would have had opportunity to return. But as it is, they desire a better country, that is, a heavenly one. Therefore God is not ashamed to be called their God; indeed, he has prepared a city for them. (Heb. 11:13–16)

In bowing to Christ as King, a person renounces sin, death and the devil and confesses that her citizenship is in heaven (Phil. 3:20). But while such a renunciation marks a transfer of allegiance, its content is only vaguely defined. It acts as a promissory note in which the Christian pledges to say 'no' to the kingdom of darkness and 'yes' to the kingdom of light.

Still, a promissory note does not eliminate the need for moral discernment, formation and struggle in the ensuing years. As in marriage, in moving through the Christian life one may have good reason to affirm both the surpassing goodness of this life as well as its poignant hardship. Many will admit, in candid moments, that they likely would not have begun following Jesus had they known the narrowness of his road. While people lay a foundation for faithfulness in covenantal promises, the shape and significance of that faithfulness comes later, as they set into the promise *keeping* by which the Lord builds his house. In conversion, a person pledges to desire the kingdom and enters into a family in whose company her desires will be transformed so that she can, with them, make good on that pledge.

What to do with what we want

Perhaps, the critic might say, the church is a big family in which a person can pretend – at least for a while – that she does not want or need sexual intimacy. In such a case, the church might offer a palliative strategy. It might delay the onset of loneliness, perhaps even stay it for quite some time. But such sublimation is false, a re-routing of desire that amounts to a foolish attempt to extinguish it. On this read, the best the gay person can hope for in the church is to fit in, but only at the expense of killing or closeting desire.

But this is to misunderstand chastity (a too common mistake), and it is to misunderstand the church. The chaste life is far from a life without desire; and the church is, if anything, 'the truly erotic mode of existence'.[18] It is that mode of existence in which people are drawn out of themselves in desiring reconciled fellowship with strangers and enemies. All other modes of existence are not truly erotic, insofar as *eros* carries a person towards that which is truly, deeply different from her; and it is only in the church that she truly learns to desire others as others. In Augustine's words, *Desiderium sinus cordis* – 'Longing makes the heart deep.' Jamie Smith makes the Augustinian point that all cultural formation, and here we may include ecclesial formation, is the formation of desire.[19] To be human, most basically, is to be a lover. Smith's zeal to put the ways, objects and ordering of our loves at the heart of anthropology – and if anthropology, then also ecclesiology – is exactly right.

The witness of single Christians, straight or gay, is to the place of desire's ultimate fulfilment, which is in the marriage of Christ and the church. Apart from this witness, Christians, who rightly exult in the gifts of God, might not be able to distinguish the gift from the Giver, and would soon enough fall into the idolatry of thinking that the uniting of a man and woman in marriage was the point of things, rather than itself an indicator of the union of Christ and the church. Single Christians, those persistently odd figures, remind the church of the passing quality of even the most beautiful and holy of marriages.

Fair enough, but what do we *do* about what we want? The Anglo-American assumption is as naïve as it is unquestioned: Express yourself! A long genealogy could be traced here, one that would include French revolutionaries, fastidious German philosophers, Romantic poets, Austrian psychoanalysts, historicists, feminists, deconstructionists, Madonna and Lady Gaga. This tradition passes on good common sense in its suspicion of the power politics in play as individuals are silenced 'for the good of the whole'. Too often, calls for the curbing of desire really amount to the curbing of *some* people's desires for the sake of the expression of others'.

But expressionism naïvely suggests that desire can be reduced to nature, with nurture left out in the cold. It fails to recognize that all desire, while having

---

18. John D. Zizioulas, *Communion and Otherness: Further Studies in Personhood and the Church*, ed. Paul McPartlan (London and New York: T. & T. Clark, 2006), p. 79.
19. James K. A. Smith, *Desiring the Kingdom: Worship, Worldview, and Cultural Formation* (Grand Rapids: Baker Academic, 2009).

roots in nature's soil, has been formed, deformed, transformed by countless influences, patterns, habits and practices. And it is this, not that I am merely 'born this way', that ennobles humanity. The Fathers 'qualify rationality with freedom: the human being is distinguished from the animals by his or her freedom to take a distance from nature and even from his or her own nature'.[20]

Some desires, broadcast as self-expression, amount to little more than what Luther calls a curving in on oneself. As such there is none of the ecstatic character of self-expression, but instead a blocking of all constraints that ends in a perverse self-exile. This kind of diseased self-expression, though touted as a courageous public act, could scarcely be more private, precisely in its refusal to speak in order to be heard. Or perhaps it is better to say that in such a moment, one speaks only in order to be heard by oneself.

Clearly, untrammelled expression is an insufficient response to repression. Critical of these poles, the Christian tradition has long recognized that human flourishing requires a fully responsible self – a self created for and called to obedience, capable of sin and invited to confession, repentance and new life in Christ. To confess before God and the church that 'I have greatly sinned . . . through my fault, through my fault, through my most grievous fault' is, perhaps surprisingly, the paradigmatic act of the responsible self. The question, then, does not concern desire's expression or repression but, antecedent to either of these relatively minor issues, its proper formation as a desire for Christ and his kingdom.

In speaking of desire's formation, we run the risk of disproportion. One of the most liberating words the church has to offer gay people is that their desires, though deep and systemic, are not the story of their lives. There is much more to them than their desires, certainly much more than their sexual desires. A delicate pastoral touch is called for in taking gay Christians seriously *as gay* while insisting, against the prevailing winds of the day, that to discover in oneself a desire is not to discover oneself without remainder. In fact, the discovery of desire is more like a question than an answer. To know myself wanting something, strongly and spontaneously, is to ask a question about who

---

20. Zizioulas, *Communion and Otherness*, p. 39. Related is Paul Griffiths' insistence that 'our desires are naturally open rather than closed, protean rather than formed, awaiting direction rather than already under orders . . . the plasticity of desire is distinctively human'. Hence the inevitability of formation. 'The weight of our catechized appetites drags us in a certain direction: The eyes of the glutton follow the food, while those of the devout seek the traces of God.' See Paul Griffiths, 'The Nature of Desire', *First Things* (December 2009).

I am, where I come from and where I am going. And this is a question best answered by the gospel.

We want so much just to get what we want, but upon doing so we offer up a lament:

> 'It wasn't what I really wanted!' is the familiar complaint of a disappointed literalism. To all desire its appropriate self-questioning: what wider, broader good does this desire serve? How does it spring out of our strengths, and how does it spring out of our weaknesses? Where in relation to this desire does real fulfilment lie? It is in *interpreting* our desires that we need the wisdom of tradition, which teaches us to beware the illusory character of immediate emotional data, helping us to sort through our desires and clarify them. The true term of any desire, whether heavily laden or merely banal, is teasingly different from the mental imagination that first aroused it. And gays have no infallible introspective certainties in relation to their desires that would put them outside the common human lot of questioning. 'I became a great question to myself!' said Augustine. And it was the question of *himself* that the gospel helped him address fruitfully.[21]

Can we know ourselves at all? As those curved in on ourselves, we sin often enough and well enough that it has become a sort of 'second nature'. Of course, that which is natural is frequently that of which we are unaware. It is that which we do almost instinctually, without reflecting on it or even noticing that we are choosing to do it. As a result, our sinning is frustratingly transparent. We miss it even when, *precisely when*, we look at ourselves; we deceive ourselves just when we seek to know ourselves. Thus, unmediated introspection can hardly be expected to yield reliable self-knowledge. To know myself, I must listen to the voice of Christ in Scripture, opening myself to him in prayer, and listen to the communion of saints in the church, opening myself to them in friendship.[22] One of the ways in which we know ourselves is in narrating our lives. As we do so, we discover who we are in reflecting on the shape of our lives and in subjecting our stories to public scrutiny. Our brothers and sisters in the church may tell us that we have told the story badly,

---

21. O'Donovan, *The Church in Crisis*, pp. 112–113.
22. Note the implicit catechesis involved here. As Griffiths writes, 'Diagnosis, whether of appetite or disease, thus begins with catechesis. Without training in the agreed list of diseases and symptoms, the diagnostician can do no work.' Paul Griffiths, *Intellectual Appetite: A Theological Grammar* (Washington, DC: The Catholic University of America Press, 2009), p. 105.

that our blindness (willing or not) has distorted or obscured the picture; and they may be right. Telling our stories thus presupposes a certain self-knowledge, but it also generates such knowledge, often precisely as others question the nature and extent of the self-knowledge we claim.

In short, self-knowledge is indirect. Since there are parts of us that we simply cannot see, we need to be told who we are. Just as Jesus heard the Father speak of and the Spirit anoint his Sonship, so we will continue to need to hear the voice of the Father in the power of the Spirit speaking of our adoption as sons and daughters of God. We need the One who made us and remade us to tell us who we are, and we need those with whom we live our new lives in Christ to tell us who we are. This will, no doubt, involve us being surprised at both the beauty and the ugliness that is revealed. It will also serve as one of the primary means of our being conformed to the image of Christ, the one true human.

Gay Christians, and all Christians, need gentle reminders that their desires are not the story of their lives. Jesus is. To look to be defined, justified, validated or propped up by anyone but him is what the Bible says it is – idolatry. This is true for me when I think a wife will make my life worth living. It is true for you who are married when you look to your spouses to provide all of your self-worth. And it is true for you who struggle with homosexual desires when you allow those desires to be the story of your life.

They are not. They are *only* desires – excruciating, confusing desires, to be sure, desires that send many gay Christians careering into self-hatred, bottomless shame and relentless, hyperventilating introspection. Desires, too, that heckle and haunt you as gay Christians, and may do so for life. But not desires that tell the story of your life. No, the story of your life, the story of my life, is the story of Jesus. It is the story of a man so convinced of his Father's love that he was able to say 'no' to every unholy desire. It is the story of a man who did not think it odd or off-putting to spend time with the least of these, who thought it more worth his time to eat with money-grubbing tax collectors and sex-drenched women of questionable character. This Jesus extends his hand to touch people no-one else touches. *That* is the way he is the faithful Son of the Father in the world. And as he calls us sons and daughters of the Father, he invites us to live like it. So we, too, embrace people we would not normally embrace. And we learn, however falteringly, to walk in the way of his Spirit, saying 'no' to every unholy desire and 'yes' to fellowship with the Father, with his Son, with his Spirit and with his family in the church. This is where faithfulness and holiness take place.

In the church, the Father disciplines us, instructing and forming us in a desire for his kingdom. He does so 'for our good, in order that we may share his holiness' (Heb. 12:10). In fact, it is by learning to desire the things of God that our sinful desires are revealed for what they are. The church is desire's hospital and its school. There the Spirit heals us as we learn to frame our stories within the story of the Bible and undergo the discipline of making another than ourselves the reference point for our lives (cf. Gal. 2:20). This takes a re-imaging of life for gay Christians, a setting and seeing it in a new context, where we learn that '[t]o renounce homosexual behavior is to say yes to full, rich, abundant life.'[23] With God's family, we learn to 'seek the things that are above, where Christ is, seated at the right hand of God' (Col. 3:1). Paul does not lapse into a striving moralism here; the reason we are to seek heavenly things is that we have been raised with Christ, having died to the world, such that our lives are now hidden with him in God. Jesus has become the measure and story of our life, and all other smaller stories must be retold in light of him. Our deepest identities, we ourselves, have been reconfigured; we have been relocated to the right hand of the Father. To continue desiring the things of the flesh is like holding out for the telegraph when you have an iPhone in your pocket. That we remain fascinated by telegraphs explains why the Father 'chastises every child whom he accepts' (Heb. 12:6).

We must be wary here, too, of an over-realized eschatology. Perfecting technique in desire's education will not bring the kingdom, nor will it necessarily banish same-sex attraction. Our corporate life in the Spirit merely, though really, anticipates the fullness of the kingdom; it does not constitute it. The Spirit cultivates his fruit over time, and we cannot expect a bumper-crop of desires native to the kingdom overnight – though in this, people who struggle with gay desires differ little from garden-variety sinners saved by the kind mercy of God.

Christians with same-sex desires are so often so afraid. They have heard the jokes, have heard how freely their friends despise homosexuality. They probably despise themselves, too. And they are afraid that they cannot trust you to care for them. Marilynne Robinson writes that '[t]he antidote to fear, distrust, self-interest is always loyalty'.[24] Just imagine: What if the church were known above all for its *loyalty* towards the gay Christians in its midst? In the life-giving context of such loyalty, perhaps then gay Christians – and all of us – would be set free to turn their attention to 'learning to *struggle well*, with others, in the presence of God'.[25]

---

23. Hill, *Washed and Waiting*, p. 77.
24. Marilynne Robinson, *The Death of Adam: Essays on Modern Thought* (New York: Picador, 2005), p. 89.
25. Hill, *Washed and Waiting*, p. 48.

Perhaps the place to begin is with lament. Lament, too, trains desire. Perhaps the formation of gay Christians in the church begins as we join them in praying with David, Jesus and all the company of saints:

> Be gracious to me, O Lord, for I am in distress;
> > my eye wastes away from grief,
> > my soul and body also.
> For my life is spent with sorrow,
> > and my years with sighing;
> my strength fails because of my misery,
> > and my bones waste away.
> I am the scorn of all my adversaries,
> > a horror to my neighbours,
> an object of dread to my acquaintances;
> > those who see me in the street flee from me.
> I have passed out of mind like one who is dead;
> > I have become like a broken vessel.
> For I hear the whispering of many –
> > terror all around! –
> as they scheme together against me,
> > as they plot to take my life.
> But I trust in you, O Lord;
> > I say, 'You are my God.'
> My times are in your hand;
> > deliver me from the hand of my enemies and persecutors.
> Let your face shine upon your servant;
> > save me in your steadfast love.
> Do not let me be put to shame, O Lord,
> > for I call on you;
> let the wicked be put to shame;
> > let them go dumbfounded to Sheol.
> Let the lying lips be stilled
> > that speak insolently against the righteous
> > with pride and contempt.
> O how abundant is your goodness
> > that you have laid up for those who fear you,
> and accomplished for those who take refuge in you,
> > in the sight of everyone!
> In the shelter of your presence you hide them
> > from human plots;

you hold them safe under your shelter
    from contentious tongues.
Blessed be the Lord,
    for he has wondrously shown his steadfast love to me
    when I was beset as a city under siege.
I had said in my alarm,
    'I am driven far from your sight.'
But you heard my supplications
    when I cried out to you for help.
Love the Lord, all you his saints.
    The Lord preserves the faithful,
    but abundantly repays the one who acts haughtily.
Be strong, and let your heart take courage,
    all you who wait for the Lord.
(Ps. 31:9–24)

© Matt Jenson, 2012

6. PREACHING

THE FREE PUBLIC SPEECH OF THE PROPHETHOOD OF BELIEVERS

Andy Draycott

In this chapter I argue that preaching is an integral part of the church's missional ethics. In doing so I am concerned that preaching be recognized as *free public speech*. I will need to establish in what way these key terms are to be understood individually and together in a way that elaborates a significant claim about missional ethics. The theological warrant for this claim about free public speech will be argued on the basis of an account of the church as the *prophethood of believers*.[1] I shall first set out a series of assumptions about preaching that I hope will command a good level of support. Having laid out my assumptions, I shall address, second, a potential problem for my argument in terms of doubts over the usefulness of the concept of the prophetic for missional ethics. This problem I propose to resolve, third, by elucidating a claim about the missional *foreignness* of the prophethood of believers in relation to Scripture and church

---

1. I intend no connection with the positions elaborated by James Luther Adams in his book of that title advocating Unitarian views on the basis of a reading of the legacy of the radical Reformation. More pertinent would be the Pentecostal New Testament scholarship of Roger Stronstad, *The Prophethood of All Believers: A Study in Luke's Charismatic Theology* (London: Sheffield Academic Press, 1999). I first came across the term as employed by Amos Yong in his *In the Days of Caesar: Pentecostalism and Political Theology* (Grand Rapids: Eerdmans, 2010), pp. 250–252.

history. Finally, I turn to contemporary possibilities for this missional ethical account of preaching as the *free public speech of the prophethood of believers*.

Assumptions

Christians must understand all creaturely speech, theologically, as enabled by the speech of the Creator God who is known in Jesus Christ through the Holy Spirit. In this way, the speech of preaching whereby this God graciously makes himself known can lay theological claim to being the paradigmatic form of creaturely speech. This speech names truth and beauty and life that are being redeemed out of the midst of brokenness and death. Creaturely speech is both responsively descriptive of and responsibly normative for living under God, as witnessed by Adam's naming of the animals in their recognized kinds. Such speech is free in its joyous delight in the abundant scope of creaturely life of God's good and orderly provision. It is public speech as it names and norms ways of living in the world. Christian preaching in light of the gospel of our redemption and adoption into the firstfruits of new creation by the Holy Spirit in Jesus Christ, the second Adam, is constituted again clearly as free and public speech. That is, preaching addresses all God's human creatures, even as human participation in divine address. Preaching is also located speech, alongside prayer and praise, which shapes all the speech of Christians in particular places. Even in this contingency, it is a core witness to the possibility of any public speech, embodying as public speech must a form of life (ethics) formed by being grasped by truth (mission).

Preaching is God's word, God's speech, God's address of which humans are creaturely ambassadors. 'We also constantly give thanks to God for this, that when you received the word of God that you heard from us, you accepted it not as a human word but as what it really is, God's word, which is also at work in you believers' (1 Thess. 2:13). Because of the historical contingency of God's self-revelation in his redemptive dealings with creation through Abraham, Israel and Israel's Messiah, Jesus, this speech of preaching as the speech of this God is bound to God's written word of Scripture. Yet as the human speech authorized by this particular divine speech, preaching is nonetheless speech for all God's creatures and therefore, rightly understood, the speech, in Christ, *of* all God's creatures. That is, within the limitations of creatureliness, preaching nevertheless is free human speech through which God speaks still.

Before proceeding to address the problem by developing a missional ethical account of preaching through the concept of prophecy, I must say more about what I do not mean by 'free speech' and 'public speech'. By the term 'free' I am not grounding the warrant for preaching on legal-constitutional provisions for what judges would or would not uphold as free speech. Preaching may or may not find itself compatible with judicial opinion in any human politico-legal order. That being said, I should readily concede that my understanding of preaching is nevertheless shaped by life lived in several national forms of liberal democratic political order such that my mode of expression may require qualification and reformulation by brothers and sisters engaging the church's mission in speech in different and more dangerous social contexts.

By public speech, I am not calling for, as do some who crave a public theology, a kind of speech that is more accessible to the public because it is neutralized of potentially offensive particularity. Without weighing into arguments beyond the scope of this chapter, and notwithstanding those elements which will arise piecemeal as I proceed, I should assert that I am unconvinced that the public forum understood as a 'naked public square' of de-particularized public speech is coherent either practically or philosophically.[2] My lack of conviction on that front is bolstered by a theological conviction on the other, already outlined in brief above, that creation is the true public forum where speech is deployed. Creation as the public for right human speech is never neutrally the forum of free speech, but always the given time and place of relationship to God the Creator.

The notion of 'public speech' happily and without much explication indicates that preaching should not be thought of as 'private' speech. This exposes the theological connections between missional ethics and ecclesiology that underlie this exploration.[3] Preaching is not a speech peculiar to a private voluntary grouping or subsection of a wider public. Rather, as the church's speech all are called to hear the gospel's address in a given time and place. The church is turned *as a* public out *to* the public *as* the public in its speech of preaching. The church proclaiming the gospel is the public transformed by the power of the word of God. Furthermore, as 'public' and therefore shared communication I intend that preaching not be conceived of monologously.[4] Certainly there is an authoritative *logos* in Scripture, but preaching, even as the word of God for this time and place, will adopt a dialogical manner as the

---

2. See the chapter in this volume by Jonathan Chaplin for more on Christian public reasoning.
3. See the chapter in this volume by Matt Jenson on the church.
4. I intend a co-incidence of concerns with Nathan Moser's suggestions, in this volume, for servant leadership in the specific sphere of preaching.

speech of a community. As a community's speech it is a phenomenon of lives lived in being-worked-out reconciliation, forming patience and perseverance in hope, whose ethical character stands to the fore. Recognition of this, I am convinced, will allow some to appreciate the truth of prophethood in which they already unwittingly participate, and encourage others to seek the Spirit's empowerment for a renewal of their discipleship in regard to preaching. 'Like good stewards of the manifold grace of God, serve one another with whatever gift each of you has received. Whoever speaks must do so as one speaking the very words of God' (1 Pet. 4:10–11a). I further believe that the emphasis developed in this chapter will liberate the church's mission from professionalization of the 'clergy' and the spectator neutrality of the 'laity'.[5] Thus eschewing a monological model of preaching will liberate Christians to discern its missional ethical significance.

The problem with prophets

As we consider the missional ethical character of preaching through the concept of the prophethood of believers several problems surface. First, we find in numerous discussions of preaching that 'prophetic' is a term that is commonly used to characterize a particular type of preaching rather than the common-or-garden variety. So preaching is judged to be prophetic as it displays a supposed commonality of ethical, social or political confrontation with that deemed to be found in the Old Testament prophets. Prophetic models are found in Samuel, Elijah or Elisha's speaking truth to power in narrative dealings with kings. This 'prophetic' strand is also to be found in the written-up speech of Isaiah, Amos and Hosea (particularly) condemning injustice and inequity in Israel/Judah or the surrounding nations. Or, last, one thinks of that New Testament flowering of Old Testament prophetic action in John the Baptist's outspokenness on the matter of Herod Antipas's marital arrangements. This characterization of the 'prophetic' along a selective reading of the Old Testament for protest speech may actually reflect other concerns that the interpreter brings with her. The problem here is that this kind of strong, challenging counter-speech to power does not lend itself

---

5. I do not want to suggest a rejection of vocational training, recognition and ordination of individuals within the church for the office of preacher, but that extremely important aspect of the ordered ministry of preaching is not the focus of my attention here.

to ready incorporation to reflections on the peaceable task of missionary proclamation of the gospel.

Second, preaching that is missional is often distinguished from the prophetic by being pastoral and invitational in its evangelistic bearing. At this point we find that the 'missional' and 'ethical' with respect to preaching are often thought of as specialist orientations of any one sermon, or perhaps different parts of the same sermon. On this understanding, preaching and the 'ethical' might align in a particular form of *prophetic* speech. Such churchly speech would be an arresting proclamation calling people in the world to repentance as apologetic preparation for good news. The missional moment would follow in the announcement of grace and forgiveness, leading into pastoral preaching for guiding and shaping saved lives. Allowing that preaching can be, on this account of the prophetic and the evangelistic, both 'ethical' and 'missional', we are a step away from the coherence sought in an exposition of missional ethics. In any case, I find this strategic subdivision of preaching into parts theologically unhelpful. While harbouring absolutely no doubt about the importance of evangelism in the life of the church's mission, I am not convinced that there is a theological division of preaching into multiple genres. That is, I am not sure of the theological grounds for dividing preaching into categories or genres as distinct from sociological or phenomenological interests. Hughes Oliphant Old in his seven-volume *The Reading and Preaching of the Scriptures in the Worship of the Christian Church* identifies five major genres of preaching, namely: expository, evangelistic, catechetical, festal and prophetic. He divides catechetical preaching into doctrinal, moral and liturgical types. On this basis our aim towards a missional ethics of preaching would be liable to fragmentation. I want to contend with theologian Oliver O'Donovan, however, that

> there is no Christian ethics that is not 'evangelical,' i.e., good news. There can be no change of voice, no shift of mood, between God's word of forgiveness and his word of demand, no obedience-without-gift, no gift-without-obedience. The gift and the obedience are in fact one and the same. They are the righteousness of Jesus Christ, encompassing and transforming our own lives, past, present and future. To preach the good news, then, is precisely what we do in expounding Christian ethics, if we expound Christian ethics faithfully. Preaching the good news is the only form of address of which the Christian church as such is capable, whether speaking to Christians or to non-Christians. When we use any other form of argument – quoting opinion-poll statistics, for example, or reporting the result of scientific experiments, or suggesting some practical compromise – the relevance of what we say depends on how well it is formed to serve the evangelical message. If the church speaks not as

witness to God's saving work but as a pundit or a broker of some deal, it speaks out of character.[6]

It is the task of this chapter to give O'Donovan's claims some substantial argumentation in relation to a more developed account of that preaching as public speech. This is what I understand O'Donovan to be claiming, especially in relation to his concern for the 'relevance of what we say'. That which Old attributes to prophetic preaching must surely belong to all preaching as the living word of God in the power of the Spirit, viz.: 'The genius of prophetic preaching is that God often has a particular word for a particular time and a particular place.'[7]

A clear example of the way in which the speech of the Old Testament prophets shapes the telling of a theological account of Christian speech today is in Nigel Biggar's *Behaving in Public*.[8] I take Biggar to be an important example of a theologian who is clear about the good of mission while deliberating about the public calling of Christian ethics in a pluralist society.[9] Biggar is against any 'sheer appeal' to Scripture in public speech, by which he means 'an invocation of authority to close down controversy, as in "The Bible says such and such; therefore, there is nothing further to discuss".'[10] Here I agree with him.

---

6. Oliver O'Donovan, *Church in Crisis: The Gay Controversy and the Anglican Communion* (Eugene: Cascade, 2008), pp. 103–104.
7. Hughes Oliphant Old, *The Reading and Preaching of the Scriptures: Volume 1, The Biblical Period* (Grand Rapids: Eerdmans, 1998), p. 16.
8. Nigel Biggar, *Behaving in Public: How to Do Christian Ethics* (Grand Rapids: Eerdmans, 2011). Biggar's approach is discussed by Jonathan Chaplin in this volume. I agree with much of his commendation of Biggar's overall approach.
9. Biggar writes extensively on witness in the power of the Holy Spirit in the present text. Mission is likewise pneumatologically framed in his 'The Value of Limited Loyalty: Christianity, the Nation, and Territorial Boundaries', in David Miller and Sohail H. Hashmi (eds.), *Boundaries and Justice: Diverse Ethical Perspectives* (Princeton: Princeton University Press, 2001), pp. 42–43. I take it that Biggar's recognition of the contribution of the Christian ethicist to the public of the church (*Behaving in Public*, pp. 46–47) would support a concern for preaching even if, as I suspect, my approach oversteps his delineations of publics. Even here though, see Biggar, ibid., p. 9: 'We live in the *saeculum*, the secular age when the tares are allowed to mingle with the wheat, members of the Church may be found in the actual world, and members of the World may be found in actual churches.'
10. Ibid., p. 67, n. 3.

Preaching's dialogical character ensures its openness as a speech into controversy without closing it down. Preaching might on my account lay claim to meet Biggar's concern for rhetorical prudence in public speech.

Biggar's careful commendation of prudence in the public speech of Christian ethicists is made the more interesting for my concerns in the way that 'prophecy' and the 'prophetic' are treated. Prophecy first arises in Biggar's treatment in a discussion of New Testament scholar Richard Hays, who claims to disavow abstract generalizing reasoning in regard to New Testament ethics by sticking close to the metaphorical, disjunctive and shocking character of the text.[11] Biggar allows that this 'prophetic mode' is an important and basic mode for Christian ethics.

> But prophecy and protest should not be the only modes of which the Christian ethicist is capable. Sometimes she will also need to think carefully and analytically about the proper responsibilities of government and about what is permissible in defense of national security and under what conditions. Sometimes she will need to shuffle off the shoes of the prophet and step into those of the policymaker.[12]

For all the clarity of Biggar's concerns, I wonder if Nehemiah, Daniel or even Jeremiah would recognize the distinction being drawn between protest and carefully considered policy.[13] Again, what Biggar regrets about Hays's insistence that general concepts not be used in favour of direct analogies from text to today is that it 'threatens to confine Christian ethics to the prophetic mode, to railing at obvious idols, while robbing it of the tools for crafting the subtle moral assessment of difficult policy choices'.[14]

Taking the individual Old Testament prophets as the model for the prophetic, even with the unsubtle reading hinted at above, also has the tendency to render prophecy an individualistic enterprise: Thus says the Lord *to me*! So Biggar decries the isolationist Christian posture that refuses to find common cause with those outside the church 'as if the only role worth playing were that of

---

11. Biggar is discussing the proposals set out in Richard Hays, *The Moral Vision of the New Testament* (New York: HarperCollins, 1996).
12. Biggar, *Behaving in Public*, p. 14.
13. Interestingly, Jim Wallis proposes precisely a recovery from a Christian public involvement characterized by protest via a 'prophetic politics' in Jim Wallis, *The Politics of God* (New York: HarperCollins, 2005).
14. Biggar, *Behaving in Public*, p. 16. It does not, however, seem to be the case that idolatry is all that obvious.

solitary prophet in sole possession of the heroic limelight'.[15] Even so, he recognizes that contradiction and denunciation must be in the armoury of a Christian voice that is shaped by Jesus. We are told that the 'prophetic strands in the biblical narrative, including the New Testament, forbid' sole recourse to 'sweet reason' in situations of evil so impervious to persuasion that 'the Christian must stop being wise man and start playing prophet'.[16]

Despite these uses of prophecy, Biggar lays the ground for rejection of his own rhetorical positioning of prophecy as individualist protest. Yet his book still closes with the following conclusion which I contend exhibits his dichotomous understanding of the prophetic and pastoral:

> An ethicist who is Christian should want to follow his Lord and Master in loving the world. And if he would love the world, he will play pastor before he plays prophet. For the only people a prophet has the right to prophesy against are those he has first cared to make his own.[17]

Nevertheless, the commendation of pastoral love, over against high-handed theological protest, is what evokes the Christian's responsibility to challenge others in the public with what Biggar calls 'discriminating prophecy'.[18] Biggar's treatment places the emphasis on the wisdom of the wise discrimination, but I wish to highlight the promise of his 'discriminating *prophecy*' for the purpose of commending preaching as integral to the church's missional ethics.

The discriminating prophecy of preaching through the prophethood of believers

Roger Stronstad concludes his Lukan study as follows.

> The Church is to be a community of prophets. But from the post-apostolic period to the present it has not functioned as a prophetic community which is powerful in works and words. In fact, in too many places the Church views itself as a didactic community rather than as a prophetic community, where sound doctrine is treasured above charismatic action. Indeed, the preaching and teaching of the word displaces

---

15. Ibid., p. 26. My emphasis.
16. Ibid., p. 73. I am not sure why wisdom and prophecy are contrasted here.
17. Ibid., p. 112.
18. Ibid., p. 99.

Spirit-filled, Spirit-led and Spirit-empowered ministry. The Spirit of prophecy has been quenched and the gifts of the Spirit have been sanitized and institutionalized. The non-Pentecostal/non-charismatic church needs to recapture its prophetic heritage, to which it is either hostile or indifferent.[19]

Continued conversation with Biggar's use of 'prophetic' will help us address some of Stronstad's concerns that seem to commend the possibly imprudent charismatic action of prophecy over more rhetorically prudent speech in the church. I shall be outlining a position that implicitly rejects Stronstad's sharp differentiation of didactic and prophetic, yet criticizes Biggar's fear of the imprudent character of prophetic speech. The problem that I encounter in Biggar's treatment is not so much a substantive one about his commendation of diverse communication approaches beyond solely counter-speech. He may very well be describing the prudential speech of encounter that is required to draw counter-speech into missional transformation and that I desire to see embodied in preaching. Yet I simply refuse to consider preaching as constitutively counter-speech. In one instance Biggar commends the role of the Holy Spirit acting in the freedom of God to shape implicit Christian behaviour outside the church.[20] That same doctrine of the Holy Spirit should correct his use of prophecy as a category within the church. The missional ethical account of preaching shaped by an understanding of 'prophecy' addresses Biggar's concerns by redirecting the 'prophetic' from the John the Baptist model to that of the Spirit-filled church. So I commend prophecy as the form of preaching and teaching as the church's free public speech.

Prophecy in Scripture

In Numbers 11 we find the New Testament's eschatological hope for prophecy on the lips of Moses in light of a scandalous prophesying within the Israelite camp. The meeting-shy Eldad and Medad should have been gathered with the other elders of the people at the tabernacle to receive a portion of the Spirit of God for their task of discriminating ruling. Instead, they had hung back with their families. The Spirit of God apportions discriminately as YHWH would give and not according to the level of eagerness or willingness of the recipients themselves and not according to social etiquette. Eldad and Medad

---

19. Stronstad, *Prophethood*, p. 123, where Stronstad also comments that Pentecostals need to learn to focus on service and not just experience.
20. Biggar, *Behaving in Public*, pp. 99–105.

receive their 'baptism' nonetheless and break forth in speech. When first a young tell-tale and then Joshua report to Moses, expecting him to disapprove of this socially misplaced manifestation of the Spirit of God, the text indicates Moses' surprise: 'Are you jealous for my sake? Would that all the Lord's people were prophets, and that the Lord would put his spirit on them!' (Num. 11:29). Precisely in this way do we find the apostle Paul in the Corinthian correspondence refusing to guard jealously his own apostolic commission against the competitive spirituality and complaints of the Corinthians. Instead, he commends to them his weakness (1 Cor. 1 – 4; 2 Cor. 1) as an expression of his love and urges them to seek to exercise this ministry of prophecy that has such high standing (1 Cor. 14). In this he is empowering them for the discriminating task of discernment and judgment (1 Cor. 2:13–16) required of those who are rich in speech (1 Cor. 1:5). God's word through Paul in these Scriptures reiterates the concern for the prophethood of believers that we find in Luke/Acts, as displayed in Peter's taking up the words of the prophet Joel at Pentecost (Acts 2:16–21).

Pentecost not only opens up the missionary ecclesial character of prophecy but also exhibits in a helpful way what the theological tradition has spoken of as the *verbum alienum*, the 'alien', external word. Speech is poured out by God's coming in the Holy Spirit. In what follows I explore this way of characterizing the unexpected grace-filled dynamic of God's speech in preaching taking 'alien' in terms of 'foreignness'.

Reading the account of the tower of Babel in Genesis 11 alongside that of Pentecost in Acts 2 is a helpful and oft-used heuristic explication of the foreignness of preaching. Babel's singular language and gathering for name-building admits no foreignness. All is commonality, an ultimately idolatrous grasping onto security in identity. Babel's identity politics is radically disrupted by God's coming down in the blessing of confusing judgment. Pentecost, likewise, sees God coming down in the pouring out of the Holy Spirit upon people of different tongues, gathered now for worship. Yet what is not restored in the disciples' prophetic outpourings heard by the crowd is a common language. Foreignness persists in multiple dimensions. This is the foreign liberating word of the gospel spoken by the redeeming God in Jesus Christ. It is furthermore the foreign word that must be spoken in testimony to the ends of the earth. That is, it must perpetually engage in its speaking and hearing in the confusion and messiness of prophets speaking as 'foreigners' in their own culture, even as Jesus recognizes in his home town: 'Truly I tell you, no prophet is accepted in the prophet's home town' (Luke 4:24; cf. 6:23). Furthermore this foreignness is lived out in New Testament prophecy as missionary travel and cross-cultural encounter, which enjoins not only patient hearing and interpretation, but also hospitality. Hence the call in 1 John 4 to test the spirits, to discern the true prophets over and against the false, not least by seeking a demonstration of true love as witness to God in Christ by the Spirit (1 John 4:13–16). What is more, this patient discernment evokes hospitality for the travelling messenger as an occasion to honour the unknown presence of an angel, the utterly foreign visitor who brings God's word (Heb. 13:2).

In the light of this community-claiming dimension of New Testament eschatological prophecy, I see no reason why the charism of prophecy, which we may readily assume as a synonym for preaching,[21] must be counter-speech.[22] The chief characteristic of prophecy, in its fullest New Testament treatment by the apostle Paul in 1 Corinthians 14, is, after all, edification, not deconstruction or critique (vv. 3, 5). Furthermore, prophecy is commended precisely for its missionary intelligibility to outsiders (vv. 24–25). This intelligibility speaks to the moral claim of Christians and others alike inhabiting one reality open to moral description and deliberation upon action. The foreignness of prophecy is a foreignness that draws near in missionary encounter, not a foreignness that parades its inaccessibility and exclusivity, as Paul fears is the case in the speech of tongues (1 Cor. 14:11).

That prospect of encounter and shared communication in intelligibility and testing means that I do not see the New Testament commending an individualist approach to prophecy. This *canard* owes much more to Max Weber's sociological categorization of the 'charismatic' than to Scripture.[23] Rather, prophecy is a shared activity of the 'prophethood of all believers' as the Spirit enables men and women, young and old to speak evangelically, to speak God's word, in the assembly and to the world (Acts 2; 1 Cor. 14).[24]

---

21. Old, *Reading and Preaching, Volume 1*, pp. 196–197.
22. As Biggar sees it in someone like Stanley Hauerwas, see Biggar, *Behaving in Public*, pp. 89–96.
23. D. Stephen Long, 'Prophetic Preaching,' in *Concise Encyclopedia of Preaching*, eds. W. H. Willimon and R. Lischer (Louisville: Westminster John Knox Press, 1995), pp. 385–389.
24. In my reading of Paul's approval of women prophets in 1 Cor. 11, and following Anthony Thisleton's interpretation of 1 Cor. 14:32a as addressed to wives (and therefore not all women), I take it that the Spirit empowers men and women to both preach God's word and weigh preaching as God's word; see Anthony Thistleton, *The First Epistle to the Corinthians* (Grand Rapids: Eerdmans, 2000), pp. 1074–1168. My reading resonates with some of the underlying concerns expressed in Sarah Ruble's chapter that follows in this volume.

Preaching as prophecy is the best way of explicating positively the tie-in of preaching to missional ethics. New Testament prophecy is not, on the whole, the lonely speaking truth to power that so fascinates the readers of charismatic preachers like Martin Luther, or his namesake, Martin Luther King Jr. Of course, there *are* those outstanding saints, and among them Stephen leads the pack in prophetic martyrdom, but the commendation of the apostles is that it is in the health of gospel speaking in congregations of ordinary men and women that the spread of the gospel to all the world is to be discerned (Col. 1:3–8). And this gospel speaking will be healthy precisely as the many participate actively in hearing and discerning, in testing the spirits, by way, in part, of observing and imitating the pattern of life lived by speakers as speakers themselves. The intelligibility of preaching is not just a grammatical, syntactical or even rhetorical intelligibility – it is a moral and thus missionary intelligibility. Know the prophet by the fruit.[25] Its shared dialogical character is not only recognized in the command to discern, test and judge words spoken to, for and by the community, but also in the theological confession that this eschatological speech of prophecy shares the already/not yet orientation of all Christian eschatology. Fullness is not yet attained even as it is tasted. So we 'prophesy only in part' and are called on to continually hear and respond to each other as a widening community of speech in love (1 Cor. 13, esp. v. 9).

Biggar's most interesting concern for Christian public speech in a pluralized secular context is to refute an overly simplistic missionary strategy of stereotyping the other. He calls for discriminating prophecy as a means to avoid hasty, stock or easy assumptions about the other encountered in the world. The patience for which he correctly calls is one he fears the prophetic mode cannot easily exhibit. In commending 'discriminating prophecy' against the blunt 'prophetic' mode he criticizes and downplays, his comments are integral to identifying a deep soteriological objection that might be laid at the door of a missional ethical account of preaching. Any form of stereotyping of others, Biggar claims, 'is to forget one's own status as *peccator* made *iustus* by God's grace, to fail in compassionate love for fellow sinners, and thereby to betray the gospel'.[26] In claiming preaching as missional, it might be objected that it precisely must not be shaped by ethical concerns. Ethical concerns, after all, are precisely the domain of so many stereotypical judgments, commands, laws

---

25. For an excellent theological treatment see R. W. L. Moberly, *Prophecy and Discernment* (Cambridge: Cambridge University Press, 2006).
26. Biggar, *Behaving in Public*, p. 99.

and norms that qualify gospel love to death. To preach ethics would imply that a gospel of works or law is being proffered rather than a gospel of grace. After all, whatever personal nuance of judgment or tone that could be offered in conversation is lost in the broad canvas, multi-person address of preaching. Preaching, it might be argued, is almost bound to stereotype – addressing teachers, or parents, or dating couples, or children – not as individuals but as categories. Preaching might do well to avoid offering platitudes and concentrate on the one stereotype guaranteed scriptural backing – the sinner called to repentance as the task of mission. Only the salvific 'for me' can be offered and heard in missional preaching, whereas the diverse freedom of the vocational 'for me' in terms of secular calling and works of love has no place here. Perhaps the ethical is withdrawn to an inner, private church instruction.

What we must protest here is a monologous description of preaching, still patently individualistic. The purifying zeal to protect evangelism as the missional speech of the church and the fear of the ethical as the address of preaching actually belongs together with a falsely pristine view of the church's identity (already touched on) as well as a professional firewall often deployed to protect the ordered ministry of preaching for the church against itself. Conversely, an emphasis on prophecy as the task of the prophethood of believers opens up the dialogical character of preaching to the foreignness of ethical concerns abroad in the world in which the church lives and ministers as prophets spread wide, as the Holy Spirit may direct.

Now we must at some point acknowledge that there is enough publicity of grievous scandal surrounding the church, as well as real experience of suffering, to support a suspicion that prophetic words are ephemerally easy and not missionally significant. Words, where preaching is precisely not seen to have been practised, are cheap. In reply we must insist that false prophets are indeed a perennial problem, and that preaching may not always be what it might make proper theological claim to be. Yet what is required is not an abandonment of speech, but what Scripture itself calls for: testing and discernment. These relational, moral judgments are called for because Christians, as those called by word to faith, cannot be constitutively suspicious of words – it is an ontological impossibility. As those so called they will be confident of the missional reach of words, even as those so morally constituted for discernment will testify to the ethical formation in the discipline of speech in community.

Prophecy in church history
I want to highlight a practice that has come to my attention through the research of my colleague, Joanne Jung, which displays the foreignness of prophecy and the prophethood of believers on multiple levels. Jung sets out and commends

a retrieval today of the Puritan practice of 'Godly conference'.[27] This practice is an outflow of a confidence that Christians are constituted as a people who are called to judge and discern the truth of God's Spirit-empowered present speech in preaching as public speech. Jung describes the development of 'prophesyings' amongst Puritan preachers in England where they would gather to strengthen each other in ministry by preaching to each other at length and in succession for several hours. These 'prophesyings' were open to the faithful laity to observe and be edified. Although eventually outlawed by Elizabeth I, a further development of the Puritan zeal for publicly proclaiming the word preached sees even greater involvement of the public in the task of preaching. What Puritan authorities referred to as 'godly conference' represented a historical example of the mutually constituting public life of the word preached in hearing and testing. It occurred beyond the walls of the meeting houses and chapels in streets, family conferences and the everyday conversation of people in public spaces. In particular, godly conference was a vehicle for the word preached to be tested in relation to the lives lived by hearers as they inquired after the well-being of each other's soul before God. In a more popular presentation of the topic of conference in a chapter of her book *Knowing Grace*, Jung defines conference as 'the intentional conversation among a limited number of people in which they integrate their growing knowledge of the Bible with their concern for another's soul'.[28] What Jung describes using the Puritans' own designation of 'conference' is a form of the ministry of prophecy that we encounter in 1 Corinthians 14. What we see is that the public of the congregational gathering for worship creeps missionally into the public life of the individual members of the church as a continuation of the dialogical character of preaching. This dialogue of agreement, testing and conferencing cannot but spill over from worship into all the areas of public life to which the word is addressed in mission. The character of these Puritan conferences is ethical formation in public. Although they take place in highways and by-ways and not in places of social prestige, this does not disqualify the public placedness of this free speech.

Beyond this historical description Jung introduces her undergraduate students to this idea of conferencing. What stands out is the comment of one such person that she reports in her 'Reflections from the heart':

---

27. Joanne Jung, *Godly Conversation: Rediscovering the Puritan Practice of Conference* (Grand Rapids: Reformation Heritage Books, 2011).
28. Joanne Jung, *Knowing Grace, Cultivating a Lifestyle of Godliness* (Colorado Springs: Biblica, 2011), p. 99.

> Conferencing seems to be a missing link in our churches. It is where the private means of grace meets the public. In the evangelical world today we have a very strong emphasis on healing and redemption. However the manner in which we carry that out is very top down. The preacher preaches and the listeners listen. Conferencing provides mutual dependency on the body for growth.[29]

Conferencing that breaks the monological 'top down' delivery of preaching is one example, it seems to me, of the proper functioning of the prophethood of believers, the weighing of prophecy as prophets confer together. The speech that preaching engenders should be neither muttered submission nor unspeakable indifference. Rather, submission will be in speech as a proving is undertaken, submitting to the responsibility in love for the public life of the mission of the church to test the preacher's claims. The missional ripples of this prophetic word of preaching as an extended and graciously abundant provision by God in the Spirit week by week and throughout the week may be truly humbling.

I recognize in this Puritan practice the prophetic task of discernment to which the entire prophethood of believers is called. Yet the foreignness of this practice speaks of the foreignness of the historical context in which we find it embedded. We would do well, however, to recognize that whatever the strange and wondrous biblical literacy we attribute to the still biblically saturated social imaginary of early modernity, the Puritans stood out. They were even – or at least felt that they were – often driven out as 'foreigners'. Our concern to explore the missional ethical character of preaching as public speech does not pretend to propose a way to make this public speech universally appealing or even widely heard, yet its effectiveness on some transformational cultural plane is not the test of fidelity the prophethood of believers seeks to discern.

In closing this section we jump forward in time from the Puritans. Hughes Oliphant Old describes a nineteenth-to-twentieth-century Great American School of preaching, which from Charles Finney onwards found itself increasingly divided by the prophetic social interests of one set of preachers and the evangelistic focus of another set. Old observes that '[b]y the time the school came to an end, the prophets and the evangelists were pretty irreconcilable. Maybe that is one of the reasons the school came to an end. The prophetic emphasis and the evangelistic emphasis lost contact with each other.'[30] I propose that talking of the missional ethical character of preaching can be held out as

---

29. Ibid., p. 109.
30. Hugh Oliphant Old, *Reading and Preaching: Volume 7, Our Own Time* (Grand Rapids: Eerdmans, 2010), p. 10.

an answer to historical failings at this point, for each school can be viewed as one speech of preaching with different emphases.

Contemporary concerns for prophecy as preaching's free public speech

In this section I outline two areas in which this prophetic understanding of preaching as missional ethical account is significant. The first addresses a theological reservation about the 'prophetic' in relating moral formation and salvation. The second is a more practical concern to allow the prophethood of all believers to overcome the ways in which preaching is experienced as alienating.

Moral formation and salvation
Preaching is formative of hearers who must then judge not by sight but rather by faith in how they are seen by God as worthy recipients of his address. Not judging by sight affirms Biggar's instinct when he dismisses stereotyping others. Biggar commends to the church a careful casuistry in its consideration of complex ethical concerns in the early twenty-first century, and avers that this is not the stuff of altar. We are not saved through appropriating moral instruction for living well in human flourishing. We are saved by Christ's righteousness, not our own. So much Biggar commends, and in doing so he is wary of preaching as a plausible form of the moral deliberation he thinks it important for Christians to entertain publicly. And yet the careful thought he seeks is the stuff of following Jesus in the ongoing making of disciples. It is precisely the genuine inhabiting of the world that is demonstrated in Scripture, precisely the moral formation required of those gathered by the word in the power of the Spirit. God's address in the gospel is one that affirms the patterns of belonging that we seek to conform to his truth even as it critiques and re-narrates them. God's address in the gospel is the declaration not only of the *peccator* but also of the *iustus*, of Christ's righteousness lived out in good works to neighbour – that most general of epithets that invites us to deliberate how we might go and do likewise. Mission and ethics, at this soteriological heart of the preached good news, belong together. The ethical, however broadly it may be addressed in preaching, is not out of place in this missional speech.

The *simul iustus et peccator* that Biggar clings to, against crass and polemical portrayals of others as simply immoral, emphasizes the complexity of the gospel claim: that the salvation wrought by Christ's death and resurrection is a vindication of the Creator's moral order, in which broken reality all humans participate as they navigate life. Biggar's recognition enjoins genuine conversational missional encounters as church speech – not the evasion of the ethical and communal, but a liberated and delightful exploration of the ethical in the light of good news. Can this encounter and conversation be entertained in preaching that is missionary proclamation? Or, another way of asking this, can the *goodness* of the good news be explored in its proclamation, or must it be trivialized into a utilitarian good as an instrument of salvation? My confidence is that exploring that goodness is precisely the public freedom of preaching as it ventures to address the kind of ethical questions that, for example, are taken up in the following chapters of this collection.

Against alienating preaching

Preaching cannot have as its goal telling people what they want to hear; it cannot aim to give people what they expect. A missional ethics of preaching is too confident of the Holy Spirit's showing up in power to entertain that notion. Preaching as a speaking and hearing task will call for discernment that may often be that of peaceful 'Amens', but even that discerning judgment must be given public time and place to coalesce and find mutual expression. The private post-sermon 'Thank you, preacher' does not do this. Preaching that is open to the surprise of the Spirit will call for a plurality of participants around the fixed and important office of the preacher.

In contrast with the temptation to stereotype, the encounter of one another as 'foreigners' brought near, to be known and loved in our difference, is important. Becoming 'members one of another' (Rom. 12:5) does not efface our difference, or rescind the challenge of needing to speak and hear, be heard and discern truth in loving judgment in the Spirit. Preaching that has as its goal to be faithful must not seek to produce fidelity by familiar repetition and nostalgia. Rather, preaching's fidelity as prophecy is opening hearers out to their own reconciled foreignness to one another as a strength that must be spoken and heard. Discernment that seeks to have the mind of Christ will do so through explicit peopled 'Amens' rather than assumed or culturally corralled endorsement. That assumed cultural endorsement can be expressed in both common silence of an 'audience' or the common talkativeness of the 'thank-you-preacher' types.

In the evangelical world our prophecy is plagued by a 'germ-free' fascination with pristine preaching that in fact distrusts the Spirit among us in prophetic discernment and speech. Preaching so often aims at an exhaustive and often exhausting comprehensiveness of exegesis and interpretation which invites participation merely as after-application, floated in the closing section of the monologous sermon. Yet where church members are not invited to exercise their prophetic calling and seek the ministry of prophecy, they are un-worded by the authoritative word that is received less as authorizing and merely as contextualizing. Hearers of the word are left as foreigners, craving encounter and interaction but stuck on the tour bus, ingesting tourist brochures and following a fixed and rigid itinerary.

This is an important failing of evangelical preaching, but there is another challenge to the missional ethical description of preaching. Could it be that, echoing in part Roger Stronstad's concern, teaching the word finds itself unable to engage the Spirit's call to discern the times in all their ethical complexity? 'Application' is the domain of action to which church members are implicitly invited between the preaching of sermons; they are not active prophetic participants in preaching. This can foster zeal to maintain a false elevation of word over action. Certainly our wider culture is not likely to idealize speech to the extent that it must be kept pristine from contagion by the messiness of everyday life. It is however conceivable that the recent preference in the church for action over words in mission is a manifestation of the zeal for purity of speech that is then only for the few illuminate; the rest of the church must engage missionally in action, apart from and unconnected to the hallowed task of preaching. The training and equipping (and privileging) of select 'sound' men for word ministry can unfortunately have the effect of un-wording others in the church and without. Practically, as this pattern of preaching is sought, this collusion in being un-worded before the select few can evidence a functional disavowal of the presence and work of the Spirit in all believers.[31] Here the speech of preaching is bound to the pattern of that which has evinced soundness before: 'Biblical preaching must be/say . . .' This is far from the free public speech we envision here. My point is that this may be a failure of expectation of hearers more often than it is of speakers. We are pointed back to the moral formation of hearers in the event of preaching as mutual prophetic task.

Conclusion: Preaching is the church's free public speech

We must hope to avoid the true bathos of the sermon hearers conjured up by Thomas Hardy. Hardy describes the Sunday habit of his characters as 'they invariably discussed the sermon, dissecting it, weighing it, as above or below

---

31. This is most obviously congruent with Sarah Ruble's chapter's discussion of the presentation of the role of women in mission in the context of the American 'evangelism vs. social action' debate.

average – the general tendency being to regard it as a scientific feat or performance which had no relation to their own lives, except as between critics and the thing criticized.'[32] Christian preaching is evangelical speech. It is the stuff of true life. It confesses and proclaims the reality of who God is in Jesus Christ. The gospel of gracious divine initiative requires that such speech be understood as Holy Spirit empowered speech. It is through the speech-emboldening-hearing-enabling Spirit that Christians are those men, women and children transformed by the good news which is truly news – free public speech.

Free

Preaching is *free* public speech as it is authorized and empowered by God. It is commissioned and need not ask permission for its way in the world. It is urgent missionary speech in the light of the eschatological reality being ushered in of the kingdom of God in Jesus Christ. For that reason it is speech bound only to today. It is a word from God for the here and now. We can do mission in no other place than the here and now of the Holy Spirit.

We cannot recognize or take seriously the here and now unless we reckon with the moral complexity and challenge that the missionary encounter assumes. The reality of speaker and hearer in preaching is the one reality being redeemed by Christ. It is not the church–world division that stands as important, but the God–world division, and this has been bridged by the one mediator (1 Tim. 2:5).[33] Jesus' vindication of created order is precisely the warrant for the evangelical speech of preaching to express its freedom in exploring for the edification of its diverse and even unknown hearers the contours of the new creation life lived in the already and not yet of the missionary age. That is, preaching will be free to joyfully tackle difficult questions as it hears Scripture not as if we were still those original hearers but in happy confidence that we are hearers of God now. Preaching will be free, furthermore, because it will not carry the burden of the moralist to have to say in absolute totality or via exhaustive biblical word-study what must be said on a matter, whether marriage, abortion, war or taxation, for all time. Any attempt to do so would trample the prophethood of believers, who must exercise their ministry of testing and weighing in discernment. Frustration with preaching's inevitable generalities is

---

32. Quoted in Roger Bowen (ed.), *A Guide to Preaching* (London: SPCK, 2005), p. 37, opening a chapter asking, 'What is preaching?'

33. Hans Ulrich, 'Waiting for the Other Word – God's Advent in Human Preaching. Considerations for a Theology of Preaching', available at www.christen-ethik.de/God%20is%20different6.pdf, p. 5, accessed 1 November 2011.

more often a function of a failure of the prophethood of believers to test out and speak over the word preached in discerning 'conference'. This speech is meant to shape the ongoing prophetic conferencing of Christians who have in any case been disciplined to carefully hear and discern the reality of missional living, borne out urgently but without inducing guilt.

Public
Preaching is free *public* speech as it opens up the Word of God to a public, the prophethood of believers, that is the church for the world. This claim's missional implication, for the world, is key. It follows on from the scope of the freedom enjoyed by evangelical speech. Hans Ulrich says that '[t]his spoken word is addressed to hearers in order to set them free of [sic] pursuing their attempts to assure their life, its sources, and its meanings, to set them free from self-justification – so that they turn to the other, become aware of the other.'[34] The one-another-hood that is the church is missional as it learns and carries out that regular relinquishing of claims for self-justification in service of the other. Preaching means that theologically. Yet how should we foster an appropriate recognition of that in church life? Regular preachers must live out what John Stott has called 'double listening'. They must hear Scripture and the world. But if double listening is mathematically correct, then the public of today is identified as the world even in the hearing of the church, as fellow prophets offering testing and discernment in their speech. I think this recognition of the public, contemporary task of fellow prophethood in listening and speaking is vital. Not only will it situate the consciousness of the regular preacher in the missional context, the task of listening and the invitation to join that speech in listening will remind fellow prophets in all walks of life in the church, and by the Spirit's wonder even outside, that they are part of the task of preaching. What this prophethood looks like will depend upon the size and community dynamic of the church in its missional location, but certainly seeing preaching submitted to the discernment of home groups would be one example. Or preaching might deliberately address a local ethical concern as an expression of its mission and open the sermon to a 'town hall' deliberation as response.

Speech
Speech is the uncontentious leftover part of my claim. Who will object to this? Yet showing how preaching as prophecy is missional speech has been my task. Most basically preaching is not just hearing, as many Christians and moreover

---

34. Ibid., pp. 10–11.

many outside the church conceive it. That it is speech in its character as theologically free and public does not detract from the affirmation of speech in mission. This itself is a testimony to the Spirit of mission, the God who acts in words and as the Word. Can we not easily imagine 'godly conference' becoming a fight, the sermon broaching ethics in any detail offending one and not saying enough for another?[35] Cannot the best-crafted sermon be misheard? Or cannot the best of prophetic testers of preaching be ignored by the vulnerable preacher determined to avoid taking 'feedback' seriously? Yet precisely in this vulnerability of speech we must commend its missional ethical character. Christians are those in the world who will not give up on speech, constitutively, as a prophethood of believers, and therefore, constitutively, as patient, bold but not all-knowing, missional ethical agents in the debates, discussions and fine-detail policy deliberations of the world as the place to which this mission is oriented in hope.

© Andy Draycott, 2012

---

35. On some of the practicalities not addressed here see Greg Forster, *Preaching on Ethical Issues* (Cambridge: Grove Books, 2010).

PART 2: ISSUES

7. PACKAGING

Sarah E. Ruble

An ethical introduction

Missional ethics, Jonathan Rowe notes in the introduction to this volume, is 'story shaped'. The story that shapes mission is, for Christians, the biblical story, the story of God's relationship with Israel and God's revelation in Jesus. Missional ethics involves evaluating whether Christian action boasts continuity with the biblical story, whether our 'fifth act' fits with the previous acts in God's unfolding drama. So far, so good. But what are we actually evaluating in light of the biblical narrative? Not simply our lives or our actions. In order to evaluate action, we must put those actions into words. We must describe them. We choose verbs, arrange details and edit extraneous information and then put that to the scriptural test. Thus missional ethics is story shaped in another sense: what we evaluate are 'shaped stories'.

This chapter[1] focuses upon that shaping, presentation or 'packaging' in order to consider how the ways in which we tell our stories both enable and impede ethical reflection. Because I am a historian, and because the tools of a historian's trade (close readings of texts, concern for context and attention to social

---

1. Adapted from *The Gospel of Freedom and Power: Protestant Missionaries in American Culture After World War II* by Sarah Ruble, copyright © 2012 by the University of North Carolina Press. Used by permission of the publisher. www.uncpress.unc.edu.

location and power) are suited to the unpacking of stories (even as they do, in turn, create new ones), I rely on historical method to explore this topic. I use a case study in 'packaging', namely, the presentation of the relationship between evangelism and what was termed service or social concern in *Christianity Today*, the most-read evangelical periodical in America. As a historian, I have an argument about that presentation (more of that anon). For the purposes of this volume, it is important to note that the historical argument has ethical import. The relationship between evangelism and service, what we might think of as the relationship between faith and works or between the vertical (God/human) and horizontal (human/human) directions of Christianity, has significant implications for how we do ministry, how we allot resources and, indeed, how we conceive of the gospel message. The study of how mission is packaged allows for ethical inquiry as well. When we think about packaging we are thinking about how to unpack the stories we have been told, explicitly or otherwise, and about how to construct the stories we tell. This chapter presents a case study in the construction and unpacking of stories. Some of the issues may be particular to a national, non-denominational magazine but many are not. For example, questions of power, be it interpretative power or the power of gender, are found wherever people of unequal power engage in mission together. Thus the particular case reveals more general issues for those concerned with missional ethics. To that case study we now turn.

A historical introduction

In 2006, *Christianity Today* (*CT*) introduced 'The New Missions Generation' to readers. Pictures of college students reading the newspaper, fixing dinner and playing on swing sets with Hispanic children accompanied an article about a generation of college students 'excited about missions'. One promoter claimed that '[t]here's a growing confidence that 2006 could be a marker year for the rebuilding of the student missions movement'. Another declared that 'a growing awareness of justice issues is the mark of this generation . . . For that reason, we are seeing more Christian graduates wanting to give some social service to people through missions organizations.' Not all of the news was good, however. An InterVarsity worker noted that 'too many college students are not convinced about the exclusive claims of Christ and the eternal lostness of humanity'. He noted that 'young people on mission trips today may not be articulating the gospel's promise of eternal salvation through Christ's death on the Cross as clearly as they are demonstrating their concern for social justice and compassion for the poor'. Jonathan Rice, the article's author, warned that such theological laxity had subverted missions before: 'A large chunk of the missionary movement of previous generations, of course, foundered on the rocks of the social gospel.'[2]

The 'of course' signalled that *CT*'s readers would know the problems the social gospel had caused for the missionary movement. While assuming that all of his readers were long-time subscribers might not have been wise, Rice was correct that long-time *CT* readers would have been well aware of what many American evangelicals considered the excesses of social concern in mission. Since its beginning in 1957, *CT* had sought to delineate *the* evangelical positions on a wide variety of issues.[3] The proper relationship between evangelism and service and social concern on the mission field was one such issue. Although the biblical commandment to love God and to love neighbour easily joined relationship with God and service to the neighbour, *CT* writers, like Rice, found that it took more than a simple conjunction to keep them in proper relationship on the mission field.

Rice's honesty about the difficulty in holding service and evangelism together had a long tradition in the magazine. Particularly after the 1970s, the magazine's writers increasingly acknowledged that evangelical missionaries struggled to hold faith and works together. Yet as *CT* revealed some challenges in the missionary enterprise, the way it described them elided persistent issues relating to power within the evangelical community. Thus the way *CT* packaged missionaries allowed readers to see some of the difficulties inherent in holding together two central aspects of the Christian life even as it obscured ongoing tensions in the evangelical world.

Service and evangelism: the *Christianity Today* debate

When *Christianity Today* began publication in 1957, it was intended to be American evangelicalism's answer to the *Christian Century*, the flagship magazine for the Protestant mainline churches. Like the *Century*, *CT* was intended to

---

2. Jonathan Rice, 'The New Missions Generation', *Christianity Today* (September 2006), pp. 100–104.
3. A quick word on sources and terms. Both the term 'evangelical' and the utility of using *Christianity Today* as a representative of it are contestable. I am not claiming that all Americans who might be considered evangelicals read *CT*, or that it spoke for the entire evangelical community. Rather, I use *CT*, a popular and influential magazine, as a case study – one that cannot reveal what all evangelicals thought, but one that can uncover dynamics germane to larger discussions of missional ethics.

engage significant theological and social issues and to mould the views of its audience's leaders. Over time, however, *CT* grew more focused on the evangelical laity and became, in a way that the *Century* never did, a popular magazine outside pastors' studies and seminary libraries.

Although *CT*'s audience and tenor changed, its commitment to being a voice of 'evangelical conviction', often in explicit distinction from what it saw as mainline laxity, did not. The discussion about the faithful relationship between service and evangelism on the mission field was one of many places where the newly created *CT* heralded a proper evangelical understanding in opposition to what it considered a wayward liberal one. *CT*, however, did not invent the evangelical problem with liberal missiology. Since at least the beginning of the twentieth century, conservative Protestants had been concerned that many mission organizations affiliated with the historic American denominations (such as the Presbyterians, Baptists and Methodists in their various denominational forms) had substituted Christian service (constructing and running hospitals, starting schools, building YMCAs and the like) for the proclamation of the gospel to sinners. In the last decade of the nineteenth century and the first decade of the twentieth, this concern had driven the creation of faith missions such as the African Inland Mission, groups focused on direct evangelization whose missionaries would rely on God to raise their support rather than on denominational funding. Over the decades, the conviction that the historic denominations were abandoning the central focus of mission, saving sinners, grew among conservatives. So too did the belief that this lack of focus stemmed from a lack of commitment to the 'fundamental' tenets of the gospel – including a final judgment after which the unsaved would go to hell. During the 1920s, conservatives in the Northern Baptist and Northern Presbyterian denominations championed resolutions that would have required all missionaries, along with all seminary professors and pastors, to affirm the 'fundamentals' of the faith. The resolutions failed, propelling many conservatives out of the mainline denominations and moving their support to non-denominational missions. The depression of the 1930s slowed conservative mission activity, but after World War II they turned their attention and their new resources to the work of spreading the gospel abroad.

So too did mainline denominations. They were also reconsidering what missions were and how they were supposed to be done in the postwar world. In the 1950s and early 1960s, mainline missiology moved away from the language of 'missions' as a separate activity performed by individuals going abroad towards the language of the one 'mission' of the church in the world. This mission would involve bringing people into the church, but it would also involve the church's other work: attending to the needs of people and society. It was to this latest manifestation of what conservatives considered the mainline's long abandonment of evangelism that the newly created *CT* spoke.

In the 1960s, writers for the magazine evinced little doubt about the proper relationship between service and evangelism or that evangelicals faithfully maintained it. Indeed, in their certainty they could even be slightly snide. Writing in August 1960, Sherwood Eliot Wirt surveyed 'The World Mission Situation'. The situation was not good. Although the number of people who needed to hear the good news was growing rapidly, many American Christians were redefining mission 'either as inter-church aid or as just about everything a church does through its total program'. Wirt lamented that 'today the overseas "heroes" are not those who strive first and foremost to bring nationals into the Kingdom of Christ's love, but social workers who teach contour farming'. And then he could not resist: 'Not that contour farming is undesirable. But the Church of Christ seems not to have discovered a divine mandate for it until our century.'[4] Armed with what he considered the original command to preach the gospel to all, Wirt assured his readers that the mainline attempt to make service the focal point of missions was an unfaithful innovation.

Yet *CT* writers did not abjure the service component altogether. The point was not that schools, hospitals and, yes, farming were bad, nor that evangelicals should care for lost souls while neglecting empty stomachs. Rather, authors asserted that a focus on the gospel would lead to service. In a 1966 round-table discussion article Dr Richard Halverson, president of World Vision and a participant in the National Council of Churches Division of Foreign Missions, claimed:

> Of course this is what missionaries have done historically. They have gone out to reach the lost for Christ and preach the Gospel to them. The lost have had sick bodies, so the missionaries have healed them and built hospitals. They've been illiterate, so they have taught them to read and built educational systems. They've been hungry, and they have fed them; naked, and they've clothed them. This has been spontaneous in the missionary activities of the church.

Another participant jumped in: 'But it's not the primary drive, is that right?' Dr Halverson responded: 'No, they go out to preach the Gospel.'[5] Halverson's confidence fitted *CT*'s general tone in the 1960s. Evangelism led to service naturally and inevitably. Missionaries with the correct priority would almost

---

4. Sherwood Eliot Wirt, 'World Mission Situation', *CT* (1 August 1960), p. 6.
5. 'Gospel and World Religion', *CT* (9 December 1966), pp. 8–13.

inevitably hold together the various parts of their task. The real danger lay in the mainline mistake – starting with social issues. Contour farming did not necessarily lead back to soul saving. But, according to *CT*, prioritizing evangelism would result in appropriate service. Those reading could take comfort that the emphasis their movement gave to conversion was both faithful and efficacious. Beginning with justification would lead to works of mercy.

CT's confident depiction waned in the 1970s. In spite of the assurance of people like Halverson, new voices within *CT* proved sceptical that conservative missionaries had really been at the forefront of caring for the needy and addressing social issues. In 'The Missionary in the Angry Seventies', David H. Adeney proposed that 'together with Asian fellow workers we should re-examine the attitude of the church toward the injustice and suffering in society' and that 'the missionary must identify himself with the members of his church in seeking to understand how to carry out the instructions given in James 2', where the apostle demands equal treatment for rich and poor.[6] Such proposals implied that many missionaries actually had not been fulfilling the social part of their mission – and needed to do so.

Adeney's claim received further support from the wider evangelical movement in 1974. That year the International Conference on World Evangelization, called by American evangelist Billy Graham, drew more than two thousand participants from over a hundred and fifty countries to Lausanne, Switzerland. The conference issued a statement, the Lausanne Covenant, which *CT* published for its readers. The covenant's section on 'Christian Social Responsibility' averred that 'here too we express penitence both for our neglect and for having sometimes regarded evangelism and social concern as mutually exclusive. Although reconciliation with other people is not reconciliation with God, nor is social action evangelism, nor is political liberation salvation, nevertheless we affirm that evangelism and socio-political involvement are both part of our Christian duty.'[7] To those *CT* readers content that evangelicals had avoided the trap of overemphasizing one aspect of the Christian life to the detriment of the other, the words of the Lausanne Covenant provided a rebuke.

Not only did the Lausanne Covenant offer a rebuke to evangelical missions, but articles about the conference witnessed to differences among evangelical leaders. *CT* provided readers with a range – albeit a small range – of evangelical opinion. Among the Lausanne articles that *CT* published was Billy

---

6. David H. Adeney, 'The Missionary in the Angry Seventies', *CT* (11 August, 1972), p. 7.
7. 'The Lausanne Covenant', *CT* (16 August 1974), pp. 22–24.

Graham's plenary address. He affirmed the covenant language, but differentiated between what missionaries specifically were called to do (evangelize) and what others in the church were called to do (engage in social concern). In the same issue featuring Graham's address, former *CT* editor Carl Henry criticized the covenant's language on social concern as 'imprecise' and 'bland'. He argued that evangelicals needed to move beyond asserting that evangelism and social concern were compatible and should query 'whether the overcoming of social alienation is not rather a necessary aspect of the evangel' and ask whether political liberation is not 'a legitimate and even intrinsic aspect of the evangel'.[8] Peter Wagner, a prominent missiologist, writing twelve months after the conference, moved in a different direction from Henry. While claiming support for the church's social action, he named an attempt on the part of delegates to 'confuse evangelism with social action' as a 'torpedo' that could have hit (but did not) the good ship evangelization. He also described 'an attempt to confuse evangelism with Christian nurture' as a torpedo and cited a quotation about Lausanne in *Time* magazine from René Padilla, Latin American missiologist and frequent *CT* contributor, as an example of discipleship nearly gaining 'precedence over winning lost men and women to the Christian faith'.[9]

Thus *CT*'s packaging of the evangelism and service debate in the 1970s both indicated and enacted a waning of evangelical assurance. By including writers and voices that suggested evangelicals had not held service and evangelism together well, *CT* indicated the presence of doubt within the evangelical movement. By publishing authors who disagreed with each other, *CT* made the matter one of ongoing debate – at least in its influential pages. Those reading the magazine would learn that evangelical leaders differed. Those differences extended beyond the Lausanne Conference. For example, a 1976 news article on a Consultation on Theology and Mission at Trinity Evangelical Divinity School claimed that 'the liveliest debate centred on how to preach the Gospel in light of the political changes going on around the world'. One speaker, J. Herbert Kane, claimed that when working under a dictatorship a missionary could decide 'either to stick to his work or to speak out against the regime and be expelled'. Since Kane averred that 'the American missionary is an ambassador for Jesus Christ, not for Uncle Sam', he recommended not criticizing the government and concentrating on preaching the gospel.

---

8. Carl F. H. Henry, 'The Gospel and Society', *CT* (13 September 1974), pp. 66–67.
9. C. Peter Wagner, 'Lausanne Twelve Months Later', *CT* (4 July 1975), p. 8. Note that Wagner did not name Padilla in his article.

Carl Henry (who had criticized the Lausanne Covenant) asserted that 'the missionary is a member of a church on the field he serves, and he or she can encourage the church as the new society to elaborate a conscious social alternative to an objectionable national milieu and thus exemplify to the world what the justice of God requires'. In this case, Henry thought that speaking against political injustice was part of Christian witness. Should the witness lead to a prison, Henry declared that jail 'is not the worst of all pulpits in the twentieth-century mass-media world'.[10] Readers could not be certain what they should expect of their missionaries: apparent quiescence in the face of political oppression, or political pronouncement that could threaten the mission.

That was not to suggest that everything was up in the air. *CT* presented a debate, but it also presented the proper evangelical debate as limited. Immediately following the report about the debate between Kane and Henry, the article emphasized shared conviction: 'Participants had little sympathy for the ecumenical funding of revolutionary movements aimed at the overthrow of unjust regimes by violence' – the evangelical critique of what it took to be the mainline position. *CT* believed that the mainline had equated political liberation with personal salvation and had taken this position to the extreme of giving money to 'violent' revolutionaries. *CT* contributor René Padilla, whose assessment of missions at Lausanne had been disputed by fellow contributor Peter Wagner, was more pronounced than Kane and Henry in his critiques of evangelical missionaries, but still affirmed the evangelical assertion that eternal salvation should not be confused with new economic and political systems. Padilla chided missionaries for separating evangelism and social concern. Yet he also wrote *CT* articles criticizing liberation theologians for, as he saw it, reducing salvation to an experience in this world. Kane and Henry disagreed on what approach to social issues was most effective for Christian witness, but they agreed that Christian witness meant bringing sinners to Christ. Even as the magazine created the possibility of disagreement within the movement, it set the limits of acceptable dissent.

In the following decades, *CT* articles continued to affirm that evangelism and social concern should be held together. They also admitted that the two often were not and that the movement remained uncertain of how to do both. An article on a 1983 Wheaton Conference on mission, for example, explained to readers that the conference had three tracks: the church in its local setting, the church in new frontiers, and the church in response to human need. For the first week of the conference, each track met separately. In the second

---

10. 'Guidelines for Mission', *CT* (20 April 1976), p. 51.

week, 'attempts to integrate these tracks were made', but the discussions proved 'premature'.[11] The ideal, *CT* once again alerted its readers, was hard to carry out on the ground.

As the twentieth century gave way to the twenty-first, similar themes were repeated, albeit with a slightly different twist. The importance of the 'whole gospel', both faith and works, remained. Some articles suggested that the issue of their dual necessity was settled while others still seemed to be trying to convince readers. In the September 2003 issues, an interviewer asked Luis Bush, a professor at Fuller Theological Seminary's School of World Mission, 'How relevant are Christians in addressing social issues?' Bush responded, 'What became clear at the Inquiry [a recent meeting of evangelicals working to establish mission priorities] was the need for the whole gospel in word and deed.' He listed hunger, community dysfunction and AIDS as places where Christians were helping. Both the question and the answer indicated a continuing tension in evangelicalism regarding social issues. The question was asked, implying that the answer could not be assumed. Bush's response indicated that missionaries were already doing significant social work, but his phrasing, 'What became clear', suggested that some evangelicals, at least, were still looking for evidence regarding the necessity of social concern.[12]

Other articles came to the issue from a different perspective. They assumed that missionaries were involved in service activities and that such involvement was good. Yet they returned to the worry from the 1950s and 1960s that social concern had overtaken evangelism in the hearts and minds of many evangelicals. Hence the fear in 'The Next Mission Generation' that evangelical missions could still sink on the shoals of a substitution of service for evangelism. A 2006 article was even more explicit. Evangelicals had lost the fear of hell and, in so doing, were condemning non-believers to it. The article acknowledged that much of what missionaries were doing was good. Service just could not be a replacement for the proclamation of Jesus' saving death and of the reality of hell.[13]

CT's packaging of evangelism and service was notable both for its change and for its continuity. The presentation certainly shifted from the confidence

---

11. Lawson Lau, 'The Great Commission in a Tense World: Wheaton '83 Ponders the State of Missions', *CT* (2 September 1983), pp. 70–71.
12. Darrell L. Bock and Luis Bush, 'The State of Missions: An Interview with Luis Bush', *CT* (July 2003), pp. 26–31.
13. J. Robertson McQuilkin, 'Lost Mission: Whatever Happened to the Idea of Rescuing People From Hell', *CT* (July 2006), pp. 40–42.

of the 1950s and 1960s to the uncertainty of the 1970s onwards. Once that shift occurred, however, the packaging was marked by continuity. The magazine published writers who affirmed a traditional evangelical understanding of salvation – repentance for sins and acceptance of Christ. Salvation defined in political terms or the substitution (as *CT* saw it) of social concern for salvation was outside the limits of acceptable evangelical opinion. Disagreement on the proper balance and combination of evangelism and social concern was acceptable. By publishing authors who disagreed, *CT* acknowledged diversity within the evangelical community, kept the debate in front of the readers and implicitly conceded that living out two of the central commands of the Christian life was difficult in practice.

That last admission had one more import – often implicit but clear nevertheless. Since justification did not seem to lead spontaneously to good works, neither for missionaries nor for converts, careful thought about missions was necessary. The persistence of the debate within *CT* showed the need for careful reflection about mission, about social concern and about the nature of the gospel itself. *CT* packaged the debate in such a way that evangelical readers would know what the gospel was not (political liberation), but would need to continue the debate about everything it entailed.

Packaging and power

CT's packaging of the discussions about evangelism and social concern acknowledged problems combining the two on the mission field, particularly after the 1960s. The magazine also publicized different opinions among evangelicals regarding how well missionaries held the two together and how they should do so. The change stemmed, at least in part, from a change in dialogue partners. As *CT* attended less to mainline mission discussions (a task made simpler by the declining number of mainline missionaries), its writers and editors increasingly attended to the church abroad. Such a shift changed the discussion from what evangelicals were doing better than mainliners to what American evangelicals were doing wrong around the world.

Neither critiques of the missionary movement nor the voices of people from abroad were unheard of in *CT*'s pages before the 1970s. Articles in the 1960s recognized changes in the postwar world, particularly growing anti-colonialism. In articles and book reviews, *CT* writers addressed accusations of colonialist attitudes among missionaries. In 1964, for example, Don K. Smith cited racism, isolationism, paternalism and urbanization as major challenges for the church in Africa.[14] He also chided the church's slow reaction to the race problem. Moreover, *CT* occasionally included non-American, non-European authors in the 1950s and 1960s. Still, such appearances were rare, and they almost always celebrated American missionary efforts.

By the 1970s, international voices were more common in *CT* and the criticisms had shifted. Although paternalism and cultural superiority were still issues, the tension between saving people's souls and living Christian lives received significant attention. Moreover, criticisms of the movement came from people abroad who were recognized as major figures within the movement. In the 1970s and thereafter, people from abroad were presented as *bona fide* Christians capable of rendering theological judgment on white missionaries.

By one reading, the growing attendance to problems on the field and to the people abroad who identified them enacted a power shift in the pages of *CT*. White Americans had once largely controlled the description of their missionary movement. They interpreted their own behaviour and people abroad. By including the perspective of people abroad, *CT* was giving interpretative power to them. They could say whether American missionaries were engendering lives of Christian discipleship. They could determine if the way evangelists lived cohered with the gospel they preached. The packaging of the evangelism and social concern debate in *CT* asserted that Christians abroad were apt interpreters of the Christian faith and of Americans abroad. Where their perspective diverged from that of Americans, they warranted a hearing precisely because they too were Christians who possessed faithful insight.

By another reading, however, the inclusion of people from abroad in the debate about service and evangelism continued to enact the interpretative power of white Americans even as the inclusion of international voices obscured that power. In the first place, voices from abroad appeared in the pages of the magazine but not in the masthead. The editorial board was still overwhelmingly white, male and American. Final edit literally belonged to them. For all of the rhetoric in articles about growing attention to the church abroad, little about the structure of the magazine changed. Power, defined as money and control and not merely the ability to offer one's own interpretation, had not shifted at all.

Moreover, those doing the interpreting had really not shifted much. Evangelicals from abroad appeared in the magazine, but the authoritative voices still tended to be white Americans. In the articles about Lausanne, for example,

---

14. Don K. Smith, 'Southern Africa: New Discovery Needed', *CT* (31 July 1964), pp. 15–16.

the perspective of Latin American theologians René Padilla and Samuel Escobar were noted. Yet they were not given without comment. Peter Wagner, who believed that Padilla's and Escobar's focus on social concern had almost torpedoed the conference, wrote the one-year retrospective on Lausanne. Padilla also wrote for *CT*, but his articles were usually near the back, in font much smaller than Wagner's and without the front-page billing. Over the decades, other international voices received greater prominence in the magazine – major articles, for example – but the people interpreting evangelicalism were, usually, white Americans.

What people could do with their interpretative power also remained constant. The people from abroad who appeared in the magazine could criticize American missionaries, but they could not go outside the bounds of evangelical belief. People abroad had interpretative power so long as they interpreted within the limits of 'evangelical conviction' set by the editors. Byang Kato, for example, a Nigerian and the general secretary of the Association of Evangelicals of Africa and Madagascar, gave a two-part interview to *CT* in 1975. While he criticized some missionary behaviours, he affirmed a key evangelical belief: the centrality of evangelism. *Contra* those in the mainline and those abroad who were calling for a moratorium on missions, Kato averred that missionaries were still necessary because evangelism was still necessary.[15]

That editors of a magazine intended for a particular audience would feature people acceptable to that audience was not surprising. But it did reinforce white evangelicals' pre-existing way of viewing the world and limit what people from abroad could challenge. Some of the people calling for the moratorium on missions were mainline American Protestants, whom *CT* had long considered suspect. Some, however, were church leaders from abroad, particularly from Africa. Referring the matter of a moratorium to an African evangelical leader such as Kato suggested that the mainline/evangelical divide that *CT* used to define many theological issues could be applied to Christianity abroad as well. Just as *CT* had no need to hear from mainline leaders on the moratorium issue, it also had no need to hear from those abroad who supported it. Subtly, *CT* delineated between what an 'outside' perspective could faithfully challenge and what it could not. The regnant understanding of what it meant to preach the gospel to all nations was something it could not. That understanding, it appeared, transcended culture.

---

15. Byang H. Kato, 'Christian Surge in Africa, Part 1', *CT* (26 September 1975), pp. 4–7; ibid., 'Africa's Christian Future, Part 2', *CT* (10 October 1975), pp. 12–16; ibid., 'Another Look at Moratorium', *CT* (2 January 1976), pp. 41–42.

There lay the great, but largely unasked, question. *CT* accurately presented evangelicalism as a worldwide movement. Many people throughout the world did practise an evangelicalism that looked much like the American version, in no small part because American evangelicals had played a significant role in spreading the Christian message throughout the world. The question was the degree to which that version of the Christian message, including its division between evangelism and social concern, was a product of a particular history, namely, the history of Anglo-American evangelicalism and its fights with more liberal Christianities.

Gender

In August 2000, the front cover of *CT* featured a woman in a calf-length skirt, white blouse and sensible shoes carrying a backpack and a suitcase. Walking alone on a dirt road, she was clearly ready for travel. The caption 'A Mission of Their Own: Rediscovering the Call of the Woman Missionary', identified the figure as a woman going to the mission field. The word 'rediscovering' indicated something that might well have surprised *CT* readers: that the call of the woman missionary had been lost.

Concern about the loss of missionary zeal was not new in *CT*'s pages. Yet the article referenced by the picture, 'A Woman's Place', differed from other articles worried about the missionary movement's health because it focused particularly on decline in *women's* involvement and because it singled out an increased focus on evangelism as one of the culprits. According to Catherine Allen, a long-time Baptist missionary official interviewed for the article, 'the urgency to get the gospel to every corner of the earth by the year 2000 has had a negative effect on women's roles in mission'. Mission historian Dana Robert expanded upon Allen's claims: 'When mission gets redefined as "proclamation evangelism", and if you say women can't be preachers, that de facto eliminates women's work in mission.' Since many evangelical groups only allowed men ordination and pastoral leadership roles, women had to serve in other ways. And that was precisely the problem: evangelicals valued service, but for many it was subordinate to evangelism. A woman's place was second.

'A Woman's Place' named gender as an important part of the service/ evangelism debate. Historically, the article accurately argued, women had been most involved in the 'social and charitable side of mission'.[16] In the late part

---

16. Wendy Murray Zoba, 'A Woman's Place', *CT* (7 August 2000), pp. 40–48.

of the nineteenth century, women had created a network of missionary societies dedicated to sending female missionaries abroad. These missionaries focused their work on women and children, combining social service with evangelistic zeal. During the early decades of the twentieth century, many of the women's missionary societies lost their independence and were subsumed by male-dominated boards. Moreover, the 1920s witnessed increasing divisions between liberals and conservative Protestants. For many conservatives, biblical inerrancy became a hallmark of orthodoxy. With inerrancy came a greater concern for adherence to passages such as 1 Timothy 2 in which the apostle Paul declared, 'I permit no woman to teach' (v. 12). Conservatives also worried that the missionary movement had become too focused on service and de-emphasized evangelism. Among many evangelicals, the dual trends of focusing on evangelism and limiting the roles of women in church leadership would continue through to the end of the twentieth century. An editorial in the same issue as 'A Woman's Place', for example, examined the 2000 Southern Baptist Faith and Message statement that had declared that only men could be pastors. Thus throughout the twentieth century women lost power over their own mission organizations and, at least in some segments of the evangelical world, also saw their historic roles de-emphasized in favour of positions they were institutionally barred from holding.

Some, of course, might argue that barring women from ordination was not the same as barring them from evangelism. Jerry Rankin, the president of the Southern Baptist International Mission Board (IMB), made that case in a letter to the editor following the 2000 'Woman's Place' story. He argued that 'every missionary with the IMB is expected to be involved in "proclamation" ministries, using whatever their assignment may be to share the good news of that gospel. There is nothing gender specific in that.' He also noted that more women had been appointed in the previous three years than during any other three-year period and that those appointments encompassed proclamation and service ministries.[17]

Rankin's letter both clarified and obscured the issue. Certainly he was correct in pointing out to readers that evangelism was not limited to preaching or ordination. Although it would have been a misreading of the 'Woman's Place' article to think so, it was possible that some could have read it as arguing that women could only participate in service positions. That was not the case (and also not the article's claim). Yet Rankin also missed part of the point. The article not only addressed questions about female presence on the mission field, but

---

17. Jerry Rankin, 'Letter to the Editor', *CT* (23 October 2000), p. 13.

also the issue of female power in mission organizations and in shaping missions theory. Rankin's letter, in many respects, perfectly illustrated the article's point: in missions, male leaders made decisions about missionaries, the majority of whom were female, and that power dynamic went largely unnoticed.

While 'A Woman's Place' focused on trends within the missionary movement, its point was germane to *CT*'s own coverage of that movement. The article named a reality: gender mattered in missionary discussions. Yet the presentation of those discussions had very often obscured that fact. In most *CT* articles 'missions' was treated as a gender-neutral and somewhat abstract category. The emphasis was not on particular missionaries but on the practice or theology of mission generally. Those general discussions rarely mentioned gender and seemed to suggest that the conversations were equally applicable to all who served. Articles around Lausanne and its covenant, for example, paid no attention to the question of who was allowed to preach. As the discussion was presented, it seemed that all missionaries, male and female, were equally able to perform evangelistic tasks. Indeed, the exclusion of gender from the discussion may well have made it appear that gender simply did not matter on the mission field at all.

At the same time, people reading the articles would have received the message that male leadership in the movement was normal, perhaps even normative. In the July 1975 edition of *CT*, which featured a one-year reflection on Lausanne, Billy Graham's address to the Lausanne Continuation Committee was the first article. He described the genesis of the meeting and dated it to a 'small group of evangelicals gathered in Montreus, Switzerland' fifteen years previously. He mentioned eight participants: Festo Kivengere, Clyde Taylor, John Stott, Stephen Olford, Bob Evans, Bob Pierce, Carl Henry and himself. All were men. They came together to plan a conference about the missionary movement, the majority of whose rank-and-file workers were women.[18]

As the 'Woman's Place' article demonstrated, there were occasional interjections of women into the missionary discussion, although such interjections did not reliably raise issues of power. In 1983 and 1984, two women, both former missionaries, wrote articles about female missionaries for *CT*. In 1983, Elisabeth Elliot wrote about Amy Carmichael, naming her as the person who influenced Elliot the most. A year later, Miriam Adeney wrote about Mary Slessor, using her as an example of what women could do with their new-found liberation. In many ways, the articles were similar. Both covered women who worked among the poor, Carmichael in India and Slessor in Africa. Both

---

18. Billy Graham, 'Our Mandate from Lausanne '74', *CT* (4 July 1975), pp. 3–6.

emphasized the good the missionaries had done in society and among needy people. Moreover, both Elliot and Adeney held up their subjects as role models for modern women. Only at that point could subtle suggestions about power be detected. Adeney, writing about Slessor, highlighted her service as the first female British vice consul in the empire. Adeney ended her article by asking her (female) readers, 'How assertive dare we be?' and then answering her own question: 'Let us be strong, creative, goal-oriented women. But not only that, let us also be liberated beyond the confines of the philosophies of our day, liberated as was Mary Slessor to the Word and to the Spirit.'[19] Elliot's article made more of Carmichael's submission to God and her willingness to serve selflessly. A reader acquainted with the two authors would have had more context for the difference – Adeney tended to the evangelical left on women's issues, Elliot to the right – but, again, the differences in the articles themselves were subtle. And in neither case do the missionary subjects protest gendered power dynamics within the movement.

Such protests did occasionally appear. In 1980, a *CT* article contained one paragraph about frustrations expressed by some women involved with the Consultation on World Evangelization (COWE). They lamented that 'their sex provided only 9 per cent of COWE's 650 participants, none of the plenary speakers, and only three of [Lausanne Committee on World Evangelization's] 50 members'. According to the article, the programme director Saphir Athyal denied discrimination and 'indicated that women were represented in the mini consultations where the real work was done, and that every effort had been made to encourage the different regions to send women'.[20] The power problem appeared in the article. It was dismissed. The women complained about several issues, including leadership. The male leader responded (or was at least reported to have responded) by asserting that who was slated to speak to the most people was relatively unimportant. He declared that women were welcome to do 'the real work'. Yet that had long been true in the movement – even if many readers of *CT* would not have known it. Women comprised the majority of people on the ground. They just could not get onto the podium.

CT's packaging of women in missions, particularly as it related to service and evangelism, largely obscured questions related to gender. Missions appeared as a gender-neutral topic. At the same time, the normativity of male leadership was reinforced as most of the articles were written about men and, particularly

---

19. Miriam Adeney, 'A Woman Liberated – For What?', *CT* (13 January 1984), pp. 28–30.
20. James D. Douglas, 'Lausanne's Extended Shadow Gauges Evangelism Progress', *CT* (8 August 1980), p. 44.

when they discussed mission theology, by men. The impression was that the movement was dominated by men. In terms of leadership, that was absolutely the case. In terms of workers on the ground, it was not.

This packaging had significant implications. A skewed view of missionary personnel meant that some relevant questions were less likely to be asked by missionary supporters. The first was a question about meaning, namely, what it meant for missions and for the church that women outnumbered men on the mission field. Was it simply a historical by-product of old practices in which mission organizations were willing to send single women, but not single men, to the field? Was the demographic imbalance a manifestation of a similar imbalance in American churches since, as historian Ann Braude has shown, women have outnumbered men in Christian churches for most of American history? If the latter were the case, what, if any, significance did it have for understanding the Christian message and the Christian community? Why did more women than men go to church, support missionaries and themselves go to the field? Was there something in the Christian gospel that was more compelling to those who had historically boasted less economic, social or political power than to those who boasted more?

The packaging also showed and created ambivalence about whether women's experience mattered in debates about a movement in which they comprised the majority of workers. The dominant presentation of the service/evangelism debate as both gender neutral and as one largely had by men, suggested that women's particular experience on the field mattered little. On the other hand, occasional reminders that some female workers (and some *CT* writers) were unhappy with the dearth of female leaders and the lack of attention to the distinctives of female service offered another (but less dominant) view. Even with the countervailing voices there was little suggestion that taking women's experience seriously might offer a way to reframe the evangelism/service debate. Whether it would have done so faithfully or effectively is, of course, another question. The point here is that by obscuring the gender question the opportunity to use the actual experience of the majority of missionaries when thinking about the debate was also lost.

Some might argue that the presentation of the service and evangelism debate rightly paid little attention to experience, particularly to gendered experience. The gospel, the thinking goes, is timeless and not altered by human vagaries. Even were the claim granted, however, it would not address the packaging concern. Failure to consider women's experience as distinct was also a failure to consider the ways in which male experience might have been shaping how evangelism and service were framed. In other words, packaging evangelism and service as gender-neutral categories did not preclude the possibility that they were being defined through the lens of male experience – it simply made it more difficult to see that the normative voices on mission were not un-gendered, but male.

A historical and an ethical conclusion

CT's presentation of the debate about evangelism and service in mission revealed and obscured. It indicated real difficulties in holding together the vertical and horizontal aspects of the Christian faith. It also acknowledged some diversity of opinion within the evangelical community regarding the faithful relationship between the two. In so doing it opened up space in which evangelicals could wrestle with commands to love God and to love neighbour. At the same time the debate obscured ongoing issues of power within the evangelical world. Although Christians outside the USA appeared in the debates, the debate was still controlled by white Americans. Likewise, the debate was most often presented as if gender did not matter even as it was conducted primarily by men about a movement numerically dominated by women.

None of this is to suggest that *CT* was deliberately obscuring power dynamics. The magazine did address questions such as women's ordination, and including writers from outside American borders was, in all likelihood, an attempt to introduce US evangelicals to new perspectives. It is to suggest, however, that power poses problems not addressed by inclusion. Power deeply shapes the stories we tell.

When the story we tell is the gospel story, the stakes are high. That is one reason why people who exercise interpretative power do not want to abandon it. They want to protect and promote a faithful version of the message. In the American evangelical tradition this has often entailed maintaining 'orthodox' belief when tempted to make it conform to human experience. The challenge lies in discerning if purported orthodoxy is itself a product of the experience of those in power, an experience that can be made to seem normative precisely because it is the experience of the powerful. When trying to discern if we are acting as story-shaped people, we must ask what has shaped the stories we are evaluating.

History can help with this challenge. History is the task of unpacking the past, of asking how things came to be. Historians explore what causes those things we consider natural, what circumstances produced what we consider inevitable and what processes occurred to obscure cause and contingency. In the context of mission, that does not mean denying God's activity. History cannot prove that God was not active in a particular circumstance. It can reveal the role of human activity. It can offer to the Christian community accounts of how things have come to be as they are and, by showing the contingent nature of what may seem given, provide space to consider whether where we are is a faithful place. History cannot tell us what the gospel is, but it can help us understand how our definition of the gospel came to be. It can help us see how our stories have been shaped as we seek to be story-shaped people.

© Sarah E. Ruble, 2012

8. FAMILIES

Joshua Hordern

Introduction

The phrase 'missional ethics' suggests two important truths.[1] First, when the gospel is preached and people are called by the power of the Spirit to follow Christ, they are called into a way of life. Mission cannot conceivably be about seeking others' mere assent to the Lordship of Christ and his saving work. Conversion involves turning comprehensively into the path which Christ has set before us. Moreover, talk about mission reminds us that this path is corporate as well as personal – we tread it with others who are followers of Christ. We are sent along it together.

Second, although mission is not always cross-cultural, the juxtaposition of 'mission' and 'ethics' raises questions about the self-consciousness of those engaged in cross-cultural missional activity. The translation of accepted – and perhaps godly – cultural norms from one part of God's world to another may be troublesome, especially when there is some expectation that converts should leave their birth community to assimilate to a foreign culture. The ethics of the missionary should not necessarily be the ethics of the people served by mission. An

---

1. I gratefully acknowledge the generous support of the Sir Halley Stewart Trust which has enabled me to conduct research for this essay and prepare it for publication.

important contemporary missiological focus for such discussion is the so-called 'Insider Movement' which, at least initially, was focused on Jesus Christ's mission among Muslims. Rebecca Lewis helpfully defines an Insider Movement as

> any movement to faith in Christ where (a) the gospel flows through pre-existing communities and social networks and where (b) believing families, as valid expressions of the Body of Christ, remain inside their socio-religious communities, retaining their identity as members of that community while living under the Lordship of Jesus Christ and the authority of the Bible.[2]

The core question raised by this movement is whether and in what way people may remain in important senses Muslim while accepting a call to follow Jesus Christ as Lord and Saviour, a question to which we shall return below.[3]

This second point is especially relevant to families. Understanding the significance of families in Jesus Christ's mission will involve reckoning both with the various forms of God's revelation and with the theological, social and political contexts Christ's mission encounters. If churches are to be faithful to Christ in their moral reflection and deliberation towards action, then they must be deeply attentive to the dual testimony of the Scriptures and creation. If such faithful churches are to engage missionally in moral reflection and deliberation towards action, then they must pay careful attention to the cultural context into which they are sent by Christ. This is the case within relatively homogenous cultures and within the highly plural settings common in late Western democracies and continental unions such as the European Union. For those who do cross cultures in mission, one must be aware both of the culture to which one is sent and, just as importantly, of one's own cultural context. This is often colloquially but unwisely referred to as the 'baggage' one carries around. 'Baggage' suggests

---

2. Rebecca Lewis, 'Promoting Movements to Christ within Natural Communities', *International Journal of Frontier Missions* 24:2 (Summer 2007), pp. 75–76.
3. The original article which launched this debate was by John Travis, 'The C1 to C6 Spectrum', *Evangelical Missions Quarterly* 34 (1998), pp. 407–408. For an introduction to the discussion, cf. John Travis, 'Messianic Muslim Followers of Isa: A Closer Look at C5 Believers and Congregations', *International Journal of Frontier Missions* 17:1 (Spring 2000), pp. 53–59. For more recent elements of the conversation, cf. Joseph Cumming, 'Muslim Followers of Jesus?', www.lausanne.org/global-conversation/muslim-followers-of-jesus.html; and Rick Brown, 'Biblical Muslims', *International Journal of Frontier Missions* 24:2 (Summer 2007), pp. 65–74, accessible at www.ijfm.org/PDFs_IJFM/24_2_PDFs/24_2_Brown.pdf.

items which are easily separable from the self, like a knapsack or valise. But familial cultural patterns are not like this. Elderly relatives not living with their children, students 'going away' to university, so-called 'bourgeois' patterns of familial respectability and, with sad irony, the tacit or not-so-tacit acceptance of widespread marital and familial breakdown – all these cultural forms are not easily popped away in the loft when one sets out on mission.

Taking together both the scriptural and cultural forms of missional attentiveness, consider the cultural contexts specifically addressed by the Scriptures. The life of the tribes and families of Israel in its Ancient Near Eastern context was known and addressed in detail by Yahweh. The patterns of Old Testament familial life shared much with that of other contemporary cultures. And yet Israel was sent as a light among these cultures. Their familial ethos was a structural feature of the prism through which the light was filtered. Perception of that light was intended to be the entry point for the nations into the global purposes of Yahweh the LORD whose own cultural knowledge emerged supremely in the New Testament mission of Jesus. For when Christ incarnate came to bring fulfilment to Israel, his own flesh and blood, he knew them well enough. But they, like all the world, did not recognize him and did not receive him.

Just as Jesus knew the missional context to which he was called, so it is part of the churches' divine calling to know the peoples among whom they are sent, in their specific cultural gifts and sins. Churches do this not simply as Jesus' followers but as the brothers, sisters and co-heirs of Christ, the firstborn from among the Father's family of the faithful dead. This eschatological horizon is ever-present in our missiological considerations, since sending logically entails an ultimate destination towards which we are sent. Faith trusts that although the mission of the churches may wander like the Israelites in the wilderness, yet that mission is providentially ordered towards the promised consummation of all things in Christ. Therefore, a descriptive understanding both of the world and the work of Christ is basic to churches' mission. Our 'missional ethics' must attend to the peoples amongst whom we tabernacle, the neighbours in their families to whom we have been sent.

Families today

But to speak of the families to which we are sent today is not to talk about one thing but many things. Article 16 of the United Nations Declaration on Human Rights, echoed in Article 12 of the European Convention on Human Rights, domesticated in UK law in the 1998 Human Rights Act, teaches us that everyone has 'a right to marry and to found a family'. However, the meaning of these words has been differently interpreted. Whether in Europe or the USA, diverse familial forms are operative, from the 'typical' family of two married heterosexual parents with children, to families with unmarried parents, to families where children are raised by a single parent with or without extended family support, to same-sex partnerships where adoption, artificial insemination or some other factor has made parenting responsibilities conceivable. Discussion of mission and family today is very obviously bound up with contests about sexual ethics and the relatively novel field of bioethics.

Beyond these traditionally Western conversations, there are other manifestations of diversity. In Pakistan and the Philippines, Islam and Catholic Christianity respectively have, in different ways, fostered an enduring consciousness of familial solidarity through the extended family of uncles and aunts, cousins and others. And now these patterns of life nurtured over centuries further afield have arrived in Europe and the United States through the rich, dynamic yet sometimes challenging or even disturbing effects of large-scale immigration. For every voice celebrating strong Muslim family bonds one hears cries of lament or anger over forced marriages, violence against homosexuals or the practice of concealing the face to preserve honour and spiritual purity. Those who rightly praise the devotion of overseas Filipino workers to their families back home also debate vigorously the issues of overpopulation, poverty, women's health and, indeed, church teaching which accompany the low use of contraception and make familial separation necessary. And in China there are the vast yet somewhat politically homogenized missional challenges with respect to family life. There, contra Psalm 127:3–5, a man's quiver is typically permitted but one arrow, although there is greater variation in family size than is often recognized. At the other end of life, the combination of breakneck-speed urbanization and the intense pressures of million upon million of Chinese pensioners is even now opening up fascinating missional opportunities as the Chinese government considers outsourcing care of the elderly to churches.

The modern West has lacked subtlety with respect to family life. The 'right to found a family' says remarkably little about what is right or desirable about any particular family, although other declared rights offer surprising details about, for example, paid holiday.[4] But even configuring family life politically is hardly uncontroversial. For some, politics is relevant to families solely with respect to criminal activity or, at most, to forms of universal social provision such as policing,

---

4. United Nations Declaration of Human Rights, Article 24, states that 'everyone has the right to rest and leisure, including reasonable limitation of working hours and periodic holidays with pay'.

education and healthcare. Politics, as the task of doing justice, some suggest, should not interfere with the form and pattern of the family. But in some forms of both Christianity and Islam – as for aspects of Old Testament Israel – the family is highly politicized. If the life of a nation depends on the stability of certain familial patterns, then coercive government should be engaged, perhaps forcefully, in so-called 'private' matters. Not for nothing is the Israelite son who rebels against his family to be condemned by the elders and stoned by all the men of the city (Deut. 21:18–21). This act of disinheritance by death is a microcosm of the larger threat of disinheritance under which Israel stands as Yahweh's adopted son.[5] Widespread concerns are present within Muslim and Christian discourse about the decay of the traditional family, whether through immigrant communities losing respect for their roots or through the perceived liberalization of the definition of marriage and family in, for example, UK and US law.

However, a modern Western *reticence* about politicizing 'the family' has, according to various feminist thinkers, entailed inattention to differences between the sexes and the emergence of what came to be called 'gender', '*the deeply entrenched institutionalization of sexual difference*'.[6] The late Susan Moller Okin called time on male, religious and academic blindness to the gendered patterns which structure contemporary social and political existence and discourse, accusing political thinkers from John Rawls to Alasdair MacIntyre of failing properly to explore how justice concerns families. Rawls's more forgivable mistake was to assume a gendered pattern of family life and leave it unchallenged by his theory of justice. For Okin, MacIntyre was altogether worse since he encouraged the West to relearn traditioned forms of patriarchal political discourse and practice, drawing directly on those (mainly Christian) sources which reinforced patterns of inequality between the sexes and sustained gendered society.[7] Despite deep gender blindness among philosophers and society at large, Okin envisaged a time when men and women would imagine the experience of the opposite sex in a way which significantly shapes political practice. Her mission was to reorder human thinking so that women would no longer be dominated by men through formal or informal social patterns, but rather have equal access to paid work and shared, equal responsibility for domestic work, including the nurturing of children.[8]

---

5. Jonathan Burnside, *God, Justice and Society* (Oxford: Oxford University Press, 2011), pp. 195–196.
6. Susan Moller Okin, *Justice, Gender and the Family* (New York: Basic Books, 1989), p. 6.
7. Ibid., pp. 43–73.
8. Ibid., pp. 105ff.

Okin's feminist passion for justice should stir Christian churches to re-evaluate their own thinking about families. An account of Christ's mission which did not pay attention to feminist analysis such as Okin's would be inadequate. 'Gendered' forms of family life are still routinely and self-consciously chosen by women and men. Some highly qualified, contemporary Western women opt out of the paid labour market and spend time at home with children. Moreover, some Muslim women seem delighted with the public wearing of veils and denounce attempts to restrict such forms of public appearance.

It is within these highly politicized contests about gender and family life which span religions, eras and sexual mores that Christian mission is situated. Missional family ethics in today's culture is inescapably bound up with diverse theological, political and social missions whose influences profoundly affect the people to whom Christians reach out in love. Churches have the challenge of learning how to speak and act in this milieu. This challenge is both ethical and missional, since churches' teaching and practice not only shape the life of Christians but also either repel or attract the people of the world, the vast majority of whom invest their humanity deeply in familial concerns.

Creation and Israel

In this situation, churches should always continue to turn to God as revealed in Scripture and supremely through Christ as the determinative authority for their life and practice. Through Christ, the firstborn of all the created order, the fulfilment of Israel and the desire of the nations, we see the display of the Godhead and discover the vocation of humanity. This vocation is, from the first, familial and missional. When the male and female are commanded to be 'fruitful and multiply, and fill the earth and subdue it' (Gen. 1:28), they are commissioned as a representative couple of a species among other species. To be familial is, therefore, of the essence of human participation in the generically and teleologically defined creation order.[9] To be familial is the given and inescapable way of being in the world. The givenness of conception, pregnancy and birth situate human creatures as interdependent beings within this

---

9. For this conception, see Oliver O'Donovan, *Resurrection and Moral Order* (Leicester: Apollos, 1994), pp. 31–52; for an account of the given, natural ordering of human, familial experience and the criticism such a notion has undergone, see Brent Waters, *The Family in Christian Social and Political Thought* (New York: Oxford University Press, 2007), esp. pp. 60–82.

wonderful and inescapable order. From the beginning, families are God's way for people to be received into the world. But people are not simply aspects of families without remainder. Although as parents we 'helped to call [children] from non-being to being, yet we did not call to them'.[10] God calls and God sends. They are known by God to be present before ever their presence is known by their parents. In that sense, notwithstanding the increased effectiveness of contraception in ordering unitive sexual love, family life is not strictly speaking 'up to us', nor is anyone reducible to their family identity. This is the missional logic of the created order itself in which each person is known and unknown, 'our' child and yet sent by God for purposes known only to God.

In Genesis we learn of God's judgment against humanity's attempt to know what should not be known and to define the terms of their life by themselves. Man and woman are sent out in a second sorrowful sense, dismissed from the experience of blessedness. The promise of fruitful begetting becomes the experience of painful labour. Tilling the earth becomes a toilsome curse. There is no way back to the blessed life with God, but only a way forward together, in which begetting and death are the constant, given theme of family life. And yet the patriarchal narratives of Genesis disclose how families, however sinful and broken, continue to be central to God's mission. Throughout Genesis, there is a progressive filling of the earth, abruptly halted in the flood before being re-inaugurated in the Noahic commission and covenant. Noah's descendants are sent out across the face of the earth in continued obedience to the commission, before assuming a cosmic significance in Abraham, whose call is God's response to the descent of humanity into sin. Through Abraham, 'all the families of the earth' will be blessed (Gen. 12:3). God does not desert his initial missional vision, but reaffirms and reorients it to bring blessing. In the story of Abram and Sarai we learn again about the givenness of children who are sent into the world by God even amidst barrenness. Abraham's and Isaac's journey to the land of Moriah illustrates precisely the way in which children are sent and received, known and unknown by their creaturely families. They are indeed 'a heritage from the LORD' (Ps. 127:3–5).

Thereafter, it is in Israel, the manifold fruits of Abraham's grandson's loins formed as a people at Sinai, that God concentrates his wisdom for families in

---

10. Paul Ramsey, *One Flesh: A Christian View of Sex Within, Outside and Before Marriage* (Grove Books, 2009), pp. 4–5; originally 'A Christian Approach to the Question of Sexual Relations outside of Marriage', in *The Journal of Religion* 45.2 (April 1965), pp. 100–118.

a fallen, Ancient Near Eastern world. In Israel, called out as a light to the nations, the familial, missional logic of the created order is given detailed social and political form. The natural, created order of the world is inter-related with Israel's life so that 'the story of universal creation is everywhere infused by Torah'.[11] The same God who created the earth also gave law fit for earthly life. The law given at Sinai 'is profoundly affirming of the emerging human sense of that which is right. Yet it is more than a mere reminder of what we already know. It deepens our understanding and fills it out.'[12] This witness to righteousness is missional, intended for the nations around who will say, 'Surely this great nation is a wise and discerning people!' (Deut. 4:6).

Good news for families today

If this is so, the missional logic of the inter-relation of created order and Torah as disclosed through Israelite family life and marriage practices should be examined. What could be learned from Israelite family practices which will assist contemporary Christian missional ethics in non-Western settings and in the robustly anti-patriarchal, anti-traditional context in which Western churches are called and sent today? Two politico-missional points suggest themselves.

Endogamy and exogamy

Israelites seem to have lived in groups called 'father's households'. A father's household, comprising all the relatives of a single living head (barring married daughters), would have consisted of several nuclear families. Several fathers' households, probably bound together by common membership of a kin-group (*mišpaḥâ*), would have formed a village.[13] These patterns gave a structure for understanding Torah and for the processes of adjudication which Torah required. Of particular relevance is the influence that kinship identity, 'endogamy' and 'exogamy' had on marriage. Endogamous marriage consists in marrying within a certain ethnic or social group and was the mandated

---

11. Burnside, *God, Justice and Society*, p. 73.
12. Ibid., p. 84.
13. Carol Myers, 'The Family in Early Israel', in L. Perdue et al. (eds.), *Families in Ancient Israel* (Louisville: John Knox Press, 1997), pp. 1–47, 37; cf. Jonathan Rowe, *Michal's Moral Dilemma: A Literary, Anthropological and Ethical Interpretation* (New York: T. & T. Clark, 2011), pp. 60–62; Christopher Wright, *God's People in God's Land: Family, Land and Property in the Old Testament* (Carlisle: Paternoster, 1990), p. 48.

practice of Israel. From Genesis to Deuteronomy, national, corporate, missional identity is safeguarded substantially through strict adherence to such practice. God's will for Israelite men is that they trust him by marrying only within the people, not going after foreign wives and so being led into idolatry. The father's household was a specific grassroots way in which endogamous relations could be grasped. Entering into sexual relationships with non-Israelites would have a negative impact on the integrity and worship of these communities. Whether or not one's spouse came from this particular group of nuclear families or other kinspeople, the principle of Israelite corporate identity was forged in these close-knit groupings.

But there are limits to endogamous marriage, especially visible in the classification of sexual offences through attention to familial affinity. Forming a faithful sexual covenant in marriage requires moving out from certain familial relationships and therefore excludes a certain range of endogamy. For example, under pain of death, a son should not have sexual relations with or marry his father's wife (Lev. 20:11) and a father-in-law should not have sexual relations with or marry his daughter-in-law (Lev. 20:12). A brother who has sexual relations with his sister shall be cut off from among the people (Lev. 20:17). The reasons for these bans lie partly in beliefs about the proper ordering of the generations and the sexes in light of the relational damage done when these are not respected. A deceased father is dishonoured if his wife is taken as a wife by his son. As in many cultures then and now, sexual relations with close kindred such as siblings are taboo. An Israelite who engages in sexual relations with a mother's or father's sister must bear his iniquity (Lev. 18:12–14). Although this is not discussed in the text, such bans on sexual relations also have empirically verifiable genetic benefits. As we will see below, such genetic concerns are particularly significant with respect to cousin-marriage, which is not prohibited by Torah and is rather practised both by the patriarchs and in Israel as an endogamous method of retaining cohesion and property (see Num. 27:1–11; 36:1–12).[14]

A limited exogamous movement, as an aspect of group endogamy, is therefore built into the fabric of Israel's instantiation of human familial life.[15] The levitical provisions about the inappropriate and appropriate forms of initiation for new unions and new nuclear families have exercised considerable

---

14. Rowe, *Michal's Moral Dilemma*, p. 146.
15. Whether genetic malformation of offspring was conceivable in a pre-fallen world with a small genetic pool is not to the point in this context, since what are at stake are specific legal provisions for a fallen world.

influence on Christian mission through the widespread acceptance by various Christian churches of a table of kindred and affinity specifying who may not marry whom. Organizing the crucial institution of marriage has become a key element of churches' mission to the world. But the critical question follows as to what difference the advent of Christ has made to the conception of endogamy and exogamy. Have churches simply taken over patterns of family life from Israel without modification by the gospel? How is the mission of Christ formative for the missional logic of Christian family ethics?

A key distinctive is the strong contrast between Israelite and Christian approaches to social endogamy. Israel were strictly forbidden from intermarrying with other nations. Moses fled to Midian and married the pagan Jethro's daughter. But Jethro effectively converted to Moses' faith before he offered the organizational advice which was so important to the proper adjudication of Torah in families.[16] For all his wisdom and proverbial instruction, Solomon's downfall was bound up with his marriage to foreign wives (1 Kgs 11:1–8), the archetype of Israelite disobedience and idolatry. But the New Testament is stunningly silent on any requirement for an ethnic test on prospective marriage partners. What is decisive is each potential spouse's faith in Christ. A person's ethnic background is of no necessary concern. Whatever Paul is talking about when he comments that believers should not be yoked (unequally) with unbelievers (2 Cor. 6:14–18) – and it may well be marriage – he is addressing a mixed Gentile–Jew Corinthian church and is therefore reorienting the meaning of Leviticus 26:12 in terms of the transnationalist expectation of Isaiah 52:11. Elsewhere Paul is clearer on the point when he advises that the widowed believer should only marry again if the man is 'in the Lord' (1 Cor. 7:39).

Gone is the need for endogamy to concern a particular tribe or nation. There is no New Testament expectation that a Jewish follower of Christ should only marry a fellow Jew. Instead there is a Christ-defined endogamy. This is now so embedded in the Western Christian consciousness as to be almost beyond notice. But it is hard to overestimate the immense missional importance of this change. Although, as we shall consider, social, ethnic or even (a limited) familial endogamy might still have value for mission, ethnic exogamy is made not only permissible but even positively beneficial in the context of Christian churches springing up among all the nations.

For this outwards, intercultural logic of mission implies both a relativizing of cultural certainties and a receptivity to diverse forms of cultural wisdom. When an Englishman marries a Scot, the differences in familial wisdom may

---

16. Burnside, *God, Justice and Society*, pp. 122–123.

be subtle, relating mainly to Rugby Union. But when an Englishman marries a Filipino, the differences are dramatic and concern obligations to the extended family, childcare and matriarchal control over family finances. Christianity both relativizes sporting rivalries and amends long-standing cultural patterns, even those specifically mandated by Torah such as food laws, so important to any domestic setting and at the heart of the transition towards mission to the Gentiles. The goodness of cross-cultural Christian marriage lies partly in the culturally destabilizing effects it brings and the new possibilities for repentance, insights and surprises which emerge. Even in marriages between spouses of similar cultural backgrounds, such as between a Scot and an Englishman, there are yet extensive possibilities for learning and adjustment, generation by generation, as expressions of family wisdom meet one another and are resolved, hopefully, by God's grace, for the better.

Of course, one must not mistake a modern, Western, middle-class preference for choice and mobility concerning marriage with an exogamous missional logic. Marriage practices, especially cousin-marriage, in majority-Muslim cultural settings bring the matter into stark relief. Where social mobility for men and women is in short supply, the possibilities for exogamous marriage and challenges to social norms or religious beliefs are severely reduced. This is a particularly pressing matter for Christian mission for two reasons.

First, there is the growing evidence that cousin-marriage, which accounts for around half of marriages in countries such as Pakistan,[17] attracts a significant increase in the incidence of congenital birth defects, up from roughly 2% to 4%.[18] And yet beneficial aspects of consanguineous marriage, including social compatibility and the strengthening of property holdings, continue to outweigh these genetic downsides. Such benefits meant that cousin-marriage was hardly unknown in Christian civilizations – most famously, Queen Victoria and Prince Albert were first cousins. Moreover, as noted above, neither biblical law nor the Christian Tables of Kindred and Affinity banned such marriages. Nonetheless,

---

17. For readily available authoritative research and statistics as well as an extensive bibliography, cf. www.consang.net/index.php/Summary, a website related to the work of Professor Alan Bittles. 'The simplest explanation for [the continuing prevalence of cousin-marriage] is that as greater numbers of children survive to marriageable age, the traditional social preference for consanguineous unions can be more readily accommodated.'

18. 'In terms of birth defects, [Bittles] says, the risks rise from about 2% in the general population to 4% when the parents are closely related.' Cited from http://news.bbc.co.uk/1/hi/health/7404730.stm.

Christian mission that is genuinely concerned for the health of neighbours across generations should take seriously the need for further research and education focusing on infant morbidity and mortality linked to consanguinity.

Second, Christian mission among Muslims has to reckon with the widespread incidence of cousin-marriage as a specific missiological challenge. This same endogamous phenomenon which supported Israel's internal cohesion and occasionally bound together royal families in Christian Europe has unsurprisingly similar effects in Muslim cultures. Of course, a narrower gene pool does not necessarily entail homogeneity of faith. However, familial pressures towards conformity are extremely strong in many Muslim settings and so it is worth considering what the impact on mission would be if cultural tendencies towards first-cousin-marriage decreased in strength. It seems possible that this would open up greater possibilities for wider patterns of social interaction, including among those who do not share the family's faith. The social restrictions which accompany cousin-marriage militate against such expansion. Accordingly, it seems reasonable that Christian mission should seek that Muslim women, a hard-to-reach group, have greater freedom to determine the range of social relations in which they engage. On the other hand, this thought must be held in tension with the missional benefits of cultural appropriateness and group solidarity which cousin-marriage among Muslim-background converts to Christ brings, benefits which are characteristically misunderstood or undervalued by those who are used to the common Western model of strangers meeting, marrying and forming more-or-less isolated nuclear families.

This is by no means a fringe missional concern considering the vast numbers of Muslims there are in the world, the importance of families in Islamic practice and the relative isolation of some Muslim women from wider social and educational opportunities. Moreover, if there is a good case for hoping for some relaxation of the tendency towards cousin-marriage, Christianity may find here the beginning of shared understanding with Okin's passionate feminism. Okin was firmly opposed to what she perceived as a Christian patriarchalism which closed down options for women. However, there is considerable diversity in the way that men exercise familial authority both between and within different forms of Christianity and Islam. The surprising point of unity between Christian mission and feminist political ethics concerns promoting exogamous marital relations as well as adapting the form of family life itself. For Okin, this freedom is critical for developing proper awareness of justice in families. If women's choices both of marriage partner and of their role within marriage are severely restricted by male dominance, this is dehumanizing for everyone concerned.

For Christianity, the freedom concerning a marriage partner is a matter of Christian liberty for, from the horizon of the new creation, Christian marriage is essentially bound up with the Christ-centred endogamy discussed above. This leads to a specific missiological challenge facing male and female converts to Christ from majority-Muslim countries who wish to remain in their home area and marry a fellow follower of Christ. For some this is simply impossible, since conversion must remain secret (C6 on Travis's scale, see Appendix below). But for others, churches have the opportunity to act *in loco parentis* in order to arrange introductions between men and women or formalize relationships already initiated. This has sometimes caused deep, long-term distress as the parents, siblings and other relatives of converts suffer shame and isolation despite continued allegiance to Islam.[19] These kinds of issues represent immense challenges to Christian mission. How are local churches, defined by allegiance to Christ, to reaffirm the creaturely gift of marriage and family life and yet overcome cultural patterns which might deny Christ-centred consensual marriage and sexual relations? The response of the Insider Movement (C5) has been to affirm good, given, natural qualities of Muslim family life and so refuse to be 'extracted' into an often Westernized ecclesial setting. To remain identifiably within their own Muslim community, following traditional familial forms where possible and yet being faithful followers of Christ is the challenging call which these Insiders believe is made upon them by Christ.

Ecclesial consanguinity

Such challenges facing Muslim background converts to Christ focus the mind on both the role of churches and the very different missional challenges surrounding family and marriage in the majority populations of the West. Jesus' death and resurrection ushered in a new form of consanguinity, not one which concerned the genetic make-up of particular sexual unions but one which ensured the permanence of a people's eschatological union. In the new covenant, being of the same blood by drinking of the one cup is the defining mark of the new communal reality which the gospel has established. Brent Waters comments that when

> a family receives the sacrament they do so as members of the body of Christ. They approach the Lord's Table not as wife and husband, mother and father, daughter and son, but as sisters and brothers in Christ. Their familial roles are decentred in sharing this eschatological meal.[20]

---

19. Brown, 'Biblical Muslims', p. 69.
20. Waters, *The Family in Christian Social and Political Thought*, p. 234.

In light of the good news of bodily membership with Christ, Waters holds that the church should not be conceptualized after the pattern of an earthly family and so overfreight the concept of family with ecclesial meaning. To do so would underplay the significance of the new community of Christ, the goodness of creaturely familial life and, indeed, the vocation to the single life which Christ himself commended and embodied and which, while dependent on family life, yet points beyond it.

The goal of the new community is not ultimately described as a family, but as a city, the New Jerusalem coming down out of heaven from God. This is by no means to set aside the truth of the fraternity and sorority of believers with Christ, but rather to situate that truth within the overriding shape of the kingdom of God. In that kingdom, there is no marriage or giving in marriage. There are no fathers, mothers, uncles, aunts, grandparents or cousins.[21] By baptism, people are born again by water as members of the kingdom and it is this second birth which is decisive for a person's identity.

But the creaturely familial affinity is not simply replaced by an ecclesial affinity. The new heaven and new earth will not blot out the memory of creaturely, familial relations. Baptism gives an indication of this, since what 'occurs at the baptismal font extends back into the family, reinforcing a sense of sojourning within a vindicated creation being drawn towards its appointed end in Christ'.[22] Being born again does not necessarily entail being borne away out of our most intimate, creaturely loves, but rather their reconfiguration according to Christ's dramatic announcement (Luke 14:26). Moreover, as he was borne away to death, he specifically made provision for the care of his birth mother (John 19:25–27). All this suggests that on the eschatological level, familial memory will be part of the glory of the Lamb whose providential care through families is basic to his mission. The cosmic significance of Abraham and Sarah attests this and, if we have eyes to see it, the narratives of our own families, whether good or bad, offer such testimony too.

So such a reorientation of affinity to Christ our brother is by no means an undermining of creaturely family life. Instead, by guarding against the idolatries which can creep into even Christian affirmations of family life, new ecclesial fellowships enable the family to be what it should be. As Waters suggests, 'The church affirms that its temporal ordering and providential witness entails [sic] the roles of spouse, parent, child, and sibling, but they are tempered, though

---

21. For the sense of parenting spiritual children, cf. Augustine, *De Bono Coniugali* (*On the Good of Marriage*), 19; 1 Tim. 1:2.
22. Waters, *The Family in Christian Social and Political Thought*, p. 234.

not negated, by their eschatological fellowship as sisters and brothers in Christ.'[23] The resurrection and ascension of Christ to the Father's right hand indicate that creaturely familial structures are incapable of capturing the purposes for which God intends human creatures. Two will be lying together – one will be taken but the other left (Luke 17:34). The creaturely marital bed cannot bear the weight of glory for which God intends the royal bride of Christ. Instead, the mission of the created family will reach its climax at the return of Christ when the children of the King are revealed.

Moral order, justice and the Insider Movement

With this eschatological horizon in mind, we can enquire with all the more confidence into the providential significance of families. Christian mission today must reaffirm the given goodness of family life in the face of widespread and deep-rooted doubts. The complexities of doing so in the contemporary West include the realities of widespread cohabitation and divorce. Moreover, in some Western contexts, the *Zeitgeist* arbitrarily prefers a plasticity in human relationships which can be moulded to suit individual preference and slavishly follows a rhetoric of rights which largely lacks sufficient content and contextualization to be plausible.

However, if mission is about the genuine conversion of people to Christ, it is also about the conversion of people to the moral order itself in all its givenness and glory, held together in Christ. This is the basic moral corollary of the good news of the incarnation, cross and resurrection. In fulfilling Israel's elected purpose as a light to the nations, the incarnate Jesus reaffirmed creaturely life in its givenness. He was sent and received by a family although, like Isaac, his particular missional purpose was anticipated by his mother from his conception. Moreover, Luke is careful to observe that, on return from his unscheduled Passover sojourn at the temple, Jesus 'was obedient' to his parents (Luke 2:51) and that he 'increased in wisdom and in years' as he grew up under their care. Although he did not himself pursue the typical Jewish life of marriage, there is nothing to suggest that Jesus' early family life did not conform to the usual pattern of obedient submission, synagogue attendance and scriptural study.

In participating in this givenness of family life within a specific cultural form, the Son of God willingly submitted himself to the created restriction of being in relationships which were involuntary. Although the Father and the Son agreed together that the Son should be born by the Spirit through a chosen woman, Mary, nonetheless, in his dependence on Mary and in being born into

---

23. Ibid., pp. 230–231.

a certain family, Jesus became related to a network of people which he – as a human – was not choosing. John the Baptist may have leaped in Elizabeth's womb, but Jesus did not stir at this strange encounter with his cousin. The recognition that God had chosen her to bear the Messiah was treasured in Mary's heart long before the foetus to be named Jesus was aware of God's mission that he be Saviour of the world.

The vindication of creaturely familial life points towards the differences between Christian mission and aspects of contemporary political theory wherein this givenness of familial life has been under-recognized. Martha Nussbaum, another feminist philosopher, has articulately explored the failings of some liberal contractarian accounts which have not attended to the infantile experience of nurture and caregiving which is basic to the humanity of all people.[24] Even liberal contractarian political philosophers, one supposes, once suckled at their mothers' breasts. But even if we take the interdependence and timeliness of humanity as a political given, there are still rival accounts of what family life should mean for the 'mission' of humanity or, on the modern liberal political level, of individual citizens.

Deuteronomy emphasizes the family and wider kinship group as the place in which the Torah is pondered and learned. Abraham, the 'wandering Aramean' (Deut. 26:5), and his family, were trained to be adjudicators of justice (Gen. 18:17–19). In the people of Israel, 'the family is at the cutting edge of day-to-day justice because it is in this setting that wisdom is internalized, with wisdom being essential to doing justice'.[25] Accordingly, if the people of Israel are to live a national life worthy of their sovereign Lord, then family scriptural study is indispensable. Moses is depicted instructing the people to 'Keep these words that I am commanding you today in your heart' and to recite and talk about them on every occasion (Deut. 6:4–9). Moreover, as already suggested, it is through the family that the work of legal adjudication is experienced at a grassroots level. Torah requires judgment in its application to the people and the 'judges at first instance' are the 'rulers of tens' (see Exod. 18:21) who are the heads of families.[26] For Burnside, 'biblical adjudication sees social order as founded on the family. This is the context for developing wisdom, informal social controls and self-restraint.'[27] The *kind of light* which Israel is to the

---

24. Martha Nussbaum, *Upheavals of Thought: The Intelligence of Emotions* (Cambridge: Cambridge University Press, 2003).
25. Burnside, *God, Justice and Society*, p. 87.
26. Ibid., p. 123.
27. Ibid., p. 141.

Gentiles is substantially determined by the familial character of the social and legal order of the people. The mission of God in Israel is deeply familial inasmuch as God's wisdom is displayed and mediated through the family structures. This pattern strongly emphasizes the importance of parental involvement in a child's moral and theological education. Accordingly, Christians will join with Okin in criticizing political theories which 'take mature, independent human beings as the subjects of their theories without any mention of how they got to be that way'.[28]

At the same time they would query that anyone should ever be called an *independent* human being. For Martha Nussbaum, the mission of family life is growth into mature *interdependence*.[29] The presupposition of Deuteronomy seems to be that the whole family and indeed the whole *mišpaḥâ* are involved in the education of children. Families were the places where people first learned the love, righteousness and faithfulness of Yahweh mediated through their parents' and wider family's teaching.[30] Moreover, they were places where expectations about appropriate forms of relationship between the sexes were explored according to Torah. The commandment to 'Honour your father and your mother, so that your days may be long in the land that the LORD your God is giving you' (Exod. 20:12) was the primary formation for the child–parent relationship. But this command made sense only in the context of the rest of Torah which the parents were meant to teach their children. The mission of Israel was dependent on families being schools of Torah.

From the perspective of contemporary political contests over the family, both Okin and Rawls believe that the family is meant to be a kind of school of political virtue, especially the virtue of justice. The form of family life in which people grow up is basic to their perception of what justice entails in the polity at large. But for Okin, Rawls's failure to question gender patterns meant that his account of justice was skewed. If oppressive subordination of females in family life is normative in a child's upbringing, then this is likely to be his or her expectation of society at large, thereby stripping away a child's potential to pursue the mission of gender justice. In summary, 'The family – currently the linchpin of the gender structure – must be just if we are to have a just society, since it is within the family that we first come to have a sense of ourselves and our relations with others that is at the root of moral

---

28. Ibid., p. 9.
29. Nussbaum, *Upheavals of Thought*, pp. 224ff.
30. Nussbaum would also rightly add that in the family one learns vulnerability, affective awareness and empathy; ibid., pp. 174ff.

development.'³¹ Accordingly, Okin challenges what she takes to be the traditionally patriarchal reality in Western societies, commenting that 'Surely nothing in our natures dictates that men should not be equal participants in the rearing of their children. Nothing in the nature of work makes it impossible to adjust it to the fact that people are parents as well as workers.'³² Her mission for justice is rooted in the perception that '[u]nderlying all ... inequalities [between the sexes] is the unequal distribution of the unpaid labour of the family'.³³

Two missional observations are in order. First, more briefly, serious questions for mission follow from Okin's account of justice and equality. For Okin, these are distinctly political terms which cohere with the wider political mission which the family can serve. Okin suggests that the hesitancy to see justice as essential to the family stems from a tendency to see justice as a remedial virtue 'called upon to repair fallen conditions'³⁴ rather than as a primary virtue at the heart of all social institutions. Christians should believe firmly in the equality of worth of both the sexes. However, they have, at least historically, been hesitant to affirm that an essential feature of the mission of Christ is doing justice through the equal distribution of the unpaid labour of the family. The tension between Okin's mission and Christ's lies not in a putative Christian oppressive mentality. Christianity has a wide tolerance of diverse, consensual familial settlements. There is reasonable disagreement among Christians about wise ways of living in a Western cultural setting in which many fathers and mothers spend less and less time bringing up their own children.

But Okin's mission to achieve strict equality is intolerant of this diversity. There is a fluidity between the familial and the political such that the former's main role is as preparation for the latter. For Okin, 'the separation of private from public is largely an ideological construct, having little relevance to actual human social life'.³⁵ The missional concern is that politics is here over-reaching its bounds and seeking to arrogate to itself both the creational role of the family and the eschatological place of the kingdom of God. When widespread in a culture, such a mindset can undermine the family as a free social organism, handicap its missional role and occlude the eschatological horizon which

---

31. Okin, *Justice, Gender and the Family*, p. 14.
32. Ibid., p. 5.
33. Ibid., p. 25.
34. Ibid., p.28; Okin here is paraphrasing Michael Sandel, *Liberalism and the Limits of Justice* (Cambridge: Cambridge University Press, 1982) p. 31.
35. Okin, *Justice, Gender and the Family*, p. 23.

promises a sunset on creaturely family life, simultaneous with the sunrise of the new heaven and the new earth.

Second, Christ's mission has specific familial content which rivals Okin's anti-patriarchal pursuit of 'a more complete *human* personality than has hitherto been possible'.[36] This missional familial content has a double aspect, one concerning common blessings and one concerning special witness.

On the one hand, there is the common blessing of families which Christians are called to safeguard. Christian mission in all cultures which is concerned for its neighbour must engage in rigorous research and analysis to ensure that evidence-based family policy is at the heart of politics so that public authorities are equipped to support marriage and family life. A number of policy avenues are normally followed at this point including, most commonly, tax advantages for married couples whose socially beneficial commitment is perversely penalized in current UK arrangements.[37] A less controversial example is a focus on the emotional development of children. The UK-based Centre for Social Justice has specifically focused on this in its reports and has brought comprehensive plans to bear in government.[38] However, evidence-based policies are unlikely themselves to resolve deep disagreements as to what forms of family life will best assist the development both of parents and children. Here is not the place to enter that particular debate, although its importance is not doubted.

Further articulation of the common blessing of families is found in the Insider Movement among Muslim converts to Christ who wish to affirm the blessing of their birth families precisely by not departing from them but rather continuing as observant Muslims where possible. Various questions would follow such a stance. How are Muslim followers of Jesus Christ to be obedient in the form of their marriage and the upbringing of their children? Is purdah a wise practice for Christian women and girls? What sexual and educational practices are appropriate in such Muslim, Christ-worshipping families? How is God calling polygamous Muslim men to follow Christ? Could Muslim culture allow for the possibility of never-married celibacy as a faithful response to Christ's call? When considering mission among

---

36. Ibid., p. 107.
37. See, for example, Don Draper et al., *The Taxation of Families, 2009–2010* (CARE, 2011), accessible at www.care.org.uk/wp-content/uploads/2010/10/CARE_Taxation-families-2009-10.pdf.
38. For a full range of reports, see www.centreforsocialjustice.org.uk/default.asp?pageRef=312.

approximately one fifth to one quarter of the world's population, these are just some of the questions which Christian family ethics will need to consider.

On the other hand, there is the special witness of families who follow Christ. Christianity affirms the equality of male and female, parent and child and yet at the same time the non-reciprocality of parent–child relations and the non-substitutability of wife and husband. Non-reciprocality is vital to the family organism, since otherwise it is reduced into a simple contest of wills. Amidst sin and abuse, the experience of being under authority in the family can, of course, be profoundly distorting for a person's experience of life. But it can also be deeply instructive and civilizing for entering into ecclesial, political and social arenas where authority is held. Non-substitutability seems to be the wisdom of Scripture in which, without advocating patriarchal domination, men and women are celebrated as equal but different. In a short piece like this, it is not possible to cover all the passages of Scripture which explore the nature of the sexes. For our purposes, it suffices briefly to examine what has been a perennially important text in the tradition, namely, Ephesians 5:21–33, wherein husband and wife are to submit to one another in love, the husband laying down his life for his wife as Christ did for the church and the wife rejoicing in his faithful service whereby she pursues whatever vocations she may have. This pattern of mutual submission and service has no definite application to the division of labour in or outside the home. Rather, it specifies the kind of witness which faithful love will give to the world as a core feature of Christian mission and offers a deep subversion precisely to the kind of abusive patriarchalism which Okin and Nussbaum so rightly condemn.

With these two missional observations in mind, we return finally to the complexities of Christian mission among Muslims. This Christian account of equality and gospel-shaped marriage presents troubling questions concerning marriage and child-rearing for Insider communities within Muslim settings. In Travis's classification, C5 converts *retain their legal and social identity within their Muslim community but reject or reinterpret any part of Islamic practices and doctrine that contradicts the Bible*. In such movements, the command of Torah to 'honour your father and mother' has a deep complexity, especially when interpreted through Jesus' teaching that 'Whoever comes to me and does not hate father and mother, wife and children, brothers and sisters, yes, and even life itself, cannot be my disciple' (Luke 14:26) and that 'there is no one who has left house or brothers or sisters or mother or father or children or fields, for my sake and for the sake of the good news, who will not receive a hundredfold now in this age – houses, brothers and sisters, mothers and children, and fields, with persecutions – and in the age to come eternal life' (Mark 10:29–30).

In Islamic contexts, such commands and promises often engender genuine life-and-death situations. The Insider Movement, by believing these words while yet hoping in Christ for his blessing of their continuing membership in their creaturely families and traditional forms of religious observance, can be understood as affirming the natural gift of social, familial life – vindicated by Christ's incarnation – as a pathway for the gospel. The question which continues to be discussed vigorously, even acrimoniously, in missiological circles, is whether retaining a Muslim cultural identity while cleaving to Christ offers a viable form of Christian life. Much has rightly been written about specific observances such as prayer, fasting and the saying of the *shahāda* ('There is no god but God, and Muhammad is a messenger of God'). But the deep reserves of Christian familial and sexual ethics have yet to be put in detailed conversation with the specifically familial questions posed by the emergence of Insider communities in Muslim contexts. Such a project seems of great importance since it would have a bearing not only on Christ's mission in such contexts, but also on what Christian wisdom can offer to complex social and political questions facing the highly plural Western polities to which Christians are also called in mission.

Appendix: Travis's scale, as summarized by Rick Brown[39]

C1 Believers are open about their new spiritual identity as disciples of Jesus Christ and citizens of God's eternal kingdom. They also have a new socio-religious identity as converts to a Christian social group. They follow primarily outsider religious practices. They use an outsider language and terminology in their meetings.

C2 They are much like C1, except that they use insider language, usually with outsider terminology.

C3 They are much like C2, except that they use many insider terms and many religious practices that seem compatible with the Bible, although not ones that are particular to the socio-religious community of their birth.

C4 They are like C3, except that they seek a distinct socio-religious identity that is neither the insider identity of their birth nor the identity of a convert to Christianity.

---

39. Brown, 'Biblical Muslims', p. 72.

C5 They are like C4, except that they retain the socio-religious identity of their birth and might use insider terms and practices particular to the community of their birth, as long as they seem compatible with the Bible.

C6 They are usually like C5, except that they are secretive about their new spiritual identity.

© Joshua Hordern, 2012

9. FRIENDSHIP

Guido de Graaff

Mission, ethics and friendship: this triad of subjects may not immediately suggest a clear or coherent theme. Things seem more manageable if we leave out the ethics (for a moment): 'mission and friendship' is a theme to which we can more easily relate. Many Christians will have thought, or heard others talk, about the role of friendship in mission and evangelism[1] – that is to say, friendship as a dimension not so much of the shared ministry of missionaries and evangelists as of the practices of mission and evangelism themselves; friendship as a means of proclaiming and sharing the gospel.

Friendship as a means of mission

The notion of using friendship in mission is particularly appealing to Western Christians living in the twenty-first century. We are no longer accustomed to, let alone comfortable with, practising mission on the grand scale seen by previous generations. The world has become suspicious of the mission campaigns once initiated by Western churches. Western society itself has grown

---

1. By 'mission' I mean primarily activities of proclaiming and sharing the gospel, and therefore *including* 'evangelism'.

weary of the 'grand narratives' that fuelled those campaigns, both abroad and at home. It is obvious why, in such a cultural climate, one of the few methods of mission still deemed to 'work' is that of friendship: sharing the good news in informal, one-to-one encounters, not just by making as many friends as possible in order to convert them, but by drawing on the relationships one already has – with neighbours, colleagues and, indeed, friends. Friendship has become our preferred method in mission. Friendship as a means of mission: it is what we hear about in sermons and evangelistic talks, and what we are encouraged to apply in our friendships.

At this point a critical question might arise. Is it right to use friendship in this way? Does this not mean that we degrade friendship, making it serve ulterior purposes rather than enjoying it for its own sake, as an 'end in itself'? This charge is justified insofar as there is indeed a danger of 'instrumentalizing' friendship: to reduce it to just a tool, a mere means. Yet this immediately begs the question as to whether the integrity of the supposed end – that is, mission – would survive such instrumentalization. The purpose of mission is the well-being of those to whom the gospel is proclaimed (albeit 'well-being' in a most profound sense), and surely 'well-being' is precisely what we seek for our friends too? Perhaps it was slightly misguided, then, to describe friendship as a 'means' of mission. It suggests there is only an instrumental, and therefore merely superficial, relation between mission and friendship; whereas, in fact, mission and friendship may well be more closely aligned, involving similar and parallel purposes, insofar as it is in both that we seek the well-being of others (or the other).

Humanly speaking, mission is about bringing the good news to our neighbour, with all that it takes: sharing the news, explaining its implications and relevance, answering critical questions, persuading and continuing witness. Friendship is arguably a natural context for such practices. For who would you first turn to, to share important or joyful news; who would you sit down with, to talk through the implications of important events; whose critical questions would you take more seriously than those asked by your friends; with whom would you be more patient, and yet who would you desire more to see things the way you see them? Add the fact that for Christians the gospel of Jesus Christ is the most important message to be shared, and we begin to see the missional importance of friendship; not just as the right tool for a twenty-first-century context, but as the platform for mission *par excellence*. In friendship we may expect to find mission unfolding at its most basic level – in one-to-one encounter, sharing and discourse. This, I suggest, is what also takes place in the following passage from the Gospel of John:

> The next day Jesus decided to go to Galilee. He found Philip and said to him, 'Follow me.' Now Philip was from Bethsaida, the city of Andrew and Peter. Philip found Nathanael and said to him, 'We have found him about whom Moses in the law and also the prophets wrote, Jesus son of Joseph from Nazareth.' Nathanael said to him, 'Can anything good come out of Nazareth?' Philip said to him, 'Come and see.'
> (John 1:43–46)

Within the Gospel's narrative, the interaction between Philip and Nathanael takes place right at the beginning of Jesus' public ministry. Jesus has begun to call individual people, inviting them to join him on his travels. In terms of mission, we could say that Jesus is calling people to what is to become the ultimate goal of mission, namely that people follow Jesus and become his disciples. Yet, while Jesus thus 'introduces' the goal of mission, it is the interaction between Philip and Nathanael that shows us the stuff much of our missional work consists of. We learn that the first thing Philip does, after accepting Jesus' invitation, is to turn to Nathanael and tell him about the new rabbi. The precise relationship between the two is not clarified. Yet, given the immediacy with which Philip turns to Nathanael, we may assume they are friends – or at least nothing less than friends. The short dialogue that follows between the two offers some examples of the kind of interaction typical of friends referred to earlier. First we find Philip breaking the news to his friend; we imagine him running into Nathanael's garden, rudely disturbing the latter while he is just enjoying a midday nap under his fig tree. However, instead of profusely offering his apologies (which, surely, you do when dealing with a mere acquaintance), Philip bursts forth: 'We have found him about whom Moses in the law and also the prophets wrote, Jesus son of Joseph from Nazareth.' Nathanael's response is as direct and unapologetic: 'Can anything good come out of Nazareth?' You do not hide your scepticism from friends! Nathanael might also be teasing Philip a bit, mocking what appears to be his latest fad. Yet Philip insists: 'Come and see.' And the next thing we learn is that Nathanael is approaching Jesus. He has given in to Philip's insistence; after all, you know when a friend is serious.

Nathanael is Philip's *friend*: the first he turns to, to share the news and ask to come and see for himself. And Nathanael quickly obliges, as you would expect from a friend. To be sure, the interaction between the two only shows the first step in the process of Nathanael becoming a disciple: while persuaded by Philip to come and see, he is yet to be won over by Jesus – which is what takes place in the remainder of the passage (John 1:47–51). Yet the first step is important, just as any human effort in mission is important, despite the obvious fact that it is God who does the converting. And nowhere is such human effort more appropriate than in the context of friendship – which, I submit, is what this Gospel passage suggests.

What I have done thus far is clarify how mission and friendship might be related. Rather than one being only a means to achieving the other, friendship and mission appear to *converge* – in terms of their purpose as well as the practices involved. In the context of mission, then, friendship is worth reflecting on in its own right. Indeed, not only can we reflect on friendship with a view to its meaning for mission, we can also reflect on mission from the perspective of friendship. In what follows I will seek to do both – to examine mission and friendship in light of each other. My specific focus will be on the social 'dynamic' in mission and friendship: how people interact. It is in this comparison, finally, that the discussion will also touch upon ethics – our third subject.

Shifting dynamics in mission

Questions about the dynamic of mission have been at the forefront of much modern theological debate. Under the influence of modernity and post-modernity, and in the light of the cultural and political shifts referred to earlier (e.g. post-colonialism, globalism), Christians have been led to question the exclusivity of the Christian religion, or its superiority to other religions and worldviews. This shift has an obvious missional 'edge', for mission and evangelism are practices through which the church traditionally encounters and seeks to convert people of other faiths. To question the exclusivity or superiority of Christianity, therefore, is also to cast doubt on the traditional dynamic of mission. Is it still acceptable, for example, to treat people encountered in mission as mere *recipients* – that is, as recipients of what the church possesses *already* (i.e. gospel, salvation, eternal life, etc.)? Should the church proclaim Christ as the *only* way towards salvation? Does it have a *unique* claim to the truth? Is it only people of *other* faiths who should convert? Many have come to answer these questions negatively, arguing that the church should instead learn to encounter people of other faiths (or none) as equals, in relationships of mutual respect and dialogue.

In line with this shift in Christian attitudes to other faiths, missiologists have redefined Christian mission as *Missio Dei*, 'the mission of God'.[2] God is the real agent of mission, which means that our missional activity involves not so much trying to convert the world as finding out where God through the Spirit

---

2. Cf. David J. Bosch, *Transforming Mission: Paradigm Shifts in Theology of Mission* (Maryknoll: Orbis Books, 1991), pp. 389–390.

is *already* at work in the world – and joining in. Some might add that this work of the Spirit among other nations and cultures may well involve genuine revelation and genuine paths of salvation, complementing the gospel of Christ and the apostolic tradition.[3] Now, to orthodox Christians the latter may be a step too far. Yet one need not be a pluralist to maintain that Christians have indeed much to learn from people of other faiths; that they should at least *expect* to learn more about the God they worship, through the unique way this same God goes with each nation and faith community. We should distinguish, surely, between God's offer of salvation and the church as a community *witnessing to* that offer. The church is an imperfect instrument of God's mission and may therefore never seek to restrict the good news to itself, or present itself as the exclusive messenger. Mission not only takes us beyond church boundaries (which arguably it does by definition); it also takes us beyond the original treasure of witness inherited by the church, involving genuine and deep engagement with the voices of other faiths.

The same goes for Christian encounters with the various 'faiths' and 'antifaiths' in modern Western society. True, it may be harder to imagine God's ways with people subscribing (explicitly or implicitly) to atheism – let alone consumerism, or Dawkinsian 'scientism'. Yet these worldviews, too, are to be taken seriously. In line with Dietrich Bonhoeffer's reflections on a 'religionless age',[4] we might say that these voices remind us that the experiences of Godforsakenness in our culture are genuine; indeed, that they are often *our* experiences too. Furthermore, they are a reminder that when God turns out to be 'with us' after all, we must acknowledge this as *God*'s doing, not the church's.

In terms of the social 'dynamic' of mission, then, what is proposed is a reimagining of mission as a *reciprocal* affair, rather than the unilateral, 'one-way' encounter of more traditional forms of mission. Mission must involve reciprocity, expressed in dialogue, respect, mutual questioning and learning, rather than simply the transmission of truth by one party to another. This is a generalization, to be sure, yet generalizations are often helpful in highlighting important differences or changes. In our case, they highlight a clear shift in the way the church (at large) practises and thinks about its mission: from executing it as unilateral endeavour, to understanding it as a reciprocal affair.

---

3. Cf. Daniel L. Migliore, *Faith Seeking Understanding: An Introduction to Christian Theology*, 2nd ed. (Grand Rapids: Eerdmans, 2004), pp. 311–314.
4. Letter of 30 April 1944. See Dietrich Bonhoeffer, *Letters and Papers from Prison*, Dietrich Bonhoeffer Works, vol. 8, ed. J. W. De Gruchy, trans. I. Best, et al (Minneapolis: Fortress Press, 2010), p. 362.

Reciprocity in friendship: Plato, Aristotle and Seneca

We have looked briefly at a shift in mission towards reciprocity. In the light of our earlier observations on the convergence between mission and friendship, the obvious next step is to examine this shift from the perspective of friendship. But first we should ask what reciprocity means in friendship itself, and whether it has become more or less important through time.

The good news is that reciprocity is a key theme in the philosophy and ethics of friendship, and has been for centuries. At first glance, it may seem obvious that friendship is reciprocal. Indeed, how could any friendship survive unless both (or all) friends contributed to it? Nevertheless, this notion that reciprocity is essential to friendship has been challenged by major thinkers, both Christian and non-Christian. Starting with some philosophers of antiquity – Plato, Aristotle and Seneca – we will see that each of them has different reasons to question, or underplay, the element of reciprocity in friendship. Yet they all reach the same conclusion: what defines friendship is the affection *I* show, independent, that is, of the affection I receive in return.[5]

Plato

For Plato, a crucial issue is the distinction between love (*eros*) which seeks gratification and love which loves something for its own sake. As he suggests in his dialogue called the *Phaedrus*, while friendships often start with the former, they can develop into relationships wherein friends learn to love each other for their own sake. They are no longer fixated on what they might 'get out of' the relationship (i.e. gratification) and begin to love each other for their intrinsic qualities – or, in Plato's case, for their intrinsic beauty.[6] Such friends begin to develop 'eros without gratification'.[7] However, according to Plato, to love a friend for his beauty is ultimately to love beauty *instead of* the friend. To recognize someone as intrinsically beautiful (rather than merely rousing one's 'appetites') is ultimately to recognize him as an expression of something more universal – the eternal and divine 'form' called Beauty. For love to attain its true object it must cease to be fixated on the beloved and focus on Beauty itself (and other

---

5. The following discussion draws on Gilbert Meilaender, *Friendship: A Study in Theological Ethics* (Notre Dame: University of Notre Dame Press, 1981), pp. 8–16, 38–40.
6. In Plato's case the context is that of Greek homoeroticism – sexual relationships between male adults ('lovers') and young boys (the 'beloved').
7. Joseph Pieper, cited in Meilaender, *Friendship*, p. 9.

forms, such as Goodness and Truth). After all, the friend is 'only' an image of the eternal Form. Certainly, in this role he remains a worthy object of love. Yet he has become a stepping-stone for attaining something higher, namely wisdom. What might have begun in physical pleasure ends in philosophy and contemplation.

It is clear that reciprocity is not a key ingredient of Plato's friendship ideal. Nor is it, in fact, a key ingredient of the more physical type of friendship: for an Athenian lover to attain his gratification, it is relatively inessential whether the object of his love loves him in return. Certainly, Plato considers it a good thing when the relationship is mutual; when the beloved not only returns his lover's affection, but also recognizes that affection for what it is – love for higher things – and learns to see and appreciate his lover in the same way. Here the lovers become real friends, encouraging each other to become philosophers.[8] Their 'platonic' love is reciprocal, to the extent that both remain attached to the other. However, as we have seen, the ultimate focus of their love is not the other but the eternal forms. Their friendship is rather a partnership in a common enterprise of attaining something that lies beyond their friendship. They will probably remain faithful to each other; after all, each played an important role in guiding the other towards philosophy. Yet, in principle, that task could have been fulfilled by *any* (beautiful) person. Their reciprocity, then, is not rooted in mutual appreciation of the other in his uniqueness or 'particularity' (as we might say about our friendships), but is instead instrumental to each friend's individual, non-reciprocal love of wisdom.

Aristotle

Turning now to Aristotle, we enter a rather different world. In Raphael's famous mural 'The School of Athens' Plato is portrayed with his finger pointing towards heaven, Aristotle with the palm of his hand turned to the ground – Plato inviting us to contemplate eternal realities, Aristotle reminding us also to examine what creeps and crawls here below. Aristotle's philosophy is more empirical than Plato's, more informed by common sense. And while he is happy to moralize from time to time, his purpose in doing so is entirely practical: to mould his students and listeners into decent citizens. This characterization also helps to highlight the difference between their respective approaches to friendship. Whereas Plato's discussion is really about philosophy and metaphysics, it

---

8. *Phaedrus*, 255b–256b; cf. Plato, *Phaedrus*, trans. Robin Waterfield (Oxford: Oxford University Press, 2002), p. xxvii.

is Aristotle who takes us to the ethics of friendship itself, including the day-to-day practicalities and problems faced by friends.

Aristotle writes extensively about friendship in both his ethical treatises, the *Eudemian Ethics* and the *Nicomachean Ethics* – although his discussion in the latter (Books VIII and IX) is best known. As a true empiricist, Aristotle seems primarily interested in describing friendship – in the various forms he finds in society. Yet, as a true philosopher, he also knows one cannot observe without a definition. And it is already here, at the point of defining friendship, that the issue of reciprocity arises. Aristotle plays with the double meaning of the Greek *philia*: he observes that while mere 'goodwill' (*eunoia*) could qualify as *philia* (derived from *philein*, 'to love'), only goodwill that is returned amounts to *philia* in its proper sense (i.e. 'friendship'). You can love wine, but that, of course, does not amount to friendship.[9] From the very outset, then, Aristotle deviates from the Platonic orientation on ever-higher objects of love. According to Aristotle, friendship consists in *mutual* goodwill: this definition is the lens through which he sets out to analyse and comment on the various types of friendship. These types include relationships we might hesitate to call 'friendship', such as the unequal relationships between parent and child, patron and client, king and subject, even master and slave. Yet for Aristotle the important thing is that in all these cases there is some form of goodwill on either side, albeit goodwill for different reasons. The client 'loves' the patron for his monetary favours, the latter 'loves' his client as an opportunity to show his magnanimity (and earn public esteem). Thus Aristotle's definition of friendship is sufficiently loose to include relationships that are reciprocal only for the sake of mutual expedience.

Some friendships, of course, are based on love that is truly for the person himself. These Aristotle labels 'virtuous' – the most perfect type of friendship. Yet even at this level, things are not always straightforward. Certainly, virtuous friends love each other for their intrinsic qualities (rather than what they gain from the friendship), recognizing in each other what they strive for themselves and thus seeking to emulate each other. The other is 'another self' (*állos autós*),[10] a phrase which suggests the strongest reciprocal relationship imaginable. Nevertheless, there are moments when Aristotle seems to let go of this reciprocity, when he suggests it is better to love than to be loved. The example he gives is of visiting a friend who is suffering adversity. It is better, Aristotle

---

9. See Aristotle, *Nicomachean Ethics*, trans. T. Irwin, 2nd ed. (Indianapolis: Hackett, 1999), VIII 2.
10. Ibid., 1166a32 (IX 4).

argues, to be the one who visits and offers comfort than to be the one who is comforted. The reason is not that it is better to enjoy good fortune than to suffer ill fortune (though Aristotle would not deny this!), but rather that offering support is better than receiving it. A virtuous man, Aristotle explains, would hate to see his friend suffer from the sight of his own suffering; he would rather keep his pain to himself. Nevertheless, the other for his part ought certainly to support his suffering friend: it is 'fitting that we should go uninvited and readily to those in misfortune'.[11] Indeed, a virtuous man should be keen to use any opportunity available to practise his virtuousness, including visiting his unfortunate friend – even if virtue prescribes that the latter is reluctant in allowing him to do so.

But there is more to it: although Aristotle does not state it explicitly, it seems that his virtuous man would simply hate to be on the receiving end of his friend's compassion. He hates to be *passive*, in terms of both suffering and receiving compassion, especially while his friend has the opportunity to practise his virtuousness – to be *active*. Using your friends as recipients of your 'beneficence' is the noble thing to do, whereas dependence on such beneficence is a matter of sheer necessity for the less fortunate.[12] Being on the receiving end of beneficence is intolerable when you are not in a position to compensate for it by showing (at least) as much beneficence in return. Suffering and compassion threaten the balance of virtuous friendship, undermining friends' tacit competition in virtue. Underneath friendship's reciprocity, then, lies rivalry.

Aristotle's ideal of friendship seems to have at least one thing in common with Plato's: the notion that friendship becomes *less* reciprocal the more it approaches perfection. In Platonic friendship, we saw, reciprocity dissolves because the ultimate object of love is impersonal (e.g. Beauty, wisdom): the friend has become a 'stepping-stone' for loving that ultimate object; strictly speaking, his loving response has become inessential. In Aristotelian friendship, on the other hand, reciprocity dissolves in the rivalry between the friends, each eager to show himself more virtuous, more active than the other. Here, the dynamic of reciprocity is eclipsed, not so much by the 'object' of love (as in Plato's case) as by the lover himself – the virtuous man who would rather show love than receive it.

Seneca
Aristotle's sensitivity to the uneasy balance between giving and receiving is echoed in the writing of Seneca, a Stoic philosopher who lived in the days of

---

11. Ibid., 1171b20–21.
12. See ibid., 1171a22–23.

the Roman Empire. Seneca is a believer in self-sufficiency, which is not so much a state of material independence as a mental state of surrendering desire; a state of not being perturbed by loss, or anything which Fortune throws at you, be it pleasure or pain. And so, when he discusses friendship in *Epistle* 9 (to his friend Lucilius), the central question for him is whether the wise man *needs* friends. According to conventional wisdom, friendship involves not only granting favours, but also receiving; not only love, but also being loved. Yet all of this implies dependence – on favours given, love returned. Not surprisingly, Seneca will have none of it: the expectation of return is what defines friendships of convenience, which are motivated by self-interest. The only sense in which the wise man 'needs' or 'desires' friends is that of needing them as the recipients of his virtuous actions, as the 'objects' of his love. The wise man wants friends 'if for no other reason than to practise friendship, not to let such a great merit lie inert'.[13] The thought still implicit in Aristotle is now made explicit by Seneca: the wise man wants friends, he argues, not in order to have someone to visit him when he takes ill, but 'that he may have someone whose sickbed he can visit'.[14] Seneca thus agrees with Aristotle that it is better to do good than to benefit from good deeds. Yet Seneca is also more radical than Aristotle. The Aristotelian friend is still engaged with his counterpart in what seems like noble competition; friendship is a practice that still 'takes two' (at least). The Stoic friend, on the other hand, while eager to show friendship, remains indifferent to any return of friendly affection. Knowing that his happiness does not (or ought not to) depend on such return, he is interested only in that part of friendship which is his own doing. Indeed, he is quite happy to be without friends; or, if he has friends, will not be shaken by losing them. Thus, bizarrely, the perfect friend has become a solitary figure.

Christian friendship

Summing up the above accounts of friendship, one could say that in each the dynamic of reciprocity is eclipsed or suppressed by a certain ideal. In Plato's case reciprocity dissolves because the particular friend must give way to a higher, impersonal object of love. In Aristotle's case, reciprocity is under pressure from the friends' moral rivalry, which demands that each seeks to outdo the other

---

13. Seneca, *Selected Letters*, trans. Elaine Fantham (Oxford: Oxford University Press, 2010), p. 17.
14. Ibid.

in virtuous practice. And in Seneca's case, finally, reciprocity simply disappears, as the Stoic wise man is interested in friends only as recipients of his good deeds. However, since our ultimate interest is in the relation (and comparison) between friendship *and mission*, we must now turn to the *Christian* tradition of reflection on friendship.

A helpful introduction into this Christian tradition is provided by the American theologian Gilbert Meilaender in his book *Friendship: A Study in Theological Ethics*. Meilaender draws on the classical tradition, yet, as the subtitle suggests, he is ultimately interested in how we as Christians might think about and practise friendship. In the light of our discussion so far, it may be no surprise to find that for Meilaender, too, reciprocity is an important issue. He discusses it in two stages: first, in chapter 1, under the heading 'Friendship as a Preferential Love', and second, in chapters 2 and 3, under the headings 'Friendship as a Reciprocal Love' and 'Friendship and Fidelity' respectively. The issues of 'preference' and 'reciprocity' are, of course, not exactly the same. To raise the issue of preference is to ask to what extent love may be selective; the love of friendship is here contrasted with universal love – love of all people, or simply 'love of humanity'. To raise the issue of reciprocity, on the other hand, is to ask to what extent we may seek and/or expect return for our love; the love of friendship is here contrasted with 'sacrificial love'. Now, strictly speaking, the answer to the first question is independent from that to the second: one might approve of preferential love, yet aspire to love in a purely sacrificial sense, seeking no return whatsoever. Conversely, one might demand universal love, yet hope for reciprocity to develop in due course. The latter, however, is practically impossible: I might try to love all human beings, yet how could I ever be *friends* with each and all of them? And therefore, in practice, it is the answer to the first question that determines whether we ask the second question at all. If we believe that our love should be universal, then the question about reciprocity has become superfluous, since to love 'universally' is to love nobody in particular. Yet if we allow for preferential love (perhaps as part of, or in addition to universal love), then the second question does arise: should we love the friends of our choice ('preference') in the same sacrificial way in which we ought to love all human beings; or may we expect – or even desire – our love to be returned?

This second question is the more important one for Meilaender. As for the first, his answer (in chapter 1) is fairly straightforward and uncontroversial – or at least from a Christian point of view. Purely universal love is both unrealistic and improper. Yes, we are called to transcend the parochial focus in our loving and befriending, seeking to imitate God's love for all his creation; friendship should be rooted in *agapē*. Yet, as Augustine reminds us, we remain finite beings, bound to limitations of time and place. Friendship, including its restricted scope, is appropriate – as long as it helps us in learning to love beyond its boundaries. Thus Meilaender speaks of friendships as 'schooling' us in love.[15]

Having established that preferential love is appropriate for Christians, Meilaender then proceeds to address the question of reciprocity, in chapters 2 and 3. Here Meilaender seems less certain: while he would like to give a positive answer (e.g. 'reciprocity is good and proper'), he struggles to find reasons for it. Yes, friendship is about receiving as well as giving, but may we also *seek* reciprocation of our love? Furthermore, is such reciprocation *constitutive* of friendship? Meilaender's hesitation at this point seems justified in the light of words spoken by Jesus himself: 'For if you love those who love you, what reward do you have? Do not even the tax-collectors do the same? And if you greet only your brothers and sisters, what more are you doing than others? Do not even the Gentiles do the same?' (Matt. 5:46–47). And then there is Paul's statement (in the NIV translation) that love 'is not self-seeking' (1 Cor. 13:5).[16] It is texts such as these that provide a powerful argument for the view that Christian friendship should be governed by *agapē*: non-reciprocal love that persists in loving even when there is no response, or when the response is hatred.

The gospel message, however, is only that we must not restrict our love to our circle of friends – *not* that we may not seek mutual love. Nevertheless, some seem to hold that Christian morality does imply the latter. Meilaender identifies the nineteenth-century theologian and philosopher Søren Kierkegaard as a key proponent of this view. In *Works of Love* (1847) Kierkegaard argues that whereas *agapē* is a Christian duty, the requirement of reciprocity is a 'contamination'. Meilaender himself is uneasy about the strong Stoic overtones of this verdict: does the Kierkegaardian friend not end up looking like Seneca's wise man, resistant to the emotions of friendship? To be sure, Kierkegaard is more humane than Seneca, allowing for at least the desire that love is returned. In fact, it is this very desire which moves the Christian to offer himself in love and service, even if friends betray him. He, for his part, will remain faithful to the friendship; or, as Kierkegaard puts it, he will 'keep the hyphen'.[17] The point is, however, that Kierkegaard insists on defining as friendship what would seem only a *precondition* for friendship (or for its restoration), namely love that is

---

15. Meilaender, *Friendship*, p. 17.
16. Cf. ibid., pp. 37, 41.
17. Cited in ibid., pp. 62–63.

stubbornly 'agapeic'. That is, even if only one party is holding the relationship, 'there is still no break'.[18]

This may sound rather unrealistic, or even absurd. Yet Kierkegaard is not alone in holding this view: in treating *philia* as identical to *agapē*, he seems to voice a sentiment shared by Protestants in general. Whereas Catholic theologians tend to follow Thomas Aquinas in regarding friendship rather as the pinnacle of love – even in human beings' relationships with God[19] – Protestants put more emphasis on sacrifice as the pre-eminent feature of love: God's love is *agapē*, 'purely sacrificial', and therefore our love should be sacrificial too. This emphasis is particularly characteristic of the Lutheran tradition. As for Luther himself, his treatise *The Freedom of a Christian* (1520) contains elements that are supportive of Kierkegaard's ideal. Here Luther famously speaks of the Christian as simultaneously free and not free, as 'free lord, subject to none' and a 'dutiful servant, subject to all'.[20] Importantly, the underlying rationale is that because the Christian is liberated through Christ *from* slavery to sin, sharing in all Christ's benefits, he is set free *for* service to his neighbour. In terms of love, since he is a recipient of God's perfect sacrificial love, the Christian is now free to pour himself out in sacrificial love for his neighbour. 'I will therefore give myself as a Christ to my neighbor', writes Luther, 'just as Christ offered himself to me.'[21] Thus a Christian's servanthood is rooted precisely in his freedom. The Christian, he concludes, 'lives in Christ through faith, in his neighbor through love'.[22]

The Christian lives 'in' his neighbour through love. A picture that might arise here is of the Christian as a mere 'conduit' of divine love: God's love, which in Christ has been revealed as purely sacrificial, always flows 'downwards' and 'outwards'. Each time it touches a human being, transforming her into a Christian, it must thenceforward 'flow through' that Christian to other human beings, who in turn must become conduits for a yet wider circle of people – and so on. In other words, having accepted God's ultimate act of love, the Christian ought always to be a *giver* of love, never a *recipient*. Indeed, to focus too much on receiving love would be to betray God's sacrificial love. Now, this picture of the Christian channelling divine love does not, in fact, do justice to

---

18. Cited in ibid., p. 62.
19. Cf. Daniel Schwartz, *Aquinas on Friendship* (Oxford: Oxford University Press, 2007), p. 1.
20. Martin Luther, *Three Treatises* (Philadelphia: Fortress Press, 1970), p. 277.
21. Ibid., p. 304.
22. Ibid., p. 309.

Luther himself. At several places in his treatise he states explicitly that Christian love is mutual.[23] Yet the picture does emerge from the writings of those who built on Luther's legacy. We have already seen how Kierkegaard – a Lutheran theologian – emphasizes the non-reciprocal 'origins' of Christian love and friendship, at the cost of their reciprocal 'fruition'. Anders Nygren, another Lutheran theologian, makes the point even more emphatically. In his *Agape and Eros* (1930–6) Nygren dismisses as non-Christian any form of love that is not strictly sacrificial. To him, the fact that friendship was a key theme in classical ethics just proves the self-seeking bent of pagan morality. From a Christian point of view, therefore, friendship is at best morally irrelevant.[24]

Meilaender himself – also belonging to the Lutheran tradition – is enough of a realist to recognize that reciprocity is simply part of our human experience, and that ideals such as Kierkegaard's and Nygren's come perilously close to Stoicism. Yet his conclusion remains rather unsatisfactory, namely that Christian friendship will always involve a measure of 'tension' between sacrificial love and a desire for reciprocal affection.[25] I will return to this tension later on, in order to formulate a more satisfactory account of how these two dynamics are inter-related. But let me first take stock of my discussion of friendship thus far, in order then to make connections with the second major subject of this chapter, namely mission.

Reciprocity: good or bad?

It is commonplace to identify a shift between the classical-pagan period and the Christian era in terms of their appreciation of friendship: while the classics championed friendship as the noblest form of love, Christians instead focused on more inclusive relationships, following Scripture in using language taken from a family context to describe their relationships (e.g., 'brothers').[26] But we should not overlook the element of continuity. Much of the Christian reservation about friendship resonates with classical reservations about reciprocity. Certainly, we have seen that the motives behind the reservations of each group

---

23. He states, for example, that each Christian 'should become as it were a Christ to the other', adding 'that we may be Christs *to one another*'. Ibid., p. 305. My emphasis.
24. Cf. Anders Nygren, *Agape and Eros*, trans. Philip S. Watson (London: SPCK, 1957), pp. 181 n. 3, 186.
25. Meilaender, *Friendship*, pp. 64–67.
26. Cf. ibid., pp. 1–2.

are not the same. Yet a common theme is that of a conflict between friendly mutuality and unilateral love – a conflict which tends to coincide with a contrast between experience and ideal.

With this observation we have arrived at a point where the comparison between friendship and mission becomes really interesting. In relation to friendship, we have seen how for Christians (or at least Protestants) the 'politically correct' position is to be suspicious of reciprocity, or to ensure that this dynamic is somehow firmly rooted in, or tempered by, the non-reciprocal dynamic of *agapē*. To befriend 'agapeically' is to follow Christ in sacrificing oneself for one's friends, rather than seeking mutual affection. Now, interestingly, when we return to the sphere of mission, exactly the opposite seems to be the case. For here the 'politically correct' position, we saw, is that mission should be based on equality and, indeed, *reciprocity*. Recall the shift identified earlier in approaches to mission and evangelism: on the back of severe hangovers from modernity, colonialism and imperialism, the church has mostly abandoned conceptions and methods of mission that assume Christians have the upper hand over those they encounter in mission – not only in the sense of political and economic supremacy, but also in terms of proximity to God, truth and salvation. Today, the norm in mission and evangelism is to engage with non-Christians as equal partners in practice and dialogue.

We also saw, at the beginning of this chapter, how friendship provides a helpful model for reimagining the practice of mission and evangelism, especially in the cultural context just alluded to. Yet, after our venture through the ethics of friendship, the question that arises concerns the implications of the Protestant friendship ideal when placed in the context of mission and evangelism. Does the demand for sacrificial love not look rather less benign once it is applied to the way the church addresses people of other faiths? Indeed, one could argue that in a missional context Kierkegaard's notion of unilateral friendship translates in a refusal to listen: 'Whatever you say, I will not be moved by your protests, criticism or indifference.' Especially when motivated by Christ's example of sacrificial love, such steely resolve seems even more disturbing, since it suggests that in imitating Christ's sacrificial love we are on the 'right side' of God – in contrast, that is, to the reluctant recipients of our sacrifices. The Protestant friendship ethic thus seems to reinforce exactly the kind of condescension which twentieth-century theologians and missiologists have worked so hard to leave behind.

Taken by itself, of course, the notion of imitating Christ's love and extending that love to others is not problematic. Yet we observed that, in a missional context, we should also be willing to receive from those to whom we minister, depending on their contributions to God's mission as much as they do on ours.

Similarly, that we should be willing to learn from them, in a dialogue that ought to be genuinely open if it is to serve the attainment of *truth*. In fact, it was because of this new outlook of mission that friendship seemed such an attractive model in the first place – that is, precisely for its *reciprocal* dynamic. Thus we face the following puzzle: when we consider friendship in itself, the ideal of non-reciprocal love seems to have much to say for it; yet when applied in a missional context, this very ideal becomes highly problematic.

Moral and epistemic

In trying to solve this puzzle, we might first try to clarify exactly what we mean by 'reciprocal' (and 'non-reciprocal') in either context – that is, in the contexts of friendship and mission respectively. Starting with the former, we should remind ourselves that the above discussion of friendship falls within the discipline of *ethics* (and *social* ethics in particular). Here we are dealing with straightforwardly *moral* questions: 'Whom should I befriend?', 'How many friends should I have?', 'What should I do if my friend betrays me?' Or questions which introduce the theme of reciprocity, and which are prominent especially in Christian ethics: 'Is it better to give than to receive?' And, 'May I look out for friends who will love me in return?' If the answer to this latter question is negative, then that is typically in view of God's *agapē*, deemed to provide the perfect example for Christian practice, including friendship.

The situation is slightly different when we turn to mission. Of course, mission can be regarded as a specific area of Christian ethics, among other areas such as family and politics. Yet within this area, I would suggest, the issue of reciprocity is primarily an *epistemic* one – that is, an issue concerning our knowledge – and ethical only by derivation. The issue of reciprocity between Christians and people of other faiths (and none) concerns questions about who possesses knowledge of the truth. In this context to commend reciprocity is to believe, for example, that Christians do not necessarily have better access to the truth than those they encounter in mission; that they are not holding the only key to salvation; that others do not always come empty handed, as junior partners bringing only 'auxiliary' wisdom.

Of course, it is hard to deny that, at a basic level, an epistemically *non-*reciprocal dynamic is intrinsic to the practice of proclaiming the gospel. Yet, as suggested earlier, there is a distinction between 'message' and 'messenger': while the message (the gospel) is deemed to contain universal truth, the messenger (the Christian proclaiming the gospel) stands *alongside* the recipient as a fellow sinner, equally dependent on the transformative power of the message. And while the recipient is dependent on the messenger for the gospel to be proclaimed, we can see how, conversely, the latter is also dependent on the former, say, for being challenged in his or her entrenched prejudices concerning the gospel. Take, for example, the spirit-matter dualism implied in the faith of many Christians: who would be better positioned to challenge such dualism than the Third World slum-dwellers to whom these same Christians would like to proclaim and explain the gospel? It is often said that the meaning of the gospel, including its universality, can only be fully known through the particular, historical embodiments of the gospel. If that is true, then we really need those to whom we minister in our mission and evangelism – for our *own* sake. The term 'recipient' applies as much to us as to them.

Friendship in mission, mission in friendship

In the context of mission, we saw that the issue of reciprocity is primarily epistemic. Only as such will it also have implications for the ways in which we conduct mission – the *ethics* of mission.[27] In the context of friendship, by contrast, the issue of reciprocity is primarily ethical, concerning the dynamics of our love (rather than our share in wisdom). Nevertheless, while this distinction between moral and epistemic reciprocity is helpful, it is not quite sufficient for solving the apparent contradiction between Christian values in friendship and mission. First of all, there is no friendship 'as such', isolated from the messy circumstances that affect mission and evangelism in the twenty-first century. Friendship can be a vehicle of mission – as we saw in the case of Philip and Nathanael (John 1). And, conversely, there are friendships that have emerged from mission and evangelism. Furthermore, moral and epistemic issues are likely to be closely intertwined, in mission as well as in friendship. I already noted that the extent to which an approach to mission is 'dialogical' will also show itself in the ethics of our mission, in the way we 'do' mission.

The same, surely, applies the other way round: moral practice in the context of friendship is likely to have certain epistemic implications (and not only in relation to mission). There is a long tradition which emphasizes that love has an epistemic dimension; that love is as much about knowing as about emotion, attraction and desire. How can we really love people – that is, *love* them rather than just have 'feelings' about them – without *knowing* them (and

---

27. It would not do to start a mission project without consulting people living in the relevant neighbourhood about their particular problems, struggles, hopes, etc.

vice versa)?[28] To be sure, this question is slightly different from the one raised earlier, about epistemic equality and interdependence. For now the object of knowledge is the other person herself, rather than the mystery of salvation that I share with her. Having said that, I should also recall how the *Christian* mystery of salvation is about a particular person – Jesus Christ. Conversely, we can say that to love another genuinely is not only to know her, but also to know her desires, needs, hopes and beliefs – that is, precisely the things we should engage with when seeking to share the mystery of Christ. In friendship as in mission, therefore, my love for my friend should be *responsive*: not just responsive to her as an abstract 'other', but to all that drives and moves her.

We are now getting closer to solving the confusing ambiguity around reciprocity. For it is precisely the *lack* of such responsiveness that makes the ideal of 'purely sacrificial' love so problematic. In his book *The Four Loves* (1960), C. S. Lewis gives the sad example of 'Mrs Fidget' – a character one hopes existed only in Lewis's imagination. Mrs Fidget manipulated her family with her relentless exercises in domestic self-sacrifice. She insisted on doing all the dishes, doing all the washing, providing a hot meal twice a day – year in, year out. She insisted on sacrificing herself for her family. Yet as a result, Lewis points out, her husband and children ended up doing things for her 'to help her to do things for them which they didn't want done'.[29] The example illustrates our capacity to 'sacrifice' ourselves in such a way that we close ourselves off to our supposed 'beneficiaries'. Mrs Fidget did not listen to her children, did not hear what her husband was trying to say. One wonders whether she really loved them at all. As Lewis explains, her 'sacrifice' was all about *her* need – her need to serve, to be valued, to make others feel guilty. This is non-reciprocal love at its worst.

The reason why we should be suspicious of overly keen display of 'sacrificial' love is basically the same, I would suggest, as the reason why we disapprove of a condescending style of mission. In both cases, we disapprove of the refusal to listen, of love that fails to be responsive. Love that is truly responsive seeks reciprocation, since it is focused on a unique and living being, a *person*. And we are ill-advised to love such a being as we might any other object – appreciating it, enjoying it, lusting after it, perhaps even sacrificing everything for it, yet from a safe distance, not really anticipating communion. To love responsively is to welcome communion.

---

28. Cf. Oliver O'Donovan, *Common Objects of Love. Moral Reflections and the Shaping of Community* (Grand Rapids: Eerdmans, 2002), pp. 1–24.
29. C. S. Lewis, *The Four Loves* (London: HarperCollins, 2002), p. 61.

But what about Jesus?

There is, however, one remaining question: What are we to make of the example of Christ? Does his ultimate sacrifice not urge us to move beyond the comfort of our friendships and risk suffering the loneliness that he suffered in extending his love to those rejecting it? Was Kierkegaard right, after all?

In response to this challenge, let us first remind ourselves that we are not Jesus: surely Jesus' sacrifice carries a 'surplus' in comparison to whatever sacrifices we might make. But still, what are we to make of Jesus' words, challenging us not just to love those who are likely to love in return? I suggested earlier that in itself this does not disqualify friendship. For a more substantive answer, however, let me return to where we began – the Gospel of John. We saw how John 1 suggests that friendship can be a vehicle for mission: Philip persuades his friend Nathanael to come and meet Jesus. As it happens, the theme of friendship becomes more explicit later on in the Gospel. In John 15 Jesus addresses his disciples as his 'friends' (v. 14), rather than as his 'servants' (v. 15). Crucially, the context to these words is Jesus' teaching of a 'new commandment', throughout John 13 – 15. This commandment is that his disciples love each another in the way he loves them. And as if to leave no doubt about how he loves them, Jesus washes their feet before they have their final supper (John 13). In John 15 Jesus goes on to explain that this sacrificial love is at the heart of their friendship with him: 'No one has greater love than this, to lay down one's life for one's friends. You are my friends if you do what I command you' (John 15:13–14). There is no ambiguity here: to be a friend of Jesus is to follow his example of self-sacrifice, even to the point of death.

Yet an important thing to remember is that Jesus is addressing his disciples *together*. In calling them his friends (i.e. plural) he is also, as it were, giving them to each other – as friends of one another. Furthermore, his commandment is not simply to 'love as I have loved you', but to 'love *one another* as I have loved you' (John 15:12). The disciples must also learn, then, to *accept from each other* what each has to offer. And that, of course, was exactly the lesson Peter had to learn, as Jesus knelt down to wash his feet (John 13:6–8).

Friendship according to Jesus' new commandment is shot through with self-sacrifice. But sacrifice made according to this commandment also welcomes the sacrifice of others. Instead of bestowing our so-called sacrificial love on whomever we like, we are to submit to friends given to us by Christ: 'You did not choose me but I chose you. And I appointed you to go and bear fruit' (John 15:16). In these words we can hear a radical reconfiguration of friendship's dynamics: since Jesus has gone before us, sacrificing himself for his friends, to seek 'purely sacrificial' friendship is to pursue a chimera. Instead, we are to practise sacrificial friendship *reciprocally* – which is to deny Meilaender's 'tension' between *agapē* and *philia*.

Finally, when Jesus says he appoints his disciples 'to go and bear fruit' there is a further hint about the relation between friendship and mission. It implies, first of all, that to befriend one another according to his commandment is to leave our comfort zones: we cannot 'go and bear fruit' unless we move beyond the cosiness of our clubs and circles. And yet, at the same time, by truly listening to and receiving from those we encounter in mission, we will practise what Jesus also commanded: to welcome and receive from those which he chose to befriend alongside us, and 'appointed' to be our friends as well.

Conclusion

Where does this leave us in relation to missional ethics? I set out to explore how the dynamics of friendship might shed light on the dynamics of mission – against the backdrop of major shifts in the practice of mission. Yet I seem to have ended up doing exactly the opposite, namely critiquing a specific Christian (or Protestant) friendship ideal, in the light of emphases in contemporary theology and missiology. But one could also look at it from a different angle: one could say these missional emphases have helped in giving voice to an alternative Christian ideal of friendship, or at least an alternative Christian perspective on friendship – a perspective which probably reflects better the reality of, and our experiences in, friendship. Looked at from this angle, contemporary experience of mission has yielded a new argument in the age-old debate concerning the two dynamics in friendship – a debate that is relevant to mission precisely because, as we have seen, friendship itself is relevant to mission. And, finally, insofar as experience in mission has successfully challenged a long-established (Christian) view on and approach to friendship, we have seen an example of how Christian ethics can indeed be 'missional'.

© Guido de Graaff, 2012

10. POLITICS

Jonathan Chaplin

Introduction

This chapter explores what a 'missional ethics' might mean for the political witness of the people of God today.[1] In nations such as the UK and USA today there are many thousands of sincere Christians active at all levels of political life who see their engagement as a unique opportunity to contribute to the common good. I want to ask what it would mean for such Christians to live a 'missional ethics', to offer some suggestions as to how the church can understand and critically support their missional vocation, and to reflect on how all of us can live faithfully as citizens even if we are not directly involved in political activity.

The field of 'politics' is so wide ranging that it is essential to select a quite narrow focus for this chapter. I will concentrate on the area of *political speech*, since that allows a closer linkage with the theme of the missionary *communication* of the gospel. I will not address any specific political issues, but rather explore how we should in general speak in public about politics. And within the area

---

1. I am grateful to participants at the meeting of the Ethics and Social Theology Group of the Tyndale Fellowship, held in Cambridge, 30 June – 2 July 2011, for valuable comments on this paper.

of political speech, I want to focus even more precisely on the theme of *political reasoning*: the nature of the arguments or justifications Christians might deploy when seeking to advance the ethical imperatives of the gospel wisely, in ways appropriate to the public realm.

Let me acknowledge at the outset that much of politics is not governed by reasoning *of any kind*. It is shaped much more by the outcomes of power struggles, between and within political parties and between government and powerful interest groups. Or it is determined by the impact of unpredictable 'events' – such as the 2008 credit crunch – which can throw the most rational of plans completely off course. And increasingly it is shaped by surges of *unreason*, as in the extremist populist movements gaining ground across much of Europe and, in England, by, for example, the English Defence League, which are choking off real debate. It has been a characteristic conceit of modern political liberalism that politics is readily amenable to rational direction. Christianity, given its frank reckoning with human fallenness, will never fall victim to this illusion. That said, it remains the case that, in several liberal democracies today including the UK, there is still significant space for the deployment of careful, reasoned deliberation about the public good, and that this sometimes makes an impact on governance. Christians should be committed to the goal of increasing the practice of wise political reasoning, even if they are also realists about the pervasive and unruly influences of ideology, power and prejudice.

What is 'Christian political reasoning'?

'Christian political reasoning' is *reasoning about the responsibility of government for promoting the public good, from the standpoint of Christian political convictions*. This definition can be clarified with the help of four further points.

First, 'government' is only one part of the state; the other is the citizenry ('the people'). The state is a political community made up of government and citizens, who are together charged with the unique mandate to promote the public good, by means of law, public policy and other actions.[2] A key part of the role of citizens, then, is to engage in political reasoning about what government should do on their behalf, and in their name, to promote the public good for the whole political community. Citizens should not view themselves as

---

2. The term 'political community' is being used here to refer not only to the nation-state but to political authorities at, in principle, any level.

passive recipients of government action but as bearers of an indispensable responsibility for determining what 'the public good' is and how it might be realized. Christians will want to bring their own, sometimes very distinctive, convictions to bear on that vital question.

The focus of this chapter is not on the reasoning engaged in by governments themselves or by public officials (e.g., legislators, ministers, civil servants or judges) but rather on that engaged in by, first, *ordinary Christian citizens*, and, second, those who seek to *represent* a Christian position in politics: in a parliament or local council or other public body, or through some campaigning group. This qualification is necessary because not everything that applies to the reasoning of citizens or representatives necessarily applies to the political reasoning of public officials. I comment on one aspect of that distinction shortly.

Second, it follows from this that political reasoning is necessarily *public* in two senses. It is, as noted, the reasoning 'of the public' (the citizenry); and it is reasoning 'about the public good'. What does it mean to reason about the public good? The agenda of the type of reasoning occurring in political settings is the unique 'good' pertaining to the public realm of the whole society. But what is 'the public good'? This is a difficult term to define precisely, and its scope and content are not fixed. We can characterize it broadly as the dense and highly complex space of interactions between individuals, associations, institutions or networks such as markets or the media. It is a space in which any member of the public can participate and which potentially impacts upon all of them. From a Christian point of view we must speak of this public realm as having a specific 'good', rather than as simply having an 'interest', as in the familiar but inadequate term 'the public interest'. This is in order to make clear that the public good should not be regarded merely as a matter of the administrative management of contending private interests, or simply as the means necessary to maintain 'social order'.

Before proceeding, we must note that it would be hopelessly naïve to assume that all governments as a matter of course sincerely intend and effectively promote the public good. Many frequently fall lamentably short. A government's performance in this respect depends on a wide range of factors. These include, first, the political culture of the nation: e.g., is there a deeply embedded sense of an impartial public good distinct to the personal interests of governors or the sectional interests of powerful groups? Are there reasonable levels of trust in government, or is it seen as an inconvenience to be circumvented? A second factor concerns the administrative efficiency of state institutions: e.g., do new laws or ministerial decisions actually get translated into executive actions, or are they blocked by bureaucratic self-interest or just sheer incompetence? How meaningful appeals to 'the public good' actually are in a particular nation depends on factors such as these. Christians, however – whatever the odds against them in their specific context – will seek to realize whatever approximation of the public good is available in their situation.[3]

As noted, the nature of the public good raises profoundly moral questions, and Christians should be among those who are constantly on the alert for such questions, resisting the reduction of the public good to purely utilitarian or technical considerations. Such moral questions about the public good will inevitably sometimes occasion wide and deep disagreement. As the leading secular humanist Polly Toynbee has rightly observed, 'Every day in parliament, fundamentally different world views do battle. Politics is all about the clash of moral universes.'[4] Now politics may not be *all* about such a clash, but there is no doubt that, today, deep moral conflict is increasingly coming to the fore in political debates in our religiously and morally plural Western (and non-Western) societies. This means that there is no longer (if there ever was) an off-the-shelf account of 'the public good' available around which everyone can rally.

Aspects of the public good that it is the unique responsibility of government to secure and promote include, *inter alia*, items which regularly appear on the formal agenda of the Houses of Parliament, the Cabinet and its committees, political party meetings, local authorities or other public bodies. Some will be mundane, others far reaching. They include matters such as the stability of a banking system, the relief of structural poverty, the proper rate of taxation, the preservation of the natural environment, the health of family life, the professional qualifications of social workers, the protection of fundamental rights, the just deployment of military force, and so on.

Yet familiar political issues like these are not the whole of what should be on the 'agenda' of politics. Political institutions have ways of keeping certain issues 'off the agenda' if they threaten to disturb the current balance of power, threaten powerful economic or professional interests, or challenge default assumptions about what is politically important. Indeed, I will suggest later that one of the most important roles of Christian political reasoning is precisely to stand ready to disturb current assumptions about political

---

3. In states where political institutions are wracked by systemic corruption or inefficiency or sectionalism, the first task may simply be to work towards a culture in which the very notion of 'public good', to which all citizens and state officials have an obligation, begins to gain some degree of acceptance.
4. *Guardian*, 25 March 2008.

priorities and to force marginalized or suppressed concerns onto, or higher up, the political agenda.

My third point of clarification regarding the meaning of 'Christian political reasoning' is likely to be more controversial for some Christians and it deserves more extended treatment than can be given here. I suggest that the 'agenda' of political deliberation – what governments talk about *officially* – should *not* include the truth of religious or philosophical doctrines. History seems to have shown that governments cannot be trusted to rule competently on such questions. To see the point, consider these hypothetical examples of illicit 'agenda items' for parliaments, cabinets, local authorities, or other political bodies:

- protocols for registrars of marriage: the merits of the biblical case for same-sex marriage;
- reforming the Financial Services Authority: applying Islamic principles;
- ministerial media briefing: how to defend the secular humanist case for abortion policy.

Would we really want political institutions to make authoritative rulings on such matters? This is not to deny that the truth or falsity of such doctrinal matters could not substantively affect the public good; on the contrary. It is only to deny that it is not *the business of political authorities* to make official rulings on such matters. Such religious or philosophical questions are best addressed in the free realm of civil society, not resolved by government. Political authorities are therefore well advised to deliberate and decide on questions such as marriage or finance or abortion without *overt appeal* to the possible sources of religious or philosophical authority on which they are thought, by some citizens at least, to depend. Of course, the freedom to appeal to 'ultimate truths' in public debate is, of course, absolutely essential if a society is to debate such issues honestly and intelligently. Such appeals are entirely legitimate on the part of *ordinary citizens or their representatives*, and they may actually shape the content of law or policy. The narrow point being made here is simply that *formal political authorities* should refrain from invoking such religious or philosophical beliefs as official justifications for their decisions.[5]

The final clarification regarding 'Christian political reasoning' is to note that it is helpful to distinguish between the *matter* and the *manner* of Christian political reasoning. The *matter* concerns the substantive ethical content of the church's

---

5. See Jonathan Chaplin, *Talking God: The Legitimacy of Religious Public Reasoning* (London: Theos, 2009), ch. 5.

proclamation in the political realm. It concerns questions such as: 'What does the Bible teach about the content of law and policy?' Or, 'What ethical implications follow from the gospel for the ordering of our political life?' There is now an extensive body of literature on this question, including:

- exegetical studies of specific 'political' passages in the Bible (e.g., Rom. 13);
- broader biblical-theological treatments of major political themes (e.g., 'law', 'Jubilee');
- works of systematic political theology (e.g., those representing broad traditions such as Augustinianism, Anabaptism, Radical Orthodoxy, etc.);
- applications of all of the above to specific geographical contexts (as in 'contextual' political theology), to key political concepts (e.g., 'authority', 'freedom'), or to contemporary political issues (e.g., warfare, debt cancellation).[6]

All of this concerns the *matter* of the church's political witness, the substantive political goals it will promote. The focus of this chapter, however, is on the *manner* of communicating such content before a wide public audience. In Western liberal democracies like the UK or USA, such an audience will be predominantly secular-minded in its political thinking and, at the same time, religiously, ideologically and morally plural in its composition. This means that such an audience cannot be presumed to regard Scripture or Christian theology

---

6. See, e.g., Luke Bretherton, *Christianity and Contemporary Politics* (Chichester: Wiley-Blackwell, 2010); Jonathan Burnside, *God, Justice and Society: Aspects of Law and Legality in the Bible* (New York: Oxford University Press, 2011); Stephen Clark (ed.), *Tales of Two Cities: Christianity and Politics* (Leicester: Inter-Varsity Press, 2005); Paul Freston, *Evangelicals and Politics in Asia, Africa and Latin America* (Cambridge: Cambridge University Press, 2001); Chris Green (ed.), *A Higher Throne: Evangelicals and Public Theology* (Nottingham: Apollos, 2008); David McIlroy, *A Biblical View of Law and Justice* (Milton Keynes: Paternoster, 2004); Oliver O'Donovan, *The Desire of the Nations: Rediscovering the Roots of Political Theology* (Cambridge: Cambridge University Press, 1996); Oliver O'Donovan, *The Ways of Judgment* (Grand Rapids: Eerdmans, 2005); Alan Storkey, *Jesus and Politics: Confronting the Powers* (Grand Rapids: Baker, 2005); Michael Schluter and John Ashcroft (eds.), *Jubilee Manifesto: A Framework, Agenda and Strategy for Christian Social Reform* (Leicester: Inter-Varsity Press, 2005); Nick Spencer and Jonathan Chaplin (eds.), *God and Government* (London: SPCK, 2009); Nicholas Wolterstorff, *Justice: Rights and Wrongs* (Princeton: Princeton University Press, 2009).

as a valid or effective authority in political matters. This will be the case even if a large minority (or, for that matter, a majority) regard these sources as authoritative in matters of belief, doctrine or ecclesial or personal ethics.

Christian political reasoning as 'winsome public wisdom'

If 'Christian political reasoning' is something like the above account, in what sense can it be 'missional'? How can the political reasoning of ordinary Christian citizens and their political representatives be seen as an expression of the church's missionary task to communicate the gospel? I want to propose that, at its best, Christian political reasoning will offer examples of 'winsome public wisdom'. Such wisdom would help bring to the fore in public debate key ethical insights disclosed or confirmed or rendered intelligible by the gospel. It would seek to clarify and illuminate the beneficial – and at times robustly challenging – contribution that the gospel can make to a society's public life. Public wisdom like this will be 'winsome' insofar as it elicits some degree of appreciation (even if reluctant) from those who do not share the deep convictions in which it is grounded. Such a response will be forthcoming if Christian-inspired public wisdom like this can show how a different direction of policy, or a different way of construing what is actually at stake in a policy debate, might resolve a serious political issue or, more broadly, contribute better to the flourishing of society.

Public wisdom offered by Christians obviously cannot expect to receive complete endorsement from the general public, but it might at least aspire to make some people curious enough to listen. Biblically, the goal of offering Christian public wisdom would be inspired by the Deuteronomist's hope that the nations surrounding Israel would be so struck by the distinctive, countercultural wisdom of God's law, as enacted in the life of the people of God, that they would begin to desire it for themselves and, perhaps, seek its source (Deut. 4:6–8). Such an audacious hope is reaffirmed in the radically different setting of the New Testament, where the apostle Peter exhorts an embattled early church surrounded by a hostile pagan empire: 'Conduct yourselves honourably among the Gentiles, so that, though they malign you as evildoers, they may see your honourable deeds and glorify God when he comes to judge' (1 Pet. 2:12).

Some might be inclined to classify what I am calling winsome public wisdom as a form of 'pre-evangelism'. But that is a misleading way to describe it, since it could be taken to imply that Christian political reasoning is merely instrumental to some other end – as if taking up our political responsibilities as citizens did not have a God-ordained integrity of its own, irrespective of what might be crudely called its 'evangelistic pay-off'. My concern is how Christian political reasoning can furnish a crucially important, indeed indispensable, complement to the explicit call to repentance and faith which is properly issued by individual Christians, or the church, in other settings.

One final qualification before I give some examples. To pre-empt misunderstanding, it is essential to note that the offering of such 'winsome public wisdom' is not only performed by Christian *political* reasoning, nor even only by Christian *reasoning*, which is only one part of the totality of Christian ethical witness. I have in mind here not only the obvious, if frequently overlooked, point that Christian ethical *practice* – especially the corporate practice of the church – is generally much more important in persuading people of the credibility of the gospel than Christian ethical reasoning. I also have in mind that there are other forms of Christian verbal (or non-verbal) communication which are not simply instances of 'reasoning'; there is also 'narrative'. There is an important element of truth in John Milbank's provocative assertion that the chief Christian task today is not, first of all, to 'out-reason' opponents of Christianity, but rather to 'out-narrate' them – to tell a better story, a story which draws them into a compelling and comprehensive vision of human flourishing and does not stop simply at presenting a rational apologetic, however important that remains in certain contexts.[7]

In what sense might Christian political reasoning furnish winsome public wisdom in the deliberative context we find ourselves in today? Many secularists hold that Christian reasoning cannot possibly be 'public' because it rests on appeals to 'tribal', or simply 'irrational', standpoints. Perhaps the best way to challenge this spurious, albeit oft-cited, claim is simply to put on display a representative example of genuinely Christian political reasoning which quite clearly is 'public'.

Nigel Biggar sets out a helpful example.[8] Contesting the secularist argument just noted, he proposes that at least some theologically grounded reasoning is, as a matter of fact, eminently accessible to the general public, even in

---

7. See John Milbank, *Theology and Social Theory: Beyond Secular Reason* (Oxford: Blackwell, 1991), p. 330. See also Samuel Wells, *Improvisation: The Drama of Christian Ethics* (London: SPCK, 2006), ch. 2. On the church's practice of ethical discernment by means of a deep exegesis of Scripture, see Brian Brock, *Singing the Ethos of God: On the Place of Christian Ethics in Scripture* (Grand Rapids: Eerdmans, 2007).
8. Nigel Biggar, '"God" in Public Reason', *Studies in Christian Ethics* 19.1 (2006), pp. 9–19. He has elaborated his case in *Behaving in Public: How to Do Christian Ethics* (Grand Rapids: Eerdmans, 2011).

conditions of pervasive secularization and deep religious and moral pluralism. Biggar illustrates this in relation to an argument against the legalization of euthanasia.[9] He shows how such an argument is deeply informed by five distinctive and explicitly articulated theological assertions and yet proceeds by way of a series of claims, the content of which should be perfectly intelligible to any thoughtful non-Christian and which some might even find illuminating or persuasive. The five assertions are set out below.

1. 'The value of the life of a human individual is conceived in terms of responsibility to created goods and to a vocation from God.'
2. 'The criticism of [consequentialist views of euthanasia] is shaped by an awareness of the limited responsibility of creatures; and that awareness in turn is enabled by the hope that there is a more-than-human power – God – who will turn evil to good where human creatures either cannot or may not.'
3. 'The decision to understand the morality of acts primarily in terms of the will's intending and accepting [rather than in terms of consequences] is strongly encouraged by a view of earthly life as a kind of preparation for the life to come after death.'
4. 'The conception of a humane society as one whose members normally support each other in adversity is shaped by [the theological assumption] that in the light of the resurrection of Jesus suffering is to be viewed without ultimate despair.'
5. 'My less than optimistic reading of the social consequences of the legalization of euthanasia is informed by an un-Enlightened assumption that even modern citizens of liberal societies remain sinful.'[10]

Biggar suggests that, at the very least, those hearers who have been raised in any historically Christian society should have little difficulty making sense of these assertions. This is a very important observation for anyone interested in 'missional ethics' in such contexts. It is indeed true that the legacy of Christendom, notwithstanding its dark side, has left many openings in public discourse for the invocation of theologically informed, yet publicly intelligible, claims. Now that legacy is, of course, fast disappearing, which is why one of

---

9. The argument is, as it happens, his own, and is developed in Nigel Biggar, *Aiming to Kill: The Ethics of Suicide and Euthanasia* (London: Dartman, Longman and Todd, 2004).
10. Biggar, '"God" in Public Reason', p. 15.

the tasks of the Christian public ethicist is to resist the intellectual amnesia that afflicts our society, by reminding it of its own formative history.[11] We can also venture that, since similar ideas have been transmitted from Western cultures to most other societies today, at least to their educated sectors, thoughtful listeners in many other contexts today would find such reasoning basically intelligible. Later I will identify a powerful theological reason why we might expect such language to be intelligible even in cultures that have experienced only minimal Christian influence.

The claim that an example of Christian public reasoning like this is after all publicly intelligible becomes clearer when we probe further into the internal processes of ethical reasoning in general. Such reasoning, when it is done well, consists of an ordered arrangement of concepts, propositions, empirical claims, arguments and so forth, such that the conclusions drawn about some aspect of right conduct flow from and are supported by those other components, and the whole reasoning process is consistent with and informed by the presuppositions from which it is mounted (presuppositions such as the stability and order of creation or the source of moral obligation in God's good purposes). Those presuppositions will be explicitly theological and, back of that, biblical. In addition to the presuppositions, some of the basic descriptive concepts employed at various stages in the process (concepts such as 'the human person', 'community', or 'rights') will also be theological. Thus in *Desire of the Nations*, Oliver O'Donovan announces that his project is the search for 'true political concepts', notions that accurately describe political reality itself (e.g., that it is necessarily constituted by 'authority'), before any flow of reasoning gets under way.

A critical question arises at this point as to whether, when and how Christians engaged in Christian political reasoning will put those theological presuppositions or concepts on display. Here we come up against the worry that not to display them might be, as O'Donovan warns, to 'veil in embarrassment' what ought to be shouted from the rooftops.[12]

Let us return to Biggar's article. The five-point argument about euthanasia he develops is, he says, a 'thoroughly theological' argument, by which he means that it is 'shaped by theology at every appropriate point in the appropriate manner'.[13] And what are the criteria of 'appropriateness'? Biggar notes that

---

11. A fine attempt to do so is Nick Spencer, *Freedom and Order: History, Politics and the English Bible* (London: Hodder & Stoughton, 2011).
12. O'Donovan, *Desire of the Nations*, p. 219.
13. Biggar, '"God" in Public Reason', p. 15.

no answer to this could ever be comprehensive, but what he does say is instructive:

> Theological arguments addressed to fellow-theologians will typically appeal directly to Scripture and to post-biblical tradition, because these are commonly recognised authorities. The argument presented here does not do much of that because it is addressed to a wider audience . . . including non-theologians who do not recognise [them] as authorities. Does that make the argument less genuinely theological? I think not. The Bible and Christian tradition are authorities because they are the source of certain truths. Once those truths have been grasped they can be affirmed and elaborated without constant reference back to the place where they were discovered – notwithstanding the fact that he who elaborates them should make regular pilgrimages to the place of discovery, in order to check his grasp for correction or improvement . . . [T]here is indeed a danger that, being distanced from their source [in the biblical story], they will be abstracted from that story, with the consequence that their meaning loses its proper shape. But a danger is not a necessity.[14]

Note especially the worry that, 'distanced from their source', Christian ethical claims will be 'abstracted' from that source so that their 'meaning loses its proper shape'. Consider an important example of how this has actually happened in the modern West. Historically, the Christian doctrine that humans are created in the image of God was a vital, perhaps the unique, foundation for what secular modernity has come to mean by the term 'human dignity' and the commitments to equality of respect and equal treatment that flow from it. Such a notion of dignity is the necessary assumption underlying modern political principles like 'democracy', 'human rights' and 'the rule of law'. But what many secular thinkers and legislators mean by human dignity today often turns out to be deeply at odds with the original meaning of 'image of God', and this makes a difference in the policies they favour. Biblically, human dignity – our status as 'a little lower than God' (Ps. 8:5) – is radically and completely dependent on humans' standing in a relationship with a Creator God who calls them into a covenant of love. Apart from that relationship, the ground of dignity seems inevitably to depend on the possession of one or other contingent human capacity, whether rationality, moral conscience, agency, personality or capacity for pleasure or pain. These, however, are highly precarious bases for defending the dignity of human beings, especially impaired ones, since it implies the view that the possession of particular capacities, at least to some minimum degree, is a *condition* for the receipt

---

14. Ibid., pp. 14–15.

of certain basic human protections and rights.[15] Modern secular humanism has, of course, not only failed to 'make regular pilgrimages' to the biblical source of the idea of the image of God, but has emphatically repudiated that source, claiming that human dignity is only adequately grounded in, for example, the capacity of human beings to exercise something like 'individual rational self-determination'. From a Christian point of view, that does not describe any basis of 'dignity', but rather discloses an attitude of profound hubris.

Yet such a caution having been entered, this does not mean that Christian ethicists cannot employ the term 'dignity' in political reasoning at all. For when they use it they have the freedom to *impart a different meaning to it and draw different policy implications from it*. Such a meaning can materially inform their political reasoning whether or not they have the opportunity to explicate its foundations and implications on any particular occasion. The worry is less about words than meanings, although it is true that in some settings, words come so loaded with meanings alien to the gospel that they must be replaced by words which convey Christian meaning better.[16] But the Christian ethicist using a word like 'dignity' in the thick of political debate need not always feel bound immediately to link it explicitly to its deeper theological grounding. One very obvious reason Biggar gives for this is that audiences in public *fora* like political institutions do not recognize the authority of the Bible or tradition on which that grounding rests. To that compelling pragmatic consideration we can add a normative one: it is an act of civic disrespect in a public political forum simply to presume that one's hearers share your own faith and so speak as if they regarded themselves as bound by it. That is no basis for the type of civil conversation that is proper to the political forum. Thus, for example, attempting to justify one's policy proposals in public simply by an appeal to the authority of the Bible or to the character of Britain as 'a Christian Nation' (and without arguing the case on its 'public good' merits) fails to meet that criterion of civil respect.[17]

---

15. See Michael Banner, *Christian Ethics and Contemporary Moral Problems* (Cambridge: Cambridge University Press, 1999), chs. 2, 3; Wolterstorff, *Justice*, ch. 15.
16. Stanley Hauerwas suggests that this is even true of central political notions in modernity such as 'freedom' and 'justice'. See his *After Christendom: How the Church Is to Behave if Freedom, Justice, and a Christian Nation Are Bad Ideas* (Nashville: Abingdon Press, 1991). I appreciate his polemical point, but am more persuaded on the substance of the issues by the Christian philosophical reconstructions of such key concepts in thinkers such as Banner, Biggar and Wolterstorff.
17. See Jonathan Chaplin, 'Can Nations be "Christian"?', *Theology* (November/December 2009), pp. 410–424.

There is a third reason why Christians need not feel bound always and everywhere to make the theological grounding of such reasoning explicit, and it arises from the very nature of ethical reasoning. Aside from what one's audience can be presumed to know or accept, the question of the suitability of 'theological candour' depends on the particular *phase of reasoning* currently being engaged in at the time. It is not normally the case that an ethicist, Christian or otherwise, when engaged in a political debate, puts on display the entire flow of reasoning from deepest presupposition through intermediate principle to practical conclusion. Much ethical reasoning, especially in political settings, consists of the presentation only of later phases of reasoning, those most germane to the 'agenda' item in question. In political debate, this is the case because the proper object of the debate is legislation or policy concerning the public good. In this *institutional context* deliberation serves the direct practical goal of reaching decisions on the public good, whereas, by contrast, in a university seminar the object is clarification and understanding, so that more expansive phases of reasoning will properly be brought into play. Once a flow of reasoning approaches its middle point, underlying presuppositions such as a particular view of the basis of human dignity will function as *presuppositions*: they will not be articulated but will be taken for granted, and reasoning will then proceed by establishing chains of logical or conceptual or semantic linkage between intermediate principles (such as 'civil liberty') or by generating specific practical conclusions (modifying prosecution policy on assisted suicide, for example).

So this is another reason why Christians engaged in political reasoning should not feel bound always or even generally to make their theological presuppositions explicit. Presuppositional candour is not a necessary condition of faithful political reasoning, Christian or otherwise. Nor is it a guarantor that others will discern the 'winsome wisdom' of one's proposals. Indeed, it may even detract from that objective. In any case, Christian political reasoners should generally gravitate towards later phases of reasoning, not in order to 'veil their convictions in embarrassment', but rather to make a difference to practical outcomes in order to advance the public good – which is the matter at hand in political *fora*. Whether such reasoning is 'missional' – whether it conveys winsome public wisdom – depends entirely on whether the Christian reasoner has been 'making regular pilgrimages to the place of discovery'. If she has, she will have been adequately replenishing her biblical and theological resources and so ensuring that when, for example, she employs terms like 'dignity' in debates about bioethics or economic justice, the connotations of what she says are as far as possible consistent with her deeper intentions. This could show itself in, for example, efforts to explain how the 'dependence' of vulnerable elderly people on the sacrificial and costly care of others is not a matter of shame and regret ('I don't want to be a burden'), but rather a sign of their true dignity as members of a totally interdependent human community.

Earlier I indicated that I would offer a specifically theological reason why it is possible for non-Christians, including those in nations lacking in any real Christian influence, to find such kinds of public and political reasoning intelligible, perhaps even plausible or persuasive. This is the biblical doctrine of creational – or 'general' – revelation, and here I want to underline the essential link noted in this book's Introduction between 'missional ethics' and 'creation ethics'. I have been speaking of the internal reasoning process in Christian political deliberation. Like all human activities, this takes place entirely within the conditioning framework of the order of creation. Reasoning is itself a created capacity, given by God to enable humans to acquire cognitive access to the order, patterns and dynamics of some or other feature of created reality. While human reasoning is also fallen and suffers all kinds of distortion, it has not lost all its illuminative powers and thus may still equip humans to know at least something of the order of creation, including its moral order (and thereby what Jonathan Rowe in the Introduction calls the 'moral goods' constituted by that order). Further, when believers allow themselves, as Paul puts it, to 'be transformed by the renewing of your minds' in Christ (Rom. 12:1–2), they are enabled to see, not some wholly other, unprecedented, moral order but, simply, *created order as it is being renewed by Christ*. Thus, as Christopher Wright powerfully argues in *The Mission of God*, 'missional ethics' is an ethics of a creation being redeemed and destined for eschatological fulfilment.[18] There is, finally, no conflict between the demands of a creation ethic and those of a kingdom ethic. If, as Hans Küng has aptly put it, 'God's kingdom is creation healed',[19] then a kingdom ethic rooted in the life and teaching of Jesus and pointing towards a new heaven and earth is, in its substantive content, fundamentally continuous with an ethic of a good creation designed for human flourishing.

Continuity, however, does not mean mere reiteration. A creation ethic does not imply adherence to a static set of invariant injunctions. God called humankind to cultivate and unfold his created goods in responsible historical action, opening up new circumstances in which new ethical insights (regarding technology or economics, for instance) were bound to emerge and new ethical

---

18. Christopher J. H. Wright, *The Mission of God: Unlocking the Bible's Grand Narrative* (Downers Grove: InterVarsity Press; Leicester: Inter-Varsity Press, 2006).
19. Hans Küng, *On Being a Christian*, trans. E. Quinn (London: William Collins, 1977), p. 231.

responses called for. Equally, the church as the primary agent through which God extends his redemptive purposes in the period 'between the times' is called to engage in fresh ethical reasoning as it pursues the one 'mission of God' in the many diverse historical contexts to which God has called it, always under the authority of what has already been given in Scripture and under the guidance and correction of the Spirit, and as mediated in part through the church as a community of ethical discernment. As N. T. Wright has put it, the church today is charged not only with performing the script laid down by the earlier acts of the biblical drama, but also with discerning the course of the final act of God's script, while it awaits the full manifestation of the kingdom of God.[20] This means that Christian ethical and political reasoning is never a matter of *merely* clarifying or interpreting a set of divinely prescribed rules or injunctions or legal precedents – in this respect Christian ethics has a very different character to, for example, much Islamic ethics – but rather of discerning, and deliberating on, how the Word of God may speak to the unique 'missional context' in which Christians find themselves. This, perhaps, is part of what is meant by the Westminster Confession when it asserts that Christians are not bound to the letter of Old Testament law but only to the 'general equity thereof'.[21] To put the point positively, this means that Christians are liberated, and not only commanded, to pursue justice ('equity') in the face of entirely new circumstances. They have genuine freedom, and responsibility, to determine what justice requires today, unconstrained by what may be a disabling conformity to specific rules derived from situations whose time has gone. One important political example of this process of historical discernment was the gradual recognition in European Christendom that monarchy was not a form of government ordained by God for all times and places, but that structures of representative, constitutional democracy could also find powerful support in the biblical tradition as interpreted in new circumstances.

Consensus or confrontation?

The foregoing prompts the important question of the degree to which the political reasoning of Christians – and Christian ethics generally – will, variously,

---

20. N. T. Wright, 'How Can the Bible Be Authoritative?', *Vox Evangelica* 21 (1991), pp. 7–32.
21. Harold Cunningham, 'God's Law, "General Equity", and the Westminster Confession', *Tyndale Bulletin* 58.2 (2007), pp. 289–312.

confirm, improve or confront the political reasoning that happens to be dominant in their culture. The doctrine of creation leads us to expect at least some instances of confirmation of prevailing public ethics, while that of the fall warns us to count on instances where such ethics will need substantial improvement or radical critique and rejection. The doctrine of redemption might enjoin any one of those three modes of engagement, and which one(s) are required at any one instance will depend greatly on the specific historical and cultural context which the gospel is encountering. We might, however, expect the radical challenge of the call to redemption to shed light most forcefully on that from which its hearers need to repent. The Bible does not imply that, when humans first encounter Christ, they meet him in a condition of comprehensive corruption, as if nothing of the original image of God remained in them or that they are incapable of any good action or motivation. Yet a genuine encounter with Christ seems most likely when the sins and brokenness which most oppress people are exposed to the light of truth. And what is true of an individual may also be true of a society. This means that Christian political reasoning – if it has indeed been making those 'regular pilgrimages to the place of discovery' – will always carry within it the possibility of exacerbating or precipitating confrontation. Christianity will then often not function as a source of social cohesion but as a source of social disruption – witness William Wilberforce's frontal challenge to the economic vested interests involved in the slave trade, Martin Luther King's confrontation with deeply embedded racism in the American South of the 1960s, and the Roman Catholic Church's courageous resistance to late twentieth-century authoritarianism in Chile, the Philippines and Poland.

It is important to consider the implications of this, not only for the identity and fidelity of the Christian community, but also for the character of the wider political community. I noted earlier that Christians engaged in political reasoning should not simply accept the existing agenda of current political discourse, but should be ready to disturb it by challenging its priorities, for example by voicing concerns – perhaps about the disabled, the elderly, the unborn, the rural poor or travellers – which have been marginalized or suppressed by political, economic or media elites. Faithful Christian political reasoning will find itself at certain times engaging in innovative, critical, indeed radical interventions that contest the prevailing directions of public policy.

Christians are not, of course, the only ones who will feel compelled at times to engage in this kind of confrontational political deliberation. As they stand against one or other 'mainstream' assumption, they will find themselves alongside (or sometimes against) a range of other minority, dissident or hitherto excluded voices. This state of affairs is inevitable in a society which is both pervasively secularized and increasingly pluralized, and it will carry consequences for how we think about democratic deliberation in general. It implies that we should prepare ourselves for a more boisterous and less sedate public square than some Christians might feel is appropriate for those called, as far as it depends on them, to 'live peaceably with all' (Rom. 12:18). It also implies that the aim of engaging in political discourse will not necessarily be the attainment of a speedy or easy consensus on matters under debate. Whatever political consensus may eventually be reached will sometimes only emerge from a protracted, vigorous, potentially turbulent, even temporarily destabilizing process of deliberation, as contending 'moral universes' run up against each other.

It is important to stress that, for Christians, the objective of theological candour, when it proves necessary, cannot be merely *expressive*, as if the point of political speech were simply to put one's religious convictions on display; that would simply be indulgent. The point of such candour is to raise the level and deepen the quality of political discourse, with a view to contributing to the public political good as this is understood from the standpoint of one's own political vision. Such candour may be seen by others as disruptive, even disrespectful; and Christians in their turn may experience the presuppositional candour of others as equally challenging. But, as Timothy Jackson has reminded us, 'It is an irony of civility that at times more sincere respect is shown to others by confronting them with revolutionary possibilities and transformative vocabularies than by assuming the status quo.'[22] The final purpose of such confrontation is not to revel in a perpetual stand-off but to facilitate more honest, more representative and, hopefully, more lasting political agreement about how to promote the public good.

It is not suggested that the 'clash of moral universes' will necessarily be to the fore in most moments of political debate. The conflict will often be concealed, or simply absent. For the hard-working Member of Parliament (Christian or otherwise) poring late into the night over the fine details of a Bill on some parliamentary committee, the matter at hand will not normally be to win some contest of moral visions (though in principle it could be), but to pre-empt a potentially costly error of legislative drafting (and to get home in time for at least a few hours' sleep). That is also faithful work done, under God, for the public good and Christians critical of, but remote from, the political

---

22. Timothy Jackson, 'The Return of the Prodigal', in Paul J. Weithman (ed.), *Religion and Contemporary Liberalism* (Notre Dame: University of Notre Dame Press, 1997), p. 197.

system should never despise it. More of the average politician's week is spent on matters like that than in leading some dramatic moral charge, as indeed is the case in most walks of life. The question of whether it is appropriate to exercise theological candour in political settings will depend greatly on the circumstances of the case. There will be many occasions on which either the internal logic of a political argument or the external conditions in which it is presented, or simply the limited capacity, skill or opportunities of the speaker (or the time of day), will caution against such candour.

The final point to add here is that decisions about whether to use theological candour must always be reserved to the speaker concerned and not be dictated either, on the one hand, by restrictive secularist notions of what counts as valid 'public reasoning', or, on the other, by misguided theological demands for incessant and explicit 'gospel proclamation' in public debate. Christian political reasoning can thus be genuinely 'missional' in character without being 'missionary' in intent.

Conclusion

In what ways does the practice of Christian political reasoning set forth above amount to a 'winsome public wisdom' that can help bring to the fore and clarify key ethical insights disclosed or confirmed or rendered intelligible by the gospel? I have suggested that Christian political reasoning is not best construed as a form of 'pre-evangelism', since this would be to reduce the God-given vocation of citizenship (of which political reasoning is part) to a mere instrument of some other purpose, however noble. Yet some might still be left thinking that, because so much of the content of Christian political reasoning described above leaves its theological groundings unstated, it is ill-equipped to commend the ethical wisdom of the gospel before an increasingly secularized and religiously illiterate society. This might be seen as especially so given the fact that such reasoning will be presented to a public audience that will generally have other things on its mind, namely some very concrete issue of public policy. How likely is it that members of such an audience will pick up the 'hints', the indirect intimations, of winsome gospel wisdom that such reasoning, at its best, can convey?

This question is inherently impossible to answer with any degree of certainty, and there is a very good reason why. The 'success' of Christian political reasoning – like the 'success' of any type of Christian missionary proclamation – can only finally be assessed by the authenticity of its content, not the effectiveness of its reception. Christian speech is tested by its conformity to gospel criteria, not by its tangible or measurable impact on its hearers. Ultimately, the church's task is but to bear witness, for it is only God who gives the growth (1 Cor. 2:6). To close, here are just two 'gospel criteria' that apply to any type of Christian ethical reasoning in the public square.

The first criterion is *fidelity to biblical truth*. To ensure as much fidelity to biblical revelation as possible when we engage in Christian public reasoning, it is, as Biggar puts it, necessary to make 'regular pilgrimages to the place of discovery'. And that means that Christian political reasoners will need to be deeply formed both by scriptural thinking and by a wide range of resources exploring the relevance and application of Scripture to contemporary public life (i.e., to the 'matter' of Christian politics). It will also mean that such reasoners will need to be sustained in their demanding and often misunderstood vocation by a community of critically supportive and informed Christians, whether their local church or some other context of fellowship.

The second criterion is *discernment of the spirits of the age*. This requires the acquisition of deep insight into the 'spirits' – religious, intellectual and institutional – shaping the direction of contemporary public life. 'Missional' Christian political reasoners must understand the hearts, minds and societal contexts of those they are called to address and must grasp astutely, sensitively and compassionately the pathologies with which their fellow citizens (and they themselves) have to deal. If they do, they will be better equipped to display the ethical implications of the gospel as winsome public wisdom.

I conclude by noting that meeting these gospel criteria for 'success' requires far greater educational, catechetical and pastoral – and liturgical[23] – challenges than most churches have yet begun to contemplate. The contemporary church needs to set about these challenges of Christian formation with much greater alacrity, and equipped with far greater spiritual and material resources, than has hitherto been the case. That is one of the key challenges facing a church committed to the promise and possibility of 'missional ethics'.

© Jonathan Chaplin, 2012

---

23. James K. A. Smith, *Desiring the Kingdom: Worship, Worldview, and Cultural Formation* (Grand Rapids: Baker Academic, 2009).

11. SERVANTHOOD

PERSPECTIVES FROM ISAIAH'S 'SERVANT OF THE LORD'

Nathan John Moser

Introduction: the need for transformed and transformational servants

In our information age, it does not take long before the scandals within the church make national headlines in every part of the globe. Less well published are the lives of the unsung heroes of the Christian faith whose sacrificial actions contribute to God's transforming mission around the world. Whether it be for good or ill, the realities of living in an interconnected and globalized world are urgent reminders to the church to take seriously what Scripture has underscored since the election of Israel, namely, who we are and how we live matter to the nations.

It is for this reason that the universal impact of the servant of the Lord in Isaiah is a promising reservoir for reflecting upon how the character of Christians can be of global significance. Who the servant *is* and how the servant *acts* accomplishes God's mission in the world. Given the missional importance of the servant of the Lord, this essay will ask the following question: Why should 'who' the servant of the Lord is in Isaiah shape our own character as servants of Jesus Christ?

I will address this question by entering into discussion with Latin American biblical scholars and theologians who have explored how Isaiah's imagery of the servant of the Lord shapes both the character and the actions of the church in the world today. Our mining of Latin American insights is not intended to limit the relevance of our study to one location, but to model how the contextual insights from scholars in one part of the globe can enrich Christians wherever they reflect upon missional ethics. We begin, then, with a brief survey of how the 'servant of the Lord' imagery has been explored by key Latin American thinkers.

Liberation historian Enrique Dussel in 'Universalism and Mission in the Servant of Yahweh Songs'[1] was one of the first to suggest that a Greco-Roman interpretation of the term 'servant' in Isaiah would only serve to perpetuate stoically passive and fatalistic outlooks on history. A more proper Hebrew understanding of the term 'servant', Dussel argued, was to understand the servant of the Lord as one who *shapes* the course of history. For Dussel, the death of the servant implies a death to particularism, which leads to an authentic global humanization of people, while the servant's resurrection is an analogy for the freedom of the poor to construct history. The mission of history building defeats the passivity and fatalism associated with being a 'servant' in contexts of oppression.

Addressing a similar concern, José Porfirio Miranda's *Marx and the Bible: A Critique of the Philosophy of Oppression* used texts relating to the servant in mission to critique 'Western' perceptions of a God who does not intervene in world history. On the contrary, Miranda argues, the servant's mission of justice (*mišpāṭ*) is not a call to contemplate juridical verdicts but a call to the sort of action that seeks the 'elimination of an injury in which the violation of justice consisted'.[2] Addressing political injustice, Jorge Pixley imaginatively argued that images of the suffering servant, taken to be pro-Persian/Cyrus propaganda that provoked violence from pro-Babylonian authorities responsible for the servant's death, resonated with the defeat of the Sandinista movement and that resurrection of the servant is an analogy for a national life that results from political martyrdom.[3]

The most exhaustive treatment of Isaiah from a Latin American perspective is that of the late José Severino Croatto. In *Isaiah: The Prophetic Word and its Hermeneutical Rereading: Liberation is Possible*, Croatto understood the first two servant songs (Isa. 42:1–7; 49:1–13) to be reflections of Israel in the Babylonian

---

1. Enrique Dussel, 'Universalismo y misión en los poemas del Siervo de Yahveh', *Ciencia y Fe* 20 (1964), pp. 419–464.
2. José Porfirio Miranda, *Marx and the Bible: A Critique of the Philosophy of Oppression*, trans. J. Eagleson (New York: Orbis Books, 1974), p. 112.
3. Jorge Pixley, 'Isaiah 52:13 – 53:12: A Latin American Perspective', in J. Levinson and P. Pope-Levinson (eds.), *Return to Babel: Global Perspectives on the Bible* (Louisville: Westminster John Knox Press, 1999), pp. 95–100.

exile while the latter two songs (Isa. 50:4–10; 52:13 – 53:12) reflect on suffering from a fourth-century BC perspective.[4] The mission of the servant is largely understood as an invitation to communities of the diaspora who, as Israel in Egypt, internalized suffering in foreign centres of power and now find themselves unable to interpret situations of oppression. The inability to reflect critically upon suffering is expressed in texts such as Isaiah 42:18–20, which describes the servant as being both blind and deaf. Finally, Carlos Mesters, a Dutch Carmelite serving in Brazil, merges the four servant songs into a single story with four 'acts' that enable the poor and oppressed to move from oppression to forgiveness. His work, *The Mission of the Suffering People: The Songs of the Servant of God in the Book of the Prophet Isaiah*, creatively places character in the service of the liberation project by highlighting how, when the offender forgives, the oppressor is made aware of his sin (cf. Isa. 52:13 – 53:12).[5]

While historically there has been more of an emphasis on how servant imagery can function to inspire political liberation from situations analogous to slavery in Egypt, liberationist thinkers like Pablo Richard have recently highlighted the impossibility and irrelevance of political power for Christians in marginalized settings.[6] Richard's concerns resonate with new endeavours by Latin American scholars to read the texts as an aid for politically impotent persons coping with experiences that echo those of the servant in either the Babylonian exile or in the Jewish diaspora.[7]

As this brief survey has shown, while the methods that seek to engage 'servant' imagery with Latin American realities are quite varied, the approaches underscore the potential of servant imagery to address the needs of those who are suffering injustice. Perhaps the natural gravitation of Latin American scholars to Isaianic servant imagery is due, in part, to the fact that the mission of the servant of the Lord in Isaiah crystallizes what theology should be about, namely, God's transformation of the world. Echoing this theological purpose, I will explore how the character traits of the servant continue and authenticate God's mission in the world today.

---

4. See José Severino Croatto, *Isaías: La palabra profética y su relectura hermenéutica. La liberación es posible. Isaías 40 – 55* (Buenos Aires: Lumen, 1994).
5. Carlos Mesters, *La misión del pueblo que sufre: Los cánticos del siervo de Dios en el libro del profeta Isaías*, trans. T. Pérez, 3rd ed. (Madrid: Ediciones Paulinas, 1983).
6. Pablo Richard, '¿Esperanza o caos?: Fundamentos y alternativas para el siglo XXI', *Relat*, online at http://servicioskoinonia.org/relat/127.htm, accessed 20 July 2011.
7. L. Rivera-Rodriguez, 'Reading in Spanish from the Diaspora through Hispanic Eyes', *Theology Today* 54 (1998), pp. 480–490.

Let us begin by proposing that 'who' the servant of the Lord is should shape our own character as 'servants' of a missional God. The following reasons can be provided for this claim: (1) the Scriptures of God extend to us an invitation to *be* the servant of the Lord; (2) the will of God to be revealed in the nations is the reason why we are to engage in the mission of the servant; (3) the Spirit of God liberates us for service and authenticates our character and mission in the world; and (4) the Son of God is our paradigm for servanthood and expresses with increasing clarity that we are to be gentle and non-imposing leaders who participate fully in the humanity of those within our missional horizon. We will now turn our attention to discuss how these aspects can shape our own understanding and practice of servanthood as we participate in mission for God among the nations today.

The Scriptures of God invite us to be the servant in mission

Isaiah's 'servant of the Lord' figure can be said to frame both the ministry of Jesus Christ and that of the early Christians. Even before the New Testament's reuse of Isaiah's servant imagery, however, the book itself had extended a literary and theological invitation to the people of God to read her own identity and mission as an extension of this mysterious *royal* figure. This innovative invitation for the people to be the servant can be seen when the servant songs are read in light of the Isaianic theme of 'democratization'. The term 'democratization' is generally used within Isaianic studies to indicate the transferring of the identity, task or benefits of the king to the wider people of God. In light of Isaiah's theme of the democratization of royalty, we are compelled to ask: How might transferring the identity and task of the king to the collective Israel (called the servant in Isa. 41:8) be significant for Christians today as they seek to extend the mission of the servant of the Lord? A brief exploration of the theme of democratization in Isaiah will point us in the right direction.

The process of democratization can be observed in various ways. As a theme, it first seems to appear on the heels of Hezekiah's prayer in Isaiah 39. The sickness and subsequent restoration of the king, as P. R. Ackroyd observed, is paradigmatic for understanding the extension of life for Judah. The life of the king represents, in some sense, the life of the people.[8] Edgar Conrad

---

8. P. R. Ackroyd, *Exile and Restoration: A Study of Hebrew Thought of the Sixth Century BC* (Louisville: Westminster, 1968).

similarly observed the transference of royal identity to the people in the reuse of literary features unique to war oracles. For instance, the phrase 'do not fear' directed to King Ahaz and his son Hezekiah (Isa.7:4; 37:6) is reformulated and applied to the servant-Israel during the Babylonian exile (Isa. 41:10).[9] God speaks to his people in exile with the same words that he had used to address previous kings. Equally notable is the way in which the servant of the Lord is seen to be doing the task once entrusted to the king, that is, establishing justice (Isa. 42:1–7; cf. 32:1). In other words, servant-Israel is now commissioned to do a royal task and is spoken to as if she were royalty herself.[10]

The association of the king's identity with that of the people in exile may also be perceived in texts descriptive of the exile outside the book of Isaiah. The gouging out of King Zedekiah's eyes in Jeremiah 52:11 by the king of Babylon may have resonated with the divine hardening and blindness in Isaiah 6:10, a condition that according to Brevard Childs was personified in wicked King Ahaz (Isa. 7 – 9),[11] and later in the blind servant-Israel (Isa. 42:18–20). That is, in some sense the experience of blindness is seen to characterize both king and people. Conversely, John Goldingay notes that the release of King Jehoiachin of Judah by Evil-merodach of Babylon (Jer. 52:31) would surely have given hope to captive servant-Israel (Isa. 42:18–20).[12] Perhaps she too, like her king, would emerge from captivity. Finally, not only do the experiences of the king resonate with those of Israel in exile, but the ideal character of the king, as one who pursues justice and truth, was similarly to characterize the collective people of God (cf. Isa. 9:6–7; 32:1–8; 42:1–7; 59:14–16). In the Second Temple period (518 BC – AD 70) the theme of democratization is more fully developed in the reforms of lay leaders such as Ezra and Nehemiah who perceive their own teaching of Torah and restoration of Jerusalem to be an extension of the servant's royal mission in Isaiah 40 – 55.[13] Equally significant is how the

---

9. Edgar Conrad, 'The Royal Narratives and the Structure of the Book of Isaiah', *Journal for the Study of the Old Testament* (1988), pp. 67–81.
10. My own understanding of 'democratization' is informed, to a large extent, by the work of H. G. M. Williamson, *Variations on a Theme: King, Messiah, and Servant in the Book of Isaiah*, The Didsbury Lectures (Carlisle: Paternoster, 1998).
11. J. Goldingay, *God's Prophet, God's Servant: A Study in Jeremiah and Isaiah 40 – 55* (Carlisle: Paternoster, 1984), p. 98; B. S. Childs, *Isaiah*, The Old Testament Library (Louisville: Westminster John Knox Press, 2001), p. 62.
12. Goldingay, *God's Prophet, God's Servant*, p. 98.
13. See J. G. McConville, 'Ezra-Nehemiah and the Fulfillment of Prophecy', *Vetus Testamentum* 36 (1986), pp. 206–224.

post-exilic period incorporates more foreign converts as the 'servants' of the Lord, an image once applied only to Israel (cf. Isa. 41:8; 56:6; 66:19–21). Finally, the theme of the servant-Israel as God's witness shapes Jesus' exhortation as he commissions his own disciples to be witnesses of his work in the world (Isa. 43:10; Acts 1:8).[14] In summary, the royal task of working for justice in the world, once given to the king and transferred to servant-Israel, is taken up by a multi-ethnic church. It has profound missiological implications for us today. As a royal priesthood and holy nation (1 Pet. 2:9) whose identity and mission are necessarily shaped by the story of Israel and of the early church, we too are called to extend the work of God's perfect servant-king, the Lord Jesus Christ.

At this point, the fluidity inherent in applying the term 'servant' to a range of referents may raise important questions. Are the texts that speak of the 'servant of the Lord' not exhaustively fulfilled in Christ Jesus (Matt. 12:15–21; Acts 8:35)? How can texts that speak about the king, Israel or the Messiah be legitimately appropriated today? Two brief points clarify the way in which Scripture extends an invitation to contemporary Christians to have both their mission and character shaped by the servant of the Lord in Isaiah.

First, the liberty with which the themes related to the servant of the Lord or the term 'servant' itself are used does not imply that all aspects of any one servant song apply to all people in the same way (Isa. 42:1–7; 49:1–13; 50:4–10; 52:13 – 53:12). Parts of Isaiah 42:1–4, for instance, are used to describe the baptism (Mark 1:11; Matt. 3:17), ministry (Matt. 12:17–21) and transfiguration of Jesus (Matt. 17:1–5). At the same time, themes from the same servant song are applied to the commissioning of the apostle Paul in an entirely different way. As F. F. Bruce noted, Paul and Barnabas are entrusted with the mission of the servant (Isa. 49:6 in Acts 13:47) and read their own call in light of the servant's commission (Acts 20:21; 26:23; Gal. 1:15–16; 2:9).[15] Paul, moreover, not only sees his own mission in light of the servant, but his own conversion is narrated in light of the conversion of blind servant-Israel (Isa. 42:18–20). David Seccombe captures Luke's use of Isaiah in the following way:

> Indications in Acts suggest that the isaianic servant songs as a whole lie in the background of Luke's presentation of the church's apostolic leaders, as

---

14. So notes David W. Pao, *Acts and the Isaianic New Exodus* (Tübingen: Mohr Siebeck, 2000).
15. F. F. Bruce, *The Book of Acts* (Grand Rapids: Eerdmans, 1968), p. 267.

> Spirit-empowered witnesses of Jesus as Lord . . . Saul's blindness points to the blindness of Israel . . . Just as servant Israel was blind and then could see and become a witness, so Saul was blind and became a witness.[16]

In other words, the servant songs can be seen as a paradigm for both the identity and the mission of Christians even when their most perfect expression is to be found in the Lord Jesus Christ. In a similar way, while the vicarious suffering of the servant in Isaiah 52:13 – 53:12 is applied to the Lord Jesus in Acts 8:28–35, its relevance for shaping Christian character is not thereby exhausted. So, too, one might think of Paul's insistence on the practical implications of living in light of the incarnation and death of Christ (Phil. 2:5–8). That is, the ontological reality of atonement, accomplished once for all by God's perfect suffering servant, can still provide a vision for shaping the character and mission of the servant's descendants (Isa. 53:10).

Second, the royal task of the servant to bring justice to the nations (Isa. 42:1–4), entrusted to the collective people of God, is to be carried out until the return of the Lord Jesus Christ. Commenting on the potential of the servant of the Lord imagery to shape the mission of the church, H. G. M. Williamson suggests there should be no difficulty 'envisaging Jesus as fulfilling that role while at the same time maintaining that it was a role first given for Israel before his time and remains open as a role to be fulfilled after his time'.[17] As W. A. M. Beuken puts it, 'So long as there is injustice, there is the need for the servant.'[18] The present need for justice in the world underscores that the task of the servant of the Lord is open until the second advent of Christ. The Christian church, then, as she lives in eager expectation of that time, should legitimately read her own identity, character and mission in light of God's ideal servant.

Having set forth some reasons that legitimate our own identification with the ideal servant of the Lord, we are now in a position to ask why Christians today should seek to have their character and mission shaped in light of these texts. Understanding the reason for the servant's mission will both aid and motivate the development of character that makes the transformational mission of the servant in the world a possibility.

---

16. David P. Seccombe, 'Luke and Isaiah', *New Testament Studies* 27 (1981), pp. 252–259.
17. Williamson, *Variations on a Theme*, p. 144.
18. W. A. M. Beuken, 'Mishpat: The First Servant Song in Its Context', *Vetus Testamentum* 22 (1972), pp. 1–30.

The will of God to be revealed in the nations is the reason for engaging in the mission of the servant

It goes without saying that even a cursory reading of texts related to the servant indicates that what the servant *does* results in a better world: justice, restoration to the land, the lifting of transgressions, universal obedience to Torah, the blind seeing and the deaf hearing. At the same time, these horizontal reasons (servant-humanity) should not eclipse the larger vertical grounds for *being* the servant of the Lord, namely, the servant is personally commissioned by God to carry out God's name-recognizing mission (Isa. 42:5, 8–12). All that the servant is to *be* and *do* relates to God's mission of being universally recognized as Yahweh. The servant is to engage in mission because of God's greater desire to be worshipped in all nations. This is God's will for the servant. As Walter Brueggemann puts it:

> The call of the servant is sandwiched to make clear that it is the will of the creator that is to be enacted by the servant. The reason the servant can traffic in covenant, bring light, cancel debts, is because it is Yahweh's will. This is what the literary arrangement of the sandwiching of the mission of the servant (42:6–7) between self-doxologies (v. 5 and vv. 8–9) communicates.[19]

The interpersonal relationship between Yahweh and his commissioned servant underscores not only that the mission is God's will, but that the mission is done *for* God. To draw on Stephen Darwall's terminology, the rooting of the servant's mission, and consequentially the servant's character, is explicitly 'second-personal'.[20] We, too, will be invigorated to do the task of the servant when we understand that our mission for God stems from a commitment to a personal and living God. This intimate relationship with God is underscored in the Hebrew text of Isaiah 42:6, where the second-person masculine pronoun is repeated no less than four times during the commissioning of the servant:

> I am the LORD, I have called you in righteousness,
>   I have taken you by the hand and kept you;

---

19. Walter Brueggemann, *Isaiah*, Westminster Bible Commentary (Louisville: Westminster John Knox Press, 1998), p. 44.
20. Stephen Darwall, 'Authority and Reasons for Acting: Exclusionary and Second-Personal', *Ethics* 120 (2010), p. 257.

> I have given you as a covenant to the people,
>   a light to the nations.

So while humanity does indeed flourish because of the character and mission of the servant, the commission to 'traffic in covenant' is intimately and divinely grounded in a 'second-personal' reason. We are to participate in mission because God has willed for his name to be universally known through the mission of the servant (Isa. 42:5, 10–12). This name-recognizing mission, however, requires that the servant have an appropriate inner character and corresponding ethical framework.

The fact that character stems from a personal relationship shared between the servant and Yahweh provides both motive for the cultivation of character (i.e., it is done *for* Yahweh) and the promise of the sustainability of character (i.e., the relationship with the Spirit who forges the servant's character is continuous). Unlike religious ideologies that separate character from service, the God-shaped character of the servant cannot be divorced from the goal of serving humanity. In fact, the ethic to be implemented within humanity is so inter-related to one's personal character and relationship to God that not to serve humanity according to justice, righteousness or truth is seen to be a personal assault on the very God personified by these traits (Isa. 59:14–15; cf. Matt. 25:45).[21] God wills for our inner character to be outwardly expressed in an ethical commitment to justice and righteousness. In so doing, we participate in Yahweh's mission to be universally worshipped as the only God in all creation.

Cultivating the character of the servant and participating in the servant's mission of justice means that who the servant is and what the servant does reveal God to the nations. The revelatory nature of the servant's character and mission is made increasingly clear in light of the anti-idol polemic that begins in Isaiah 41:21. In particular, the servant's unique second-personal relationship with divinity contrasts with the Babylonian idols, which do not relate to the gods they supposedly represent. It is Israel's special relationship with God that makes her 'imaging' God to the nations a plausible reality. This status has been brought out helpfully by Richard Clifford, who notes that the servant in Isaiah functions as the icon of God.[22] Clifford observes that the larger literary

---

21. Jan L. Koole, *Isaiah. Part 3. Vol. III, Isaiah 56–66* (Kampen: Kok Pharos, 1998), p. 195.
22. Richard J. Clifford, *Fair Spoken and Persuading: An Interpretation of Second Isaiah* (New York: Paulist, 1984); 'The Function of Idols Passages in Second Isaiah', *Catholic Biblical Quarterly* 42 (1980), pp. 450–464.

environment of the servant song (Isa. 42:1–7) underscores a concerted effort to contrast Israel and her God with the idols of Babylon and the gods they represent. Sarah Dille likewise picks up on the contrast between Yahweh and the gods by noting how the silence of the gods functions as a foil to make the 'noise' of a pregnant and fighting Yahweh all the more glorious (cf. Isa. 42:13–14).[23] While the silent gods of Babylon are incapable of transmitting their glory to their representative mute and ineffective idols on earth (Isa. 41:22–29), Yahweh transmits his presence to his icon servant-Israel in whom he is glorified (Isa. 49:3).

Likewise, our character and mission is to reveal the character and mission of the triune God to the nations. God's desire to reveal his glorious presence and mission to the world was most fully accomplished in the person and work of the Lord Jesus, God's new servant-Israel, his perfect icon (Col. 1:15). Having been grafted into this special relationship with Christ (John 17; Rom. 9 – 11; Gal. 4:28), Christians are constituted as iconic representatives of God on earth (Isa. 43:10; Acts 1:8). Yet to be the icon of God does not imply reflecting the image of a static God incapable of intervening in the affairs of earth. As Miranda noted, we are not called merely to contemplate the juridical verdicts of God but, to draw on Clifford's terminology, we are constituted as the '*icon-in-act*' of God. The servant is the image of God because the servant *acts* for God in history and, in so doing, brings about real change.

To be an *icon-in-action* (cf. 2 Cor. 3:2–3) is potentially transformative in contexts such as Latin America where, as Severino Croatto notes, themes of divine suffering and death permeate icons and religious imagery to such an extent that passivity in the face of suffering would seem to be legitimated by God.[24] The servant as the *icon-in-act* of God, however, is not the passive *object* of human history. Rather, to build on the analogy of Rubem Alves, the servant suffers and is glorified as the *subject* of human history.[25] God changes history *through* the mission of the servant. Thus, the invitation to *be* the servant of the Lord is a call to action that results in God being universally worshipped and acknowledged.

By way of summary, the reason why we must participate in the servant's mission in history is because it is the will of God who has personally

---

23. Sarah J. Dille, *Mixing Metaphors: God as Mother and Father in Deutero-Isaiah* (London: T. & T. Clark, 2004).
24. J. S. Croatto, 'Popular Religion: An Attempted Statement of the Problem', *Ministerial Formation* 29 (1985), pp. 18–19.
25. Rubem Alves, *A Theology of Hope* (Washington: Corpus, 1968).

commissioned his church as his 'iconic' agent in the world (Isa. 42:6–7; 2 Cor. 5:19–20). Thus, the servant's character and mission provide a picture, an icon as it were, of God for the nations, and to the extent that we cultivate the servant's qualities we will also be an icon of God for people from every nation. Our striving after a godly inner character then is important because the church, however poorly she reflects God, is nonetheless a picture of the Lord Jesus on display for the nations. This high and heavy iconic calling drives us to an important question: How is the ever-important character needed to represent God to the nations cultivated? If the servant is a painting of God for the nations, what are the broad strokes of the Spirit as he paints the canvas? It is to this dynamic process of character formation to which we now turn our attention.

The Spirit of God liberates us to be the servant and shapes our character for mission

How is inner character – who we are – forged in a way that is coherent with public ethics – what we do? Opting for public ethics versus inner virtue is an issue within the church. Pedro Zamora, commenting on the trend of the evangelical church in Spain, having been liberated from Franco, to opt for the imposition of public ethics rather than the pursuit of a coherent inner life, writes:

> I believe that our society demands from the Church, not a determined campaign for determined public ethic, but a *simple faith* capable of generating a *simple life* that is, at the same time, a truly human life.[26]

Perhaps the same demand is made by the nations who are said to *hope* for the servant's mission (Isa. 42:4), yet implicitly desire that what the servant does flows into the public arena from a richness of character marked by compassion and humility.

Surprisingly, however, both God's ideal servant-Israel, for which the nations long, and empirical servant-Israel both highlight the dilemma that grips contemporary society and the church, namely, the lack of coherence between who we are (character) and what we do (mission/ethics). Like Israel, the present dichotomy between the church's character and her ethics renders her morally

---

26. My translation of Pedro Zamora, *La fe sencilla: Reflexiones sobre la vida* (Madrid: Ediciones Fliedner, 2011), p. 18.

impotent in the world she seeks to transform.[27] What the character of the servant should be (Isa. 42:1–7) is not reflected in the present reality (Isa. 42:18–20). It is this very tension that makes the servant songs such appropriate conversation partners for Christians in the public arena today. Where then is the dilemma facing empirical servant-Israel? From what does Israel need to be liberated in order to fulfil her mission? What must the Spirit of God do to bring about authentic servants who transform the world?

Liberation

R. Melugin notes that while the servant-Israel is commissioned to implement justice in the nations, she is obviously far removed from the experience of justice (cf. Isa. 40:27).[28] While ideal Israel is to delve into the public arena by giving sight to the blind, the real Israel is described as being blind, deaf and unresponsive to God. Ideal Israel is to liberate the captives, but empirical Israel is presently trapped, captive to Babylon (Isa. 42:1–7; 42:18–20). As Melugin underscores, Israel has not experienced those things which she has been commissioned to do as the ideal people of God. Positively, however, the fact that Isaiah pictures the servant (or the personification of Israel) as implementing justice, giving sight to the blind and liberating the oppressed implies what Melugin terms a 'dual administration' of justice. That is, justice will be both given *to* Israel and distributed *by* her. Grace, however, must come first. Given the servant's role in implementing justice, we can assume that God will have done a gracious work in servant-Israel. Having received justice, the prophet perceives Israel as growing into her missional role among the nations, even if it means, as Williamson notes, radically redefining who Israel actually is (cf. Isa. 49:3).[29]

The exclusive work of God in liberating his people prior to entrusting them with a mission resonates with the overarching story of Scripture: redemption must come before the forging of character which, in turn, authenticates public ethics (mission). Just as liberation from Egypt comes before the giving of the law and call to missional holiness, liberation from Babylon frees God's citizens to internalize the inner ethics of Zion (Isa. 35:8; 52:11; 61:3; Rev. 18). More gloriously, God's divine judgment and redemption manifested in the cross of

---

27. In distinguishing between 'ideal Israel' and 'empirical Israel' I am drawing on the work of Williamson in *Variations on a Theme*.
28. Roy F. Melugin, 'The Servant, God's Call, and the Structure of Isaiah 40 – 48', in E. H. Lovering, Jr (ed.), *Society of Biblical Literature 1991 Seminar Papers* (Atlanta: Scholar's Press, 1991), pp. 21–36.
29. Williamson, *Variations on a Theme*, pp. 150–154.

Christ liberates from sin and empowers the disciples of Jesus to live out the ethics of the kingdom in coherent ways (Matt. 5; Col. 2:1–25). In summary, God's liberating work in salvation is a non-negotiable 'first' in the forging of character needed for authentic mission in the world today. Character formation for mission, then, is first and foremost rooted in the salvific work of God. At the same time, however, character formation is dependent upon the dynamic second-personal relationship shared between the servant and the Spirit of God. It is this relationship that empowers and sustains the character Christians need to participate in mission with authenticity in God's world.

The Spirit

While the person and work of the Spirit of God has been active in the reversal of destinies and in the liberation of the people that marks the new order (Isa. 32:15–20), the Spirit equally engages in the preparation and authentication of the servant in the world. The character and ethics needed to function as God's icon to the nations is a work of the Spirit who is upon the servant (Isa. 42:1; 61:1). As Wonsuk Ma observes, the same Spirit that gave leaders a sense of ethical and moral qualities in the first part of Isaiah is now seen to enable and authenticate the servant's mission in the world.[30]

Introducing the first servant song, Isaiah 42:1 suggests that it will be the Spirit who forges the consistent character choices of non-violence and compassion the world desperately longs to see (cf. Isa. 2:2–4; Gal. 5:22). Consequently, one can appreciate the literary progression that evidences growth in the empirical servant's inner disposition and mission. As Willem A. VanGemeren notes, the servant becomes increasingly resilient (Isa. 49:1–13), is willing to suffer persecution for the weary (Isa. 50:4–10) and prays with eschatological confidence (Isa. 63:15ff.).[31] Having been liberated by God, empowered and authenticated by the Spirit, the servant is now prepared to cultivate an inner disposition needed for mission, namely, the disposition to learn from Yahweh.

The school of suffering

To build on Melugin's analogy of the dual administration of justice, one might say that teaching Torah to the nations (Isa. 42:4; cf. 2:2–4) implies the servant's

---

30. Wonsuk Ma, 'Until the Spirit Comes: The Spirit of God in the Book of Isaiah', *Journal for the Study of the Old Testament* Supplement Series 271 (Sheffield: Sheffield Academic, 1999), p. 92.

31. I am indebted to Willem A. VanGemeren of Trinity International University for this observation.

own need for schooling, for the servant will need to internalize the Torah he teaches. Read sequentially, the flow of themes within Isaiah paints a picture of a deaf and blind Israel (Isa. 42:18–20), unresponsive to the Word of God, emerging as a 'student-servant' who wakes up every morning for his lesson in moral education (Isa. 50:4–10). Unlike most trends in contemporary theological education, however, the servant is being educated for the specific purpose of sustaining the most vulnerable in society. More specifically, the servant has his eyes and ears open to learn how to accept suffering (cf. Isa. 6:9). Childs summarizes the flow of the text as follows:

> What the servant learned was not information, but to accept the experience of suffering and shame. Earlier (49:4) he had confessed his failure to persuade a resisting people. Now, the negative response intensifies into physical violence from which the servant did not retreat ... the one who became the 'learner', who had assumed the role of the servant to restore the remnant of Israel (49:3,6) is now led along a new path of suffering and deepest humiliation. When seen in the larger context of the narrative movement within chapters 40 – 55, there is a clear transfer from Israel, the servant nation, to Israel, the suffering individual who now embodies the nation's true mission.[32]

The student-servant, then, places himself in a position to be taught by God and in so doing he learns to suffer so that he can comfort the weary and sustain the weak (Isa. 40:27–31; Matt. 11:28). It is not surprising that the willingness to suffer is being forged within the character of the student-servant, since it will be suffering humanity that emerges onto the servant's pastoral horizon (Isa. 42:2–4).

Suffering, of course, is a familiar Christian virtue (Heb. 2:9; 1 Pet. 2:19; Jas 5:13). In fact, it was desired so intensely by some that Church Fathers such as Clement of Alexandria had to teach against needless suffering and martyrdom.[33] Today, however, it would seem that the church may need to reconsider suffering as part of her Christian experience, especially in the light of 'prosperity gospel' teaching. While many in the majority world suffer daily for their Christian faith, many Western Christians seem to have followed the ancient ideological lead of the Targum which disassociates suffering from the Messiah in the fourth

---

32. Childs, *Isaiah*, pp. 394–395.
33. S. Rosell, 'Loving God ... unto death: The witness of the early Christians', *HTS Teologiese Studies/Theological Studies* 66.1 (2010), online at http://www.hts.org.za/index.php/HTS/article/view/301/1069, accessed 21 October 2011.

servant song (Isa. 52:13 – 53:12). It is here, Croatto helpfully notes, that the New Testament sheds light on how ancient texts of Scripture are actualized in ways that preserve their core meaning.[34]

While a text may be recontextualized in any number of ways – as in the Targum – the death and resurrection of the Messiah in the New Testament points the interpreter forward in ways that preserve the original sense, namely, redemption is always forged in and through suffering. Thus redemptive history can never be unrelated to suffering, and Christian discipleship must be propelled by identification with the suffering servant (1 Pet. 2:19–25) and linking the realities of suffering to one's faith. Having been redeemed by God's perfect Israel, the Lord Jesus, we are equally called to suffer persecution for our faith in him (Isa. 50:4–10; John 15:18; Col. 1:24).

If Isaiah 50:4–10 initiates the servant in the school of suffering, the theme of suffering is most prominent in Isaiah 52:13 – 53:12. While the two texts approach suffering from different angles, they both underscore the impossibility of thinking of the mission of God apart from suffering. John Walton's suggestion that the imagery of the substitute king ritual lies behind the fourth servant song (Isa. 52:13 – 53:12) provides an important lesson for student-servants enrolled in the school of suffering. By way of summary, Walton suggests that the servant song is a reflective transformation of widely practised 'substitute king rituals' in the Ancient Near East ranging from the second millennia BC to the time of Alexander the Great.[35] Broadly speaking, when omens threatened the life of a king, a substitute king would be chosen, largely from the 'dispensable' members of society, to be sacrificed for the redemption of the real king. The uniqueness of Isaiah 52:13 – 53:12, Walton concludes, is that a real king, clothed as a servant, does not demand the death of a member of society for his own redemption. Instead, a real king dies for the benefit of his people. The transformation of this imagery contributes to the general theme of democratization but, in a new way, namely, a real king extends the benefits of his death to the people, even to the vulnerable of society.

The transformation of substitute king imagery underscores the importance of character formation in the following way. Given that our identity is subsumed in that of the servant-king, the imagery of actively suffering for the marginalized and alienated should compel us to break with elitism that so tragically marks

---

34. J. S. Croatto, *Hermenéutica bíblica: Para una teoría de la lectura como producción de sentido* (Buenos Aires: La Aurora, 1984), p. 56.

35. John Walton, 'The Imagery of the Substitute King Ritual in Isaiah's Fourth Servant Song', *Journal of Biblical Literature* 122 (2003), pp. 734–743.

both the world and the Christian church. The 'stepping down' of a royal figure for the benefit of those who might otherwise be sacrificed for the upper echelon of society is potentially transformative. The imagery of a servant-king who dies for the marginalized compels us to eschew all elitism and class divisions in order to serve the poor so that they, too, can receive the life of God.

To recapitulate, the character needed to participate in the mission of God has as its starting point the liberating and salvific work of the Spirit God. At the same time, the presence of the Spirit upon the servant forges the character of the servant and authenticates the servant's mission. Finally, the servant grows in resilience and is willing to suffer for the faith so that the poor may share in the life of God. Having been liberated and enabled for service, we will explore how the Lord Jesus Christ, who ministered as the ideal Servant of the Lord, provides a practical paradigm for those called to be missional servants today.

The Son of God is our paradigm for servanthood

One of the enduring legacies of liberation theologies is the need to read texts from the perspective of the marginalized and for their benefit. The gospel of the servant is, after all, to be proclaimed to the poor in holistic ways (Matt. 11:5; Luke 4:18; 7:22). This pastoral commitment resonates with the missional activity of the servant as well who is called to share the life of God with 'bruised reeds' and 'dimly burning wicks' (Isa. 42:1–7). How then are we to proceed in being the *icons-in-act* of God for the marginalized and poor of the world? The witness of Isaiah 42:1–7 in the life and mission of the Lord Jesus underscores the characteristics that are to mark authentic Christian servanthood, namely, a non-imposing and gentle manner of leadership, and being a full participant in humanity. I will suggest ways in which these character traits might be contextually translated by the church in mission as a paradigm for expressing missional servanthood today.

Non-imposing leadership
Whether it is Rome's Constantine, the Crusades, the Spanish Inquisition, the Protestant colonization of the Americas, or the ideological culture wars of the mainline or fundamental branches of the Western church, the history of Christendom is one marked by imposition by Christian leaders. Ironically, the servant's way of doing 'God's business' seems to be bypassed in every generation, including his own.

In ancient times when peoples were conquered, the victor parading in the streets would typically oblige those he had recently subdued to accept the new religion.[36] The servant, however, presents us with a different way of doing God's work. John Goldingay puts it like this: 'The Man of War leads us to Jerusalem but the Man of Sorrows leads us to God.'[37] In contrast to Ancient Near Eastern victors – with the possible exception of the religiously tolerant Cyrus (though see Isa. 45:1) – God's victorious agent will have nothing to do with imposition of religion. This countercultural form of the servant's leadership style is highlighted by the repetitive use (six times) of the negative adverb in Hebrew (*lō'*, 'not') in Isaiah 42:2–4:

> He will not cry or lift up his voice,
>   or make it heard in the street;
> a bruised reed he will not break,
>   and a dimly burning wick he will not quench;
>   he will faithfully bring forth justice.
> He will not grow faint or be crushed
>   until he has established justice in the earth;
>   and the coastlands wait for his teaching.

In this way, the text defines the servant's character *in contrast* to images of leaders of the day who sought to legitimate their religion through violent means. The contrastive nature of servanthood is equally drawn upon by the Gospel of Matthew to describe the ministry of the Lord Jesus. In contradistinction to his opponents, who imposed their views, Jesus went about his ministry in a remarkably quiet fashion. Richard Beaton notes that the scribes and Pharisees are seen imposing their views by making a lot of noise in public, either scorning Jesus for healing the lame or quarrelling with his disciples for picking grain. Jesus, on the other hand, withdraws into silence and brings healing and liberation to those oppressed under the religious rule of the day.[38] More specifically, the reuse of the first servant song (Isa. 42:1–4) in Matthew draws the distinction between Jesus and the religious leaders by pointing to contrastive uses of the law.

Immediately after the healing of the withered man's hand on the Sabbath (Matt. 12:1–17) and prior to the healing of the demonized man (Matt.

---

36. Edward Young, *The Book of Isaiah: The English Text, With Introduction, Exposition and Notes, Volume 3, Chapters 40 – 66* (Grand Rapids: Eerdmans, 1965), p. 112.
37. John Goldingay, 'Man of War and the Suffering Servant: The Old Testament and the Theology of Liberation', *Tyndale Bulletin* 27 (1976), pp. 76–113.
38. Richard Beaton, 'Messiah and Justice: A Key to Matthew's Use of Isaiah 42:1–4', *Journal for the Study of the Old Testament* 75 (1999), pp. 5–23.

12:22–27), the Evangelist quotes Isaiah 42:1–4. Matthew, however, intentionally quotes the Greek Septuagint rather than the Hebrew text. Perhaps one of the most significant changes between these versions is that the Hebrew text of Isaiah 42:4 reads that nations wait *'in his Torah'* while the Greek text reads that nations wait *'in his Name'* (Matt. 12:21). Don Carson helpfully notes that Matthew opts for 'Name' rather than 'Torah' precisely to underscore his point that the law (Torah) is to point people perfectly to Jesus Christ.[39] The overall effect of placing this text in between two Sabbath healings is to draw a distinction between how Jesus and the religious leaders of the day understood the law. To draw on Peter Berger's terminology, while the law interpreted by the religious leaders of the day legitimates the status quo of oppression and infirmity, the Evangelist sees the law as a means to point people to Jesus, the gentle liberating Servant of the Lord.

As disciples of Jesus, we too are to minister in ways that contrast with the religious leaders who legitimate situations of oppression for the weak and vulnerable of the world. But what might Isaiah's vision of a non-imposing liberator who gently ministers to the oppressed look like in Latin American contexts? What is the landscape of leadership in which the Isaianic vision of servanthood is be nurtured and developed? Examples of patrimonial figures may be seen across the political landscape of Latin America expressing a general trend of *caudillismo*. From Cuba's Castro to Venezuela's Hugo Chavez, strong and charismatic leaders take upon themselves the frustration and needs of the masses, promising to intervene in life-threatening situations.[40] *Caudillismo* also permeates popular Protestantism, which Pablo Deiros describes as generally revolving around a charismatic leader who, being totally uncommitted to traditional ecclesiastical structures, places himself in front of the masses and with great personal sacrifice creates organizations which could never function apart from his presence or influence.[41] Such a landscape of political and religious leadership begs the question: How might we engage the ancient vision of Isaianic leadership with contemporary expressions of *caudillismo*?

---

39. D. A. Carson, *Matthew*, Expositor's Bible Commentary, vol. 8 (Grand Rapids: Zondervan, 1984), p. 396.
40. S. Torres Ballesteros, 'El populismo: un concepto escurridizo', in J. J. Álvarez and D. Alfín Castro (eds.), *Populismo, caudillaje, y discurso Demagógico* (Madrid: Centro de Investigaciones Sociológicas, 1987), pp. 159–180.
41. Pablo A. Deiros, *Historia del cristianismo en América Latina* (Buenos Aires: Fraternidad Teológica Latinoamericana, 1992), p. 176.

On the one hand, Isaiah's vision of the servant clashes with various aspects of *caudillismo*, not the least in the caudillo's demand for blind allegiance from the poor who require the patrimony of the father figure for spiritual or political survival.[42] In contrast to this, the covenant benefits mediated by the servant leader in Isaiah benefit his people (Isa. 42:6) even when there is a critique of leadership (Isa. 40:27; 50:4–10) or outright rebellion (Isa. 53:5–6). Moreover, related to the problem of a single 'patron' who demands blind allegiance is the creation of an organization or institution that can only function in the presence or under the influence of the self-made *caudillo*. Mission that is entirely tied to a single personality (termed *personalismo* in Spanish) appears to be in conflict with the Isaianic vision of democratization that transfers both the identity and mission of the leader to the masses under his care.

On the other hand, personally assuming the needs of the masses and striving to meet these needs through great personal sacrifice (Isa. 53:4–6), even if it means breaking with traditional established structures of religion, echoes in many respects the mission of the servant of the Lord and enriches its application in contemporary society. This aspect of Isaiah's servant of the Lord who assumes the needs and the struggles of humanity leads us to our final point, namely, the servant of the Lord identifies with humanity to the fullest extent.

Being human

In a beautifully woven arrangement of Hebrew poetry, a chiasm presents the servant as having the same humanity as the weak to whom he seeks to minister. The vulnerable are described as a:

Reed about to break
   //**Wick** that is faintly burning.

The servant is also referred to as a reed and as a wick, but in a slightly different way. In the Hebrew text, the servant is presented as a:

Wick not faintly burning
   //**Reed** not about to break.

---

42. Eugene Nida, *Understanding Latin Americans: With Special Reference to Religious Values and Movements* (Pasadena: William Carey Library, 1969), p. 146.

The literary structure describes both the servant and the people as reeds and wicks. That is, they are of the same substance.[43] In the same way that the suffering servant is a Lamb slaughtered for sheep that have gone astray, Isaiah 42:2–4 presents the servant as a bright candle for those candles that need light; a strong reed for reeds that are nearly broken.[44] In other words, not only does the servant take upon himself the wounds of humanity (Isa. 1:5–6; 53:4–5), he *shares* in the humanity of those he serves. The difference, however, is not one of humanity but of being sustained by God. Both the servant and the vulnerable are wicks subject to the same winds.[45] However, the servant has a continual supply of oil because the Spirit of God is upon him (Isa. 42:1; 61:1).[46] As J. Alec Motyer notes, both the servant and the vulnerable are reeds that receive blows and bruises, but the bruises do not paralyse the servant as they do the vulnerable. Rather, the inner qualities generated by the Spirit enable the servant to face the pressures that lie ahead.[47] For this reason, it was necessary to develop character and learn the importance of suffering. The servant will be dealt heavy blows but, through it all, will prove to be unflinching and resilient (Isa. 50:4–10). As someone who suffers in life, the servant is in a unique position to share what sustains him with the vulnerable. He shares the life of God with those who are just like him. Their wicks can also burn from a continual supply of oil.[48] They, too, can receive the inner qualities that enable one to face suffering because they share in the same Spirit. The one with a royal task is commissioned to share his source of strength with those who are just like him.

Sharing in humanity is, however, something of a forgotten inner quality among ministers or missioners today. Enrique Dussel reflects on the problems clergy have in coming to grips with their own humanity in the following way:

> To be a part of a social class is to enjoy the fruits of its culture and the benefits of its power . . . when a clergyman has to go to a municipal office for some reason, he is often invited to leave the long line of people waiting for service and to come right to the front. He readily avails himself to the offer, pretending that it is a mark of respect for the Church or God's ministers. In reality, he is enjoying the privilege of a class

---

43. Koole, *Isaiah*, p. 223.
44. Goldingay, *God's Prophet, God's Servant*, p. 97.
45. J. Alec Motyer, *The Prophecy of Isaiah: An Introduction and Commentary* (Downers Grove: InterVarsity Press, 1993), p. 320.
46. Koole, *Isaiah*, pp. 223–224.
47. Motyer, *The Prophecy of Isaiah*, p. 320.
48. Koole, *Isaiah*, p. 223.

that has social power. Such power, insofar as it exerts domination over others, is sin. Clergymen make full use of their political power shared by their class when they jump in line or use their muscle in administrative details.[49]

In many respects, elitism among clergy is symptomatic of larger cultural trends in Latin America where there is still a marked distinction between the 'high class' and the 'low class', despite a growing middle class. Yet surprisingly, many clergy have emerged from working-class backgrounds only to find that vocational ministry elevates them to a class that separates them from the poor they first sought to serve. Dussel continues:

> [Many] priests and religious [workers] in Latin America . . . come from a working-class background and it was there that their Christian vocation developed. Then, they went through a period of training . . . when they returned to work among the labouring class, they found they no longer spoke the language or lived in the same mental framework.[50]

The same distancing between evangelical religious workers and the people they are commissioned to serve was observed by Samuel Escobar, who noted the tendency of vocational workers to develop 'middle class' mentality.[51] The result is that theology is no longer done to address the needs of the poor, something described by Nuñez and Taylor in the following way:

> A disturbing pattern emerges in the new members of the rising middle class. Most of them have come from families which a generation ago formed part of the 'popular classes'. You would expect that they, having risen on the scale, would be more sensitive to those who remain on the underside . . . The 'new rich' have short memories and readily adopt the value systems of the elite, forgetting their roots.[52]

Antonio González has observed that these sorts of class divisions may contribute in part to the widespread phenomena of speaking in tongues among

---

49. Enrique Dussel, *History and the Theology of Liberation: A Latin American Perspective*, trans. J. Drury (New York: Orbis, 1976), p. 161.
50. Ibid.
51. Samuel Escobar, *Evangelio y realidad social* (El Paso: Casa Bautista de Publicaciones, 1988), pp. 21–22.
52. Emilio A. Núñez and William D. Taylor, *Crisis and Hope in Latin America: An Evangelical Perspective* (Pasadena: William Carey, 1996), p. 122.

Latin American Pentecostals.[53] If everyone has the same gift, class divisions begin to blur as everyone is found to be on the same playing field. In light of class divisions too obvious to comment, the vision of the Spirit of the Lord upon collective Israel, democratized with the task formerly given to elite royalty, provides an alternative vision for the equality and empowerment of *all* the people of God.

Of course, the Isaianic vision of leadership is not only a call for humility, but equally speaks to the need for the ethical integrity of ministers who imagine themselves as having been ordained into a higher-tiered Christianity. Eugene Nida noted some time ago the acceptance of the 'amoral' nature of the priest in some popular expressions of Latin American religion.[54] Given that the efficacy of sacraments does not depend upon the minister but upon Christ and his Word (*ex opere operato*), the day-to-day ethics of the priest may be perceived as irrelevant because he has been ordained as a perpetual channel of sacramentally infused grace. The mission of the priest (who he is) would appear to be unrelated to his personal ethics (what he does), a problem that has been thoughtfully addressed by several Roman Catholic leaders.[55]

Such a critique, however, may equally speak to non-sacramental expressions of Christianity in Latin America that similarly divorce the inner character of the 'pastor' from a corresponding coherent ethical framework. All too often Christian leaders are exempt from ethics because they have been 'anointed by the Spirit', so that regardless of immoral behaviour they are still thought to be channels of the Spirit. But whether it stems from erroneous perceptions of sacramental theology or pneumatology, the ethical exemption of ministers is a critical issue that can be addressed by Isaianic servant imagery for the following reason: the humble servant of the Lord is as equally praised by God *for his mission* as he is *for his personal character and ethics* (Mark 1:11).

Conclusion

In this chapter I have suggested ways of linking the ancient vision of Isaiah's servant of the Lord with some of the contemporary realities and concerns unique to Latin American contexts. In so doing we have sought to show how

---

53. Antonio González, *The Gospel of Faith and Justice* (New York: Orbis, 2005).
54. See Nida, *Understanding Latin Americans*.
55. See, for instance, Norbert J. Rigali, 'Moral Theology and Church Responses to Sexual Abuse', *Horizons* 34 (2007), pp. 183–204.

'who' the Servant of the Lord is should shape our own character as 'servants' of a missional God. There are four reasons: (1) the Scriptures of God extend to us an invitation to *be* the servant of the Lord; (2) the will of a personal God, whom we represent, to be revealed in the nations is the reason why we are to engage in the mission of the servant; (3) the Spirit of God liberates us for service, shapes our character and authenticates our mission in the world; and (4) the Son of God, as our paradigm for servanthood, expresses with increasing clarity that we are to be gentle and non-imposing leaders who participate fully in the humanity of those within our missional horizon. It is our prayer that these aspects of servanthood within Isaiah will not only enrich the Latin American church in mission, but equally provide paradigms for Christians anywhere in the world, because who we are and how we live matters to the nations.

© Nathan John Moser, 2012

12. MONEY

Sean Doherty

Introduction: a critique of insufficiently critical contemporary approaches

I begin by levelling an accusation which I will not fully substantiate, although I will at least try to explain why I do not substantiate it. Despite noble intentions, a great deal of Christian economic ethics has been lamentably supine and bland. Take the venerable theological ethicist Duncan Forrester, who contends on the one hand that theological contributions to the notion of justice 'come from a coherent view of reality'.[1] On the other hand, he is concerned that an overly comprehensive Christian approach would be 'unlikely to find general acceptance' in contemporary society.[2] Instead of a comprehensive approach, Forrester offers what he calls 'theological fragments'.[3] This rather vague tactic flows from the notion that public consensus is a determinative objective of theological ethics, hence my charge that it makes theological ethics rather supine.

---

1. Duncan Forrester, *Christian Justice and Public Policy* (Cambridge: Cambridge University Press, 1997), p. 3.
2. Ibid., p. 195.
3. Ibid., p. 3.

This is also the dominant social ethical approach of the public work of my own denomination, the Church of England. Peter Sedgwick, formerly with the Board for Social Responsibility (now the Mission and Public Affairs Division of the Archbishops' Council), speaks of the 'great benefits provided by the next stage of global capitalism. The churches need to remain part of the debate on reforming and humanizing that world, and not abandoning it for a rhetoric of Christian identity over against that world. Such a task will appear compromised, but . . . it can also be immensely worthwhile.'[4]

Kathryn Tanner's *Economy of Grace* is an honourable exception in several respects. She forthrightly sketches the characteristics of a genuinely theological economy and argues that 'theological economy encroaches on and enters within the territory of the economy it opposes'.[5] But even she makes the fatal mistake of assuming that a theological economy is so far removed from the reality of our world, so that if it simply opposes the world as it is, it will be 'sterile' because it would therefore 'leave the world to its own devices, without practical counsel for realistic change . . . Its only advice would be the complete overhaul of the present system, the simple replacement of the present system with a wholly different one.'[6] Shying away from this, she instead observes that matters such as wages, tax, inflation versus employment, protectionism and so on are 'up for grabs' within the basic structure of capitalism.

So what I find supine is this. On the one hand, many theologians acknowledge the radical incommensurability between a theologically constituted economy and the existing global capitalist order. On the other hand, the tendency is to sacrifice this radicalism on the altar of improving the way things actually are. The argument seems to be that since we cannot abolish capitalism,

---

4. Peter H. Sedgwick, *The Market Economy and Christian Ethics* (Cambridge: Cambridge University Press, 1999), pp. 272–273. More recently, Malcolm Brown, the current Director of Mission and Public Affairs for the Church of England, has sought to bring together the 'liberal' (his terminology) commitment to dialogue with economics as a discipline with its own integrity, with the theological robustness of the more 'communitarian' approach of Alasdair MacIntyre, Stanley Hauerwas, the Radical Orthodoxy movement and so on. I am not convinced that this is sufficient to liberate him from the supine posture I am criticizing here, because he remains highly critical precisely of their insistence on operating in exclusively theological terms. See Malcolm Brown, *After the Market: Economics, Moral Agreement and the Churches' Mission* (Bern: Lang, 2004).

5. Kathryn Tanner, *Economy of Grace* (Minneapolis: Fortress, 2005), p. 89.

6. Ibid., pp. 87–88.

we must work within its precincts, to ameliorate its unfortunate corollaries, to make as good a job of it as possible in the circumstances. Thus Christian economist Donald Hay takes as his methodological point of departure Jesus' statement to the Pharisees that Moses allowed divorce 'because you were so hard-hearted' (Matt. 19:8). The principle of monogamous lifelong union is the ideal in creation, but we must 'look for a *second best* in a fallen world, while continuing to affirm God's first best'.[7] His yardstick for arriving at this second best is 'what is practicable in a fallen world'.[8] He therefore compares capitalism and communism from a Christian perspective (as if those are the only two options available) and it is hardly surprising when he concludes that a suitably rehabilitated version of capitalism is this second best. It is by no means perfect, but it is vastly preferable to the political and fiscal evils of communism. No doubt that is entirely accurate as far as it goes. But is that as far as we should go? To put it another way, it does not seem to me that Jesus' description of this Mosaic law as a concession to sin is the right methodological starting point for Christian social ethics. In fact, quite the reverse: Jesus explicitly contrasts the way this segment of Torah grounds marriage in the tragedy of fallen reality with God's original intention in creation. It is clearly the latter which Jesus regards as morally definitive.

So even those who perceive that capitalism is deeply problematic lack a robust constructive theological agenda for economics. Other Christian thinkers do not even consider that it is problematic in the first place. A number of Christian bankers, notably Lord Green of Hurstpierpoint (formerly chief executive of HSBC, also an Anglican priest), Lord Griffiths of Fforestfach (vice-chairman of Goldman Sachs) and Ken Costa (recently chairman of Lazard), perhaps stung by popular accusations of hypocrisy or materialism, have written spirited apologias, displaying a strong degree of theological learning and sophistication in their vindication of their professional lives in terms of Christian vocation.[9] Here again we meet the view that capitalism is imperfect but necessary in the circumstances. Ken Costa admits, 'Over the years I have had my doubts about the market economy . . . This particularly

---

7. Donald A. Hay, *Economics Today: A Christian Critique* (Leicester: Apollos, 1989), p. 311.
8. Ibid., p. 311.
9. See, e.g., Brian Griffiths, *The Creation of Wealth* (London: Hodder and Stoughton, 1984); Stephen Green, *Good Value: Reflections on Money, Morality and an Uncertain World* (London: Penguin, 2009); Ken Costa, *God at Work: Living Every Day with Purpose* (London: Continuum, 2007).

troubled me in recent times, when there seemed to be a headlong, compassionless pursuit of financial reward without restraint.'[10] Elsewhere he puts this even more strongly: 'The capitalist economy relies on holding money tightly. Christ's economy is different.'[11] This latter phrase is telling: he recognizes that Jesus has an economy, and he perceives that it is different from capitalism. Yet he concludes, somewhat incongruously, 'These questions remain: but I have not found a better system [than capitalism].'[12]

This truncated survey will have to suffice, and I ask for forbearance for offering a sweeping generalization with such little evidence. By way of an apologia of my own, I have chosen not to spend more time substantiating my critique, in order to avoid falling into the same trap, namely to fail to propose a constructive theological alternative. To summarize these claims, my worry is that, in their eagerness to engage in constructive dialogue with the discipline of economics, some Christian thinkers have signally failed to prioritize theology and have therefore been congenitally hamstrung from developing a stout and properly Christian ethical response. For my own Anglican social tradition, the missional aspect of ethics means taking one's place as a dialogue partner in the contemporary world. It is missional in the sense that it is at the interface between theology and economics, seeking to make a significant contribution on the 'macro' level to social structures and systems, with all the mess and imperfection which that entails. For the reasons I have just identified, I suspect that this is biting off more than we can chew theologically. At this lofty social-structural plane, compromise seems to us in our context all but inevitable. Perhaps we will be more successful if we begin by trying to be faithful to the teaching of Jesus on the more modest level of old-fashioned individual discipleship, where we can describe 'Christ's economy' (Ken Costa's phrase) in theological terms and actually expect to put it directly into practice.

In other words, I think the problem is precisely that we have been working with an inadequate concept of mission. I am not suggesting that theology should abandon the structural sphere. That is part of God's mission. I am suggesting that we are so dilapidated in this area because we have not laid good foundations on which to construct something more ambitious. Rather than turning to contemporary economic theory, then, the proper methodological step for a missional ethic of money will be a return to the biblical and historical traditions of Christian thought. A missional ethic of money will resist the

---

10. Costa, *God at Work*, p. 6.
11. Ibid., p. 168.
12. Ibid., p. 6.

impulse to begin with constructive dialogue with economic science. This may come later. But the opening moves will be to proclaim the good news, to call people to repentance and costly discipleship, and to draw on the transforming power of the gospel. My hope is that the following sketch will show the inherent promise of this approach above that of the regnant paradigm.

The goodness of money

I have described one trend in recent Christian economic ethics which endorses wealth and capitalism far too readily. But this is in itself an over-reaction to an equally problematic ascetic denial of the goodness of money. The immense dangers of money are clearly alluded to in Scripture, but we should not be so hypnotized by them that we fail to give a suitable account of its goodness, or at the very least an account of its moral neutrality.

Material goods are called 'goods' for good reason. In the creation narratives of Genesis 1 and 2, we hear of the goodness of the world and are shown that God himself is the abundant source of material gifts. He creates humans as physical creatures with physical needs and the capacity for physical enjoyments, and he himself provides the means by which we might satisfy these needs and enjoy ourselves. Such needs are not spurious. They are part of our bodily nature, which is described as 'very good' (Gen. 1:31). Even the epistle which so famously states that 'the love of money is a root of all kinds of evil' (1 Tim. 6:10) is the same one which condemns those 'who forbid marriage and demand abstinence from foods, which God created to be received with thanksgiving . . . For everything created by God is good, and nothing is to be rejected, provided it is received with thanksgiving' (1 Tim. 4:3–4). In the earthy and rather carnal narratives of Genesis 1 and 2, physical enjoyments of food and sex pre-date the fall and are not sinful. This context explains why Scripture does not seem to regard having or using money as such as problematic.

Then God gives humanity work to do in cultivating the garden. The human vocation is to tend something which is already good and fruitful. Little support here, therefore, for a doctrine of wealth creation, but support aplenty for an emphasis on the goodness of human work. The goal of work is not simply to make money. Work is good in itself; it is part of the way in which God has made us, in contrast to Greek philosophy where the goal is unlimited leisure to pursue the higher things in life such as contemplation and virtue. Indeed, even after the fall, the first thing God does for Adam and Eve is to provide them with physical clothing. Again, meeting material needs is no sin – it is God who does it.

In the Gospels, while there is plenty of emphasis on giving up one's wealth in order to be Christ's disciples, neither is there an ascetic ethic. Jesus feeds people in large numbers and turns water into a vast quantity of wine. He enjoyed a good party, was accused of being a glutton and a drunkard. On one well-publicized occasion he even allowed a woman to waste a lavish amount of pricey perfume on a pedicure. He and his followers shared a common purse and received support from wealthy benefactors. He may even have owned a house. Yet he seems not to have sought or accumulated money and luxuries, and when he sent his followers out on itinerant mission he required of them a particularly strict level of material discipline.

So money in itself is not bad. Indeed, it can be put to genuinely good uses: to meet our legitimate needs for food and clothing, to succour the needy, to spread the gospel. In the words of the adage, money is a good servant, even perhaps a servant of God, but it is a bad master.

This polarity is particularly encapsulated in the Sermon on the Mount. Jesus tells us quite unabashedly that we should ask God for our daily bread. Not all interpreters have understood his words this way. Origen claims that 'daily bread' is not a reference to material, physical bread, but to spiritual sustenance. Cyprian hedges his bets and says it is both. But John Chrysostom is surely nearer the mark:

> What is daily bread? Just enough for one day. Here Jesus is speaking to people who have natural needs of the flesh, who are subject to the necessities of nature. He does not pretend that we are angels. He condescends to the infirmity of our nature . . . [which] does not permit you to go without food. But . . . it is not for riches or frills that we pray. It is not for wastefulness or extravagant clothing that we pray, but only for bread.[13]

What I find so salutary about Chrysostom's line of thought is its insistence that there is no spiritual advantage in the false modesty of pretending we are other than needy physical mortals. Such a pretension would in fact be an idolatrous denial of our creaturely humanity. 'Is not life more than food, and the body more than clothing?' (Matt. 6:25). Life is more than these things, but it is not less than them.

Let us avail ourselves of a Reformation perspective here as well as a patristic one. Martin Luther had little time for the wealthy. Yet he ferociously opposed the mendicancy movements, in their debased forms, which treated poverty as

---

13. In Manlio Simonetti (ed.), *Ancient Christian Commentary on Scripture, Ia: Matthew 1 – 13* (Downers Grove: InterVarsity Press, 2001), pp. 135–136.

meritorious. The work of historian Carter Lindberg has been particularly seminal here in exposing the way in which the pre-Reformation system of piety doubly reinforced the conditions of the poor.[14] By their poverty, the poor were beneficiaries of God's favour and the rich could receive his approval by giving alms to the poor and thus alleviating their plight. Help for the poor was therefore immediate but very temporary, and theologically speaking there was no need for a structural and durable solution to the causes of poverty. Everyone had a vested interest in the status quo. While Luther was under no illusions as to the possibility of the eradication of poverty, he was nevertheless characteristically pugnacious about this state of affairs. In his lectures on Deuteronomy, Luther offers the following comment on God's famous promise in Deuteronomy 15:4 that 'there will be no poor among you':

> All who display, and boast of, external poverty are disciples and servants of Satan, who rage directly contrary to the Lord and His Christ . . . Poverty, I say, is not to be recommended, chosen, or taught; for there is enough of that by itself as [Jesus] says, 'The poor you always have with you' . . . But constant care should be taken that, since these evils are always in evidence, they are always opposed.[15]

Poverty exists, but that does not make it meritorious or beneficial. In Luther's exposition of the Sermon on the Mount, he admits that princes in particular need a moderate amount of money.[16] But even this seeming concession is morally configured, as he simultaneously insists that such assets are bestowed for the express purpose of looking after one's subjects properly. That is, even wealth is construed in terms of one's vocation and responsibility towards others. Luther's view is therefore that while Christians should not accumulate wealth, neither should they be poor. They may use their money for two things: to benefit others and to meet their own needs. When he says 'needs', he means 'needs'. Luxury is ruled out.

To return to our reflections on the Sermon on the Mount, Jesus offers us a rationale for the prayer for daily bread, namely that we can trust God to meet our material needs. 'Therefore do not worry, saying, "What will we eat?" or "What will we drink?" or "What will we wear?" For it is the Gentiles who strive

---

14. As well as numerous shorter articles on this topic, see especially Carter Lindberg, *Beyond Charity: Reformation Initiatives for the Poor* (Minneapolis: Fortress, 1993).
15. Martin Luther, *Luther's Works*, 55 vols. (Philadelphia: Fortress; St Louis: Concordia, 1955–86), vol. 9, p. 148.
16. See ibid., vol. 21, p. 171.

for all these things; and indeed your heavenly Father knows that you need all these things' (Matt. 6:31–32). We are not to seek after them, then, but to receive what God gives us to meet our needs. Indeed, the subsequent verse makes this promise even more bluntly: 'Strive first for the kingdom of God and his righteousness, and all these things will be given to you as well' (Matt. 6:33). A missional ethic of money will make no bones about a frank appeal to self-interest – but only self-interest which is configured by the kingdom of God and his righteousness is true self-interest.

The danger of money

With this point we begin to approach the other flank of our polarity. Jesus not only promises that God will meet our material needs – he also warns of the terrible danger of serving money. Indeed, it is his laser focus on the trustworthiness of God as *Abba* Father which means that he is so caustic about hoarding wealth. If we trust God to provide for us daily, on the basis of this promise we will have no need to store up wealth for tomorrow. I find absolutely no basis in the Sermon on the Mount for the ethic of cautious stewardship which is currently bedevilling the church. Quite the opposite: 'Do not store up for yourselves treasures on earth, where moth and rust consume and where thieves break in and steal' (Matt. 6:19). Jesus demands of us a dynamic of reckless generosity: 'If anyone wants to sue you and take your coat, give your cloak as well . . . Give to everyone who begs from you, and do not refuse anyone who wants to borrow from you' (Matt. 5:40–42). Our posture towards worldly goods should fundamentally be one of not holding on to them. We can have things, but we cannot keep them. But this seeming recklessness is undergirded by a more fundamental self-interest. This posture of freely giving away things which appear to be to one's benefit will ultimately be of far greater benefit.

What benefit exactly? For Chrysostom, Jesus' instruction not to worry about money is not a benign and gentle piece of uplifting advice intended to help us live more rounded lives or some such. It is intended to ensure that we are not damned. The motive for avoiding anxiety is as follows:

> The hurt you receive is . . . in the subversion of your salvation, casting you as it does away from the God who made you, cares for you and loves you . . . Only after Jesus has shown the hurt to be unspeakable, then and not before does he make the instruction stricter.[17]

---

17. Quoted in Simonetti, *Ancient Christian Commentary, Ia.*, p. 144.

The escape route from service of Mammon is not to be anxious, and the strictness of Jesus' instruction is for our own eternal good.

This is particularly well elucidated by Luther. He avers that the two most dangerous forces in Christendom are false teaching, because it corrupts faith, and greed, because it corrupts the fruit of faith.[18] This connection between faith and one's handling of money enables Luther to resolve a vexed point in biblical interpretation. Why does the Bible, and Jesus in particular, seem to imply that the rich cannot be saved (e.g., Mark 10:23–27 and pars.; Luke 14:33; 16:19–31)? We know that we are justified by *faith*. The question follows: If you have faith, how can you fail to be saved even if you are greedy or rich? Can Luther of all people really mean that you are, after all, saved by works?

The answer, of course, is no; and the explanation, of course, is this: the way you handle your possessions is directly related to whether you *trust God*. As is often stated, faith is not mere mental ascription to a set of correct doctrinal propositions, important as that may be. Rather, faith is a deep trust in God's goodness towards his creatures. If you see God as someone who is active in the world, someone who is loving and caring, you can trust him to provide for you. If you do not, you will try to provide security for yourself. This inevitably results in hoarding worldly goods in case you need them in the future. Greed is therefore an enslavement from which we need to be liberated by trusting God to care for us and meet our needs. Only this frees us from the neurotic compulsion to acquire more and more in order to be secure.

So greed originates in a lack of trust in God, that is, a lack of *faith*, a lack precisely of the attitude by which one is made right with God. Hence, according to Luther, a greedy person cannot be justified and therefore cannot be saved, because a greedy person does not trust God. It is not that you earn merit by giving away your possessions. It is that your behaviour discloses the fundamental orientation of your heart. Greed with respect to your money is the correlate of unbelief with respect to your God. For Luther, then, it is absurd to distinguish between trusting God to meet one's present needs and trusting him to save one's soul. They are both expressions of the same thing:

> They fear that they would die of hunger or be ruined entirely if they were to obey God's command and give to everyone who asks of them. How then can they trust him to maintain them in eternity? Those who will not trust God in little temporal things must at last despair also in those matters that are great and eternal.[19]

---

18. See Luther, *Luther's Works*, vol. 21, p. 167.
19. Ibid., vol. 45, p. 281.

If you do not trust God, you will inevitably be greedy and not generous. You will try to provide for yourself, rather than allow God to look after you. The unspeakable danger of this pseudo-faith is therefore the false assurance which it gives.

The seeming paradox here is only such if one construes 'faith' as a purely intellectual state, a theoretical or mental agreement with particular propositional statements. Such pseudo-faith would of course be entirely compatible with not trusting God to provide for you and meet your needs, and therefore compatible with greed. This is, of course, the point at issue in the letter of James: even demons have a cognitive belief in God, and this is perfectly congruent with failing to help the needy. To quote another epistle about which Luther was not entirely complementary, the faith which pleases God is not simply holding the opinion that he exists, it is believing that he rewards those who earnestly seek him (Heb. 11:6). Famously, of course, in Luther's early days faith in God was for him at times a monstrous and terrifying affair, given his acute awareness of his failure to measure up to the required standards and his corresponding fear of God's righteous wrath.[20] The breakthrough for him was the recognition that God is *pro me* and *pro nobis*. This is the difference between faith which condemns and faith which justifies. Justifying faith believes that God is for me, that he will care for me and act on my behalf.

Thus, in his lectures on Genesis, commenting on the story of the fall in Genesis 3, Luther portrays the essence of sin not as *superbia*, as Augustine did, nor as a lack of belief in God, but as Adam's and Eve's lack of trust in God's settled intention of goodness towards them. The strategy of the serpent is to cast aspersions on the goodness of God's intention in prohibiting Adam and Eve from eating the fruit of the tree of knowledge, suggesting that God has a sinister ulterior motive behind his command: 'Satan said this to stir up resentment against God . . . that in this way Eve might begin to hate God as though he bore them too little good will.'[21] Sin arises not so much when Adam and Eve eat the fruit, as when they cease to believe that God has given them the command in order that they might flourish and be blessed. The essence of faith is trusting that God actually wants what is good for you, even if to human perception it may seem otherwise. Faith in this sense of trust in God's settled goodness (not in some abstract sense, but his goodness *pro nobis*) cannot coexist with greed, because greed is the compulsion to secure one's future well-being through one's own efforts rather than trusting that God will continue giving you your daily

---

20. See, e.g., ibid., vol. 34, pp. 336–337.
21. Ibid., vol. 1, p. 158.

bread. Greed is a manifestation of fear of the future and therefore of unbelief. Luther's conclusion is therefore that if you are greedy, you do not have faith. Hence his seemingly counterintuitive conviction that the greedy will not be saved is not a return by the back door of justification by meritorious deeds, but an insistence that greed and saving faith are incompatible.

But, Luther goes on, there is a further danger here too. Greed also *feeds* unbelief, because attachment to possessions distracts your heart from God. So a particular reason to flee from greed is that greed affects your faith and therefore your salvation. Thankfully, the opposite is also true: losing or giving money away can help one *exercise* and *strengthen* one's trust in God. Our hearts are incapable of extricating themselves from their enchantment to worldly goods. But when these goods are stripped away, we are prevented from relying on them and forced to trust God instead. Giving things away will not secure your salvation as a matter of reward, but will help to foster faith, the basis of salvation and spiritual growth. A member of the church at which I served my curacy put it to me in this memorable way: 'When I'm worried about money, I give some away.'

Luther therefore describes wealth as a false economy. The cost of being wealthy is in fact greater than the profit: 'What will it profit them to gain the whole world and forfeit their life?' (Mark 8:36). Again, there is a frank appeal to self-interest here, properly understood. Jesus does not instruct his followers to give away their money simply because they ought to. They should give away their money because it is good for them. Mammon is not a good master: on earth, moth and rust destroy and thieves break in and steal. Instead, we are besought to lay up for ourselves treasure of a far better quality and order.

Earning money

Here again is our polarity. Money is not evil. I would go so far as to say that it is a gift of God. But it is also dangerous. Like all God's gifts, it can be perverted. So, if money can be acquired and used in perverted ways, our next task is to sketch out how it can be acquired and used rightly. Let us consider therefore two points: earning and giving.

In fact, we immediately discover that these are not two points, but one. The biblical *locus classicus* here is Ephesians 4:28: 'Thieves must give up stealing; rather let them labour and work honestly with their own hands, so as to have something to share with the needy.' Even in the height of the early church's fervent eschatological expectation, St Paul (I am assuming that he wrote Ephesians and the Thessalonian correspondence) insists that manual labour is not degrading or pointless. But neither is its purpose to enrich oneself, to accumulate money for one's own indulgence and comfort. The purpose of earning money is to help others. The very goal of acquiring money is so that you can give it away. Paul's own period as a tentmaker provides a good example in this regard: working and earning money is no sin – indeed it is compulsory – but the money he gains is used to support his missionary efforts. While money is dangerous, as we have seen, it is also a potential tool in God's own missional purposes. It can be used by him to enable proclamation of the good news, feeding the hungry, clothing the naked and so on.

This does not mean that money can be made any old how. Just as some theologians have been hypnotized by the evil which money can do and have therefore denounced it in an unmitigated fashion, others have been seduced by the sheer power of money to accomplish things. The danger of this is an implicit authorization of a consequentialist moral paradigm where the goal of doing as much good as possible with money justifies the means of making as much of it as possible. This reasoning appears in the notion that because of capitalism's efficiency with resources and harnessing of incentive to generate vast wealth, it enables philanthropy on a colossal scale which would be quite impossible under socialism. I suspect that is entirely accurate, as far as it goes. But it disregards the fact that while money may be good in itself (or at least morally neutral), it can be acquired in sinful ways. We must interest ourselves not only in what people do with the money they have got, but in how they get it in the first place.

This is another point of intersection between mission and ethics: the invocation of mission as a justification for Christian involvement in a particular way of getting money. But is this what we should mean by mission? Certainly there is no sin in being a Christian merchant or artisan. But this lazy misappropriation of Luther's concept of vocation as a blanket authorization for involvement in almost any occupation does not stand up to scrutiny. Few of us would accept the need for Christians to become drug dealers or abortionists in order to be salt and light in such worlds. If an activity is inherently wrong, the proper course of action is to call those engaged in it to repent and make amends, and to offer them God's forgiveness. Similarly, if an activity is not inherently wrong but is currently being performed in an unjust way, the solution is not to participate in the unjust form with a view to reforming it, but to find wholesome alternative ways of acting – even if this means foregoing mainstream participation. We need to make up our minds as to the morality of a particular way of earning money as a preliminary to evaluating the validity of Christian involvement in that sphere, rather than taking such involvement as legitimate or necessary and therefore retrospectively justifying its activities.

Let us take a moment, then, to reopen this question. It is not at all transparent that Christian involvement in certain financial industries is an acceptable thing. We do not have space for a full-blown analysis, but let me enumerate some concerns. First, financial practices which rely on or enhance the accrual of capital on a large scale seem questionable in the light of the teaching of Jesus against hoarding which we have just explored. This is also suggested by various aspects of the Torah, which allow the incentive of profit arising from hard work and innovation, but only on a very limited scale and not at the expense of anything but minor levels of inequality. The jubilee legislation in particular, in the name of curbing inequality, would have repressed the things which we would consider indispensable for economic growth and development, such as the accumulation of capital in order to facilitate investment to increase efficiency and specialization. The jubilee legislation would have acted against inequality in two ways: by redistributing profit and by ensuring that everyone had access to the means of supplying their own livelihood rather than being permanently dependent on charity or servitude.[22]

Second, the Christian tradition has in the main been opposed to receiving a profit by lending money at interest, and it does not seem to me that the theological and exegetical reasons advanced against this view by Calvin and his supporters are persuasive.[23] I have addressed getting money and earning it, as circumlocutions for the far more popular phrase 'to make money', which I have sought to avoid. This is to make the point that money should not in fact be made by money, but earned by productive work. Luther in particular disliked the practice of making a guaranteed return on lending because it forced the debtor to cover any losses when they were the one who could least afford to do so, while the superior wealth of the creditor put them into a position in which they could take advantage of the debtor without any risk to themselves. This would be ruled out by Christ's commands to give to everyone who asks and to lend without expecting anything in return (Matt. 5:42; Luke 6:35), and even more fundamentally, to love one's neighbour as oneself.

Hence, for Luther, the golden rule functions here as a rule of thumb to check if a transaction is just, by envisioning a reversal of situations. If the

---

22. For an empirical sociological approach which reaches the same conclusion, see Richard G. Wilkinson, *The Impact of Inequality: How to Make Sick Societies Healthier* (New York: New Press, 2005); and more recently Kate Pickett, *The Spirit Level: Why Equality is Better for Everyone* (London: Penguin, 2009).

23. For an overview, see Joan Lockwood O'Donovan, 'The Theological Economics of Medieval Usury Theory', *Studies in Christian Ethics* 14.1 (2001), pp. 48–64.

creditor would not want to trade places with the debtor, then the creditor is taking advantage of him. If the potential debtor is in need, the putative creditor should simply give him his surplus money. And if the potential debtor is not in need, then the creditor should give his excess money to someone who is, rather than lend it out in order to further enrich himself. For this older school of Christian thought, money should be earned by making something or providing some service which is actually of direct benefit to another person – I suspect the thinkers whom I have interacted with here would hardly have been convinced by the theory of benefit by trickle-down!

Counterintuitively, this rejection of involvement in many aspects of the current financial system is a profoundly missional claim. In contrast to the indiscriminate ethic of involvement which I have criticized, the medieval approach which I have advocated claims that the financial arena belongs to Christ at a far more fundamental level. Rather than envisaging it as an essentially wicked sphere into which Christians must venture in order to improve it and rescue unbelievers through conversion, the traditional Christian approach assumes that the whole thing already belongs to Christ and that activity within it *should therefore conform to his teaching* right now and not to some alien interim ethic. This is not to disapprove of attempts to reform this sphere or to convert its occupants. It is to say that we may not treat the commands of Jesus as an impossible and idealistic bit of hyperbole, nor are we at liberty to pretend that as grown-up Christians we cannot avoid a compromise with the way the world actually is. In any interaction with another person, we must not put ourselves above them, but should love them as ourselves, emptying ourselves and taking the very nature of a servant in order to benefit them, as Christ has done for us. Self-interest and profit are ruled out as motives and replaced with the intention that our neighbour should flourish.

So, let us summarize our comments about earning. While we have discovered Paul's emphasis on earning money in order to give it away, we have argued that this does not offer authorization either for earning a particularly large quantity of money, or for earning it in an illicit way, which I suggest includes most forms of lending at interest, though not investment where the risk is shared. While money can indeed be a tool of God in his missional purposes, the good it can accomplish does not give *carte blanche* as to how it is accrued.

Giving money

Before we end, let us make some brief comments about giving. We have noted the dangers in hoarding money. The natural question to ask is, therefore, how much money should we give away? It is important to be concrete about this, and not vague, and help is at hand from the masterly pen of St Thomas Aquinas. Thomas is fairly upbeat about the notion of property as such, although like Luther and Paul he configures it in terms of responsibility towards others. He is unambiguous in his disapproval of theft as an intrinsically evil act which can never be justified. Yet he goes on to make the following claim. If someone in needs asks you for food and you refuse it, but they then take your food (or take money in order to buy food), they have done no wrong. He explains it as follows:

> In cases of need all things are common property, so that there would seem to be no sin in taking another's property, for need has made it common . . . Inferior things are ordained for the purpose of succouring man's needs by their means. Wherefore the division and appropriation of things which are based on human law, do not preclude the fact that man's needs have to be remedied by means of these very things. Hence whatever certain people have in superabundance is due to the purpose of succouring the poor.[24]

So the one who took what they urgently needed has not committed theft. But Thomas presses his claim further: the person who originally refused to help the needy one *has* committed theft, because they have deprived a person of what they are rightfully due. The allocation of goods is a human matter which cannot over-rule the original divine purpose in giving these material goods to humanity in the first place, hence Thomas's claim that whatever one has left over after meeting one's own needs is 'due to the purpose' of helping those who need it. He therefore quotes Ambrose as follows: 'It is the hungry man's bread that you withhold, the naked man's cloak that you store away, the money that you bury in the earth is the price of the poor man's ransom and freedom.'[25] Indeed, in cases of 'extreme indigence' Thomas considers it praiseworthy even to forego your own requirements in order to help others.[26]

It is not difficult to see some burning implications of this in a world in which not only relative but also absolute poverty is rife, where literally millions of people have nowhere to live, no electricity, no access to basic sanitation, and where over a million people die each year from lack of access to safe drinking

---

24. Thomas Aquinas, *Summa Theologica*, 2nd rev. ed., 22 vols., trans. Fathers of the English Dominican Province (London: Burns, Oates & Washbourne, 1912–36), 2a 2ae, q. 66, a. 7. Consulted online at www.newadvent.org/summa/, accessed May 2011.
25. Ibid., 2a 2ae, q. 66, a. 7.
26. See ibid., 2a 2ae, q. 32, a. 6.

water and another million due to easily preventable diseases. The amounts we spend on bottled water, perfume, fizzy drinks and pet food, let alone on nuclear weapons, dwarf the sums needed to change these realities, for example, to pay for basic education, sanitation, food and drink for all. The logic of capitalism tells us that 'it is not as simple as that', and that if we give our money away the system would simply collapse and everyone would end up worse off. And of course there are political reasons, as well as corruption and waste, which prevent charity actually helping those who need it. Prudence has a role to play in enabling wise decisions about how and where one gives, and a particularly good example of this can be found in the 'Giving What We Can' movement set up by utilitarian philosopher Toby Ord (www.givingwhatwecan.org), which takes empirical research seriously in ensuring that charitable giving is as effective as possible.

However, the ideology of capitalism blinds us to what we *can* do and are obliged to do, because it operates on this macro-utilitarian level of trying to secure the optimal long-term consequences for the whole world and indeed for history itself. The more we spend on luxury goods, the more we will help the poor – eventually. Of course, it takes time for improvements to trickle down, but this will be for the greater good in the long run as it will prevent people from being dependent on handouts. It is poverty which is natural, not wealth, and so instead of blaming the rich for the condition of the poor and handing over our wealth to them, which would be counterproductive, we should help the poor create wealth for themselves. But this seems difficult to reconcile with the biblical witness to the original abundance of creation and the analysis of the causes of poverty offered us by the biblical prophets. Certainly it did not convince Chrysostom, who was adamant that scarcity was always caused by sin. To an economist this view appears roughly as credible as the opinion that the world was created in six literal days, and it is very difficult for us to stop ourselves from investing the discipline of economics with neutral scientific status. But even if we ignore the material implications this logic has for the needy, we should not ignore the damage it will do in the meantime to our very souls. Again, the golden rule applies here: if we were destitute (either in relative or absolute terms), we would want those with means at their disposal to offer us immediate and not deferred assistance, rather than spending their money on things which they do not strictly need and of which we could only dream.

Conclusion: what makes this ethic missional?

Let us draw this rather contentious essay towards a close with some reflections on what it might mean to be missional in this area. The ethic I have sought to propose is missional because it claims the territory of money as Christ's territory. It is not grubby or ignoble, but part of his good creation. Thus we see that the problem with accounts of economics which assume that we need to make compromises with the way things are is not that they are excessively positive about money. The problem is quite the opposite: they are insufficiently aware of its goodness and therefore make insufficient moral claims with respect to it.

This ethic is also missional because it joyfully and vigorously proclaims the good news, namely that we can trust God to look after us, right here, and right now. This is crucial because, in the face of the sheer magnetic power of human greed, ethics will tend to quail and water itself down to a more manageable standard unless it is undergirded by substantial and potent theological realities. Luther saw that Pelagianism can manifest itself in two related ways. Confronted with God's seemingly unattainable moral standards, the first and more familiar instantiation of this heresy pretends that with effort, human abilities can meet the requisite level of obedience. Yet Luther perceived that the likely outcome of this was Pelagianism's more subtle tendency, namely to dilute the required moral standards to a more practicable level. A seemingly legalistic façade hides an antinomian reality. Only greater confidence in God's freely given and abundant forgiveness and transforming power will liberate us to acknowledge the height of his commandments.

This transforming power is needed in other ways too. Our greed means that we cannot simply set out the right norms and follow them. We first need to be set free from our white-knuckle grip on possessions. This is given to us in faith, which of course is a posture of receiving rather than earning. We receive from God abundantly, so we can give away generously. Faith thus has concrete economic implications.

Again, this makes our point that a theological economic ethic is viable only if it is undergirded by a good theology and missiology. Hilary of Poitiers declares that Jesus 'removes all concern for things of the present' on the basis that we are 'thunderstruck by the hope of the future'.[27] It is the dynamic connection between these two things which we have sought to explore here. The failure of much Christian economic ethics to draw on the moral stipulations of the New Testament is perhaps a result of its failure to draw on the eschatological hope of the New Testament and the transforming resources of the gospel. It is not enough to simply tell people what to do. This will not only fail to change their behaviour, it will also tend towards the subversion of the

---

27. Quoted in Simonetti, *Ancient Christian Commentary, Ia.*, p. 123.

moral standards themselves. So an ethic of money which is not missional in this robust theological sense will not be very ethical either. To be ethical, our ethic of money *needs* to be missional.

This is why Jesus' teaching suggests that our missional ethic of money must be missional not only in the wide sense that *Missio Dei* carries of serving the world, loving our neighbour, caring for creation and so on, but also in the classic evangelistic sense of concern for people's eternal salvation. In particular, those of us called to the pastoral and teaching offices of the church must be entirely candid with those for whom we are responsible about the eternal risk which wealth carries. We have had cause to remind ourselves that money and material possessions are not bad in themselves. There is no sin in eating and enjoying food or wearing clothing, perhaps no sin in owning a car or a house. But we must remain acutely aware of how dangerous is the love of money. Money, sex, power, food and so on are all good gifts of God, intended for our enjoyment and to enable us to flourish, but they are perilous to the point of perdition when loved too much and so misused. And indeed the risk of owning too much is so high that we must ourselves err on the side of caution, and encourage others to do the same.

13. IMMIGRATION

LOOKING AT THE CHALLENGES THROUGH A MISSIONAL LENS

M. Daniel Carroll R.

Introduction

Human history is, in large measure, the story of migrations, both large and small, ranging from short distances to the crossing of continents and oceans, undertaken in peace and vulnerability, or involving entry by force. Today it is estimated that internationally more than 200 million people are on the move from their places of origin to new lands. To include internal migrations would add many more to this already sizeable number. The reasons for this movement are the same as they have been since time immemorial: political unrest, war, natural disasters, hunger, the lack of viable and dignified work, and religious, political and racial persecution.[1] The sheer size of this transfer of populations in our day is overwhelming, its worldwide scope unprecedented. This is a challenging and inescapable dimension of modern socio-economic, political and technological globalization.

Many nation-states feel threatened by this influx of outsiders (both actual and potential). Their presence is perceived to be a menace to national identity, cultural mores, societal infrastructures, ecological integrity and economic

---

1. A helpful, accessible survey of current issues is Khalid Koser, *International Migration: A Very Short Introduction* (Oxford: Oxford University Press, 2007).

stability. Not surprisingly, immigration discussions increasingly focus on legality and border security. Debates centre on quotas and other filters for access, increased and more sophisticated vigilance, penalties for violations and possible connections with terrorism. In contrast, immigration advocates, while not ignoring the importance of these pragmatic matters, prioritize the human rights and needs of immigrants, whether documented or undocumented. The rhetoric is heated, as these two opposite poles on the immigration issue dig in to defend their 'just' cause.

This historical juncture provides an opportunity for Christians and the church to offer a unique perspective, one self-consciously informed by the breadth of Scripture and the resources of Christian traditions and history.[2] More specifically, an explicitly Christian position on immigration should be located within a *missional* framework. That is, it should be analysed and grounded in the *Missio Dei*, the work of God through the people of God in the world. Its relevance for mission is reflected in a recent Lausanne statement, *The Seoul Declaration on Diaspora Missiology* (November 2009), and *The Cape Town Commitment of the Third Lausanne Congress on World Evangelization* (October 2010). A section in this latter document is dedicated to migration ('Love Reaches Out to Scattered Peoples', II.C.5).

The international context of contemporary migration coincides with recent missiological emphases on the implications of the interplay of the global and the local (neatly coined as 'glocal') in the *Missio Dei*. First, the wide span of topics that are now brought into consideration is broad enough to include one as volatile as immigration. This 'glocal' thinking is generating fresh and creative reflection. This volume is a testament to that fact. Second, and very importantly, this issue cannot be viewed merely as mission *to* immigrants or missional and ethical insights *about* immigrants and immigration. That is just one part of the equation. The immigrant situation itself is a rich context for biblical, theological and pastoral thinking and action, so those from majority cultures do well to

---

2. For a fuller discussion and survey of the biblical material on immigration, see M. Daniel Carroll R., *Christians at the Border: Immigration, the Church, and the Bible* (Grand Rapids: Baker Academic, 2008). Other key sources for our discussion are Christopher J. H. Wright, *Old Testament Ethics for the People of God* (Leicester: Inter-Varsity Press; Downers Grove: InterVarsity Press, 2004); *The Mission of God: Unlocking the Bible's Grand Narrative* (Downers Grove: InterVarsity Press; Nottingham: Inter-Varsity Press, 2006); *The Mission of God's People: A Biblical Theology of the Church's Mission* (Grand Rapids: Zondervan, 2010).

hear *from* those voices.³ The amount of theological and pastoral work on immigration, both from 'above' and 'below', as it were, and from across the ecclesiastical spectrum, is exploding.⁴

This chapter will highlight four biblical themes that are foundational for developing a missional ethical point of view on immigration. This presentation makes no pretence of being comprehensive. It is hoped, however, that it will prove a fruitful orientation for further reflection and praxis.

Missio Dei, the human person and migration

The place to ground an approach to immigration from the perspective of the *Missio Dei* is Genesis 1. That is, we begin at the beginning, with the creation of humankind. The text states that every person is created in the image of God, and that includes immigrants. For some, this fundamental fact might seem obvious and overly simplistic, but it is crucial in current debates.

Immigrants, especially the undocumented, are labelled an 'invading horde' or a 'tidal wave' or worse. They are commonly stereotyped in derogatory fashion as 'those people' or stigmatized as 'lawbreakers'. Many occupy low-wage jobs,

---

3. This is the challenge, from different perspectives, of Al Tizon, *Transformation after Lausanne: Radical Evangelical Mission in Global-Local Perspective* (Eugene: Wipf & Stock, 2008); Jehu Hanciles, *Beyond Christendom: Globalization, African Migration and the Transformation of the West* (New York: Orbis, 2009); and Soong-Chan Rah, *The Next Evangelicalism: Freeing the Church from Western Cultural Captivity* (Downers Grove: InterVarsity Press, 2009). Also note Craig Ott and Harold A. Netlund (eds.), *Globalizing Theology: Belief and Practice in an Era of World Christianity* (Grand Rapids: Baker Academic, 2006).

4. Examples of this growing bibliography include: Churches Commission for Migrants in Europe, *Theological Reflections on Migration: A CCME Reader* (Brussels: Churches Commission for Migrants in Europe, 2008); Ben Daniel, *Neighbor: Christian Encounters With 'Illegal' Immigration* (Louisville: Westminster John Knox Pres, 2010); Miguel De La Torre (ed.), *Trails of Hope and Terror: Testimonies on Immigration* (New York: Orbis, 2009); *Erga migrantes caritas Christi* (Vatican: Pontifical Council for the Pastoral Care of Migrants and Itinerant People, 2004); Daniel G. Groody and Gioacchino Campese (eds.), *A Promised Land, A Perilous Journey: Theological Perspectives on Migration* (Notre Dame: University of Notre Dame Press, 2008); Nick Spencer, *Asylum and Immigration: A Christian Perspective on a Polarized Debate* (Cambridge: Paternoster, 2004).

live in poorer neighbourhoods and tend to congregate in enclaves of like backgrounds. Consequently, they are often regarded as uneducated and uncultured in comparison with the host culture. This serves to reinforce negative perceptions of the 'other' and results in their marginalization.

The truth that they, too, are made in the image of God should change the tone and direction of the immigration debate, at the very least among those who claim the Christian faith, and this in at least two ways, each of which depends on a particular understanding of the meaning of this image (Gen. 1:26–28).[5] The first is the ontological view. This interpretation argues that the image concerns what individuals have and are in unique measure in comparison to the rest of creation: they have a mind, emotions, will and a spiritual dimension or soul. The lesson is that every immigrant has incalculable worth in the sight of God and, therefore, should also have value in the sight of all persons. The fact that Jesus Christ gave his life for all, including immigrants, adds another layer of supreme worth for each immigrant.

A second way to look at the image is the functional view, which highlights the words that follow the declaration that humans are created in the image of God. Humans are given the charge to 'subdue' the creation and 'have dominion' over the other creatures (cf. Gen. 2:15). In the ancient world kings set up images of themselves in territories under their control as visual witnesses to their authority. In like manner, humans are living representatives of God, the great heavenly King. They are to serve him and preside over and actively care for his creation as his vice-regents. This responsibility means that humans have incredible gifts and capacities to fulfil their God-given tasks. This truth about the image, of course, also applies to immigrants. They not only have value (the previous point); they have incredible potential. They, too, are capable of ruling the earth. What this means is that immigrants should not be maligned as an unwelcome weight on society. Conversations can now focus on what they can contribute to the common good and how to facilitate their becoming all that God has designed them to be. This perspective on immigrants is dramatically different from what can dominate public discourse.

A *Missio Dei* perspective for the majority culture does not allow for disparaging attitudes and behaviour that excludes immigrants as less than fully human persons. Migration is about people, individuals of divinely bestowed worth and talents. In the United States, many denominations recognize this and have begun to establish outreach ministries to these outsiders, to plant churches and

---

5. The Lutheran relational view is a third option. It reinforces this paragraph's statement about human worth grounded in the cross.

to develop leadership training and aid programmes. Sadly, there is a divide between the perspectives in denominational offices and those of many in the pews. While the leadership appreciates this new opportunity for mission, lay people react negatively to the newcomers in their midst. This pattern, however, is not repeated everywhere. A recent study in Great Britain reflects a greater openness to immigrants among churchgoers.[6]

For the immigrant population, the Genesis passage stands as an encouragement. They are not less than those among whom they live. They have worth and the aptitude for moving ahead and making an impact on their new surroundings. Their ethnicity and experiences no longer have to be a source of shame, but rather an exceptional provision (and responsibility) given by God to participate in the *Missio Dei*. This will not be easy. Life in 'diaspora', to which we will return below, is often marked by a crisis of identity and a variety of obstacles and challenges. This biblical framework does not minimize the difficulties in trying to accommodate to the host culture, but it can help immigrants to appreciate themselves as uniquely empowered to influence it.

Blessing, mission and migration

The biblical narrative after Genesis 2 is a tale of spiralling into the devastating results of sin. The core of the temptation in the garden was to be like God (Gen. 3:5). God's motives are questioned and the delegated responsibility to serve God as an obedient vice-regent is set aside. The warning had been that defiance of his parameters would bring immediate death (Gen. 2:16). The fulfilment of those words unfolds in surprising and unexpected ways.

Death, at least physical death for the couple, does not come quickly. In the curses of Genesis 3:14–19 there is a line about returning to the earth and to the dust from which the man had been taken (Gen. 3:19), but neither Adam nor the woman die at this point. In fact, when the man names the woman, he calls her 'Eve', since she was to be 'the mother of all living' (Gen. 3:20). There are predictions of an existence marked by conflict and pain (Gen. 3:15–19), the sacrifice of an animal to cover the humans' nakedness (Gen. 3:21) and

---

6. Darrell Jackson, 'Europe and the Migrant Experience: Transforming Integration', *Transformation* 28.1 (2010), pp. 1–15. Response to immigrants varies, of course. Note the report by Gerrit Noort, 'Emerging Migrant Churches in the Netherlands: Missiological Challenges and Mission Frontiers', *International Review of Mission* 100.1 (2011), pp. 4–16.

finally the irrevocable separation from the presence of God when the couple is expelled from Eden (Gen. 3:23–24). No death here! Genesis 4 actually begins with the birth of two sons with the help of Yahweh (Gen. 4:1–2).

Death does arrive, however, in dramatic fashion. Cain murders Abel (Gen. 4:8) and then worries that he in turn will be killed as he wanders, or migrates (Gen. 4:14–15). His descendant Lamech boasts of his insatiable violence (Gen. 4:23–24). In Genesis 5 we hear the refrain 'and he died' numerous times. Perhaps those in this list fell to old age and disease. In Genesis 6 the text states that the world was 'filled with violence' and 'corrupt', as humanity actively sought evil (Gen. 6:5, 11). And then death comes upon all living creatures by the hand of God through the flood (Gen. 7:11–24). Only Noah and his family survive, along with a select group of animals. Now the reader realizes the significance of what God had said. The words 'in the day that you eat of it [the tree of knowledge of good and evil] you shall die' foretell the unleashing of death into every dimension of human existence. Humans would kill each other, they would die from natural causes, or God would take their lives.

After the flood there is hope that this Noah, whose name is a play on the Hebrew verb 'comfort' (Gen. 5:29), would launch a new beginning and a brighter future. But in the end he lies passed out drunk in his tent, violated in some fashion by his son Ham (Gen. 9:20–23). Human failure climaxes at the Tower of Babel (Gen. 11:1–9). Echoing the temptation in Eden, humanity tries to make a name for itself by constructing a tower 'with its top in heaven', where God is. This hubris is coupled with rebellion, the refusal to fill the earth as commanded by God. His judgment is the scattering of these people and the confusion of tongues in order to neutralize humanity's unfathomable potential for evil.

With this scattering are born the nations of the world. Genesis 10 provides details about where these sons of Noah and their descendants spread. The phrase 'according to their languages' (Gen. 10:5, 20, 31) connects that Table of Nations to the judgment of Genesis 11:6–9, which is chronologically prior to the dispersion described in Genesis 10. This phrase signals to the attentive reader that Babel is their mother; there the nations of the world had their birth and, therefore, at the heart of every people is the lure of arrogance. In the canonical story, the history of the nations begins at Babel. And there it will end. Humanity will gather one last time at the final Babel with fists raised against God (Rev. 17 – 18).

Mission and migration in Genesis
By Genesis 11 the creation is cursed and humanity characterized by pride, violence and death. This is the context in which the *Missio Dei* takes shape. For

what lies ahead Yahweh does not choose one of the peoples whose roots are at Babel. He cannot. Instead, God calls one person and then forms a people (Gen. 12:1–3). This people is created for mission.[7] Their mission, the very reason for their existence, is to be God's means of blessing 'all the families of the earth'. The word 'families' is an important lexical link to the nations listed in Genesis 10:5, 20, 31. That is, those very peoples who sprang from the rebellion at Babel are the target for mission. And, unlike the rebellious goal of Babel, the 'name' of God's people will be great as they serve God and fulfil the *Missio Dei*.

In Genesis the concept of blessing is both spiritual and material. It involves pointing those with whom they come in contact to Yahweh their God through the construction of altars where they call on his name (e.g., Gen. 12:7–8; 13:4, 18; 21:33; 26:25), the confession of their faith before others (e.g., Gen. 31:5–13, 42; 33:10–11; 41:16; 50:20), prayers for their neighbours (Gen. 18:22–33; 20:7, 17; 32:9–12) and speaking words of blessing (Gen. 14:22; 47:10). It also has physical elements. It is about having children (e.g., Gen. 13:5–6; 15:1–6; 16:11–16; 21:1–3; 35:11), finding water (Gen. 26), multiplying flocks (Gen. 29 – 30) and administrating a government office to save a nation from famine (Gen. 41, 47). In sum, the blessing of God is about life in all its fullness: relationship with him and participation in the bounties of his creation. These are things the people of God can enjoy, but they are to be the channel of these blessings to all. The fulfilment of this mission depends on their obedience. So the Genesis narrative is also about doing what God demands in order to be that people of blessing (Gen. 18:17–19; 22:15–18). It recounts their pilgrimage of faith. Sadly, there are multiple disappointments (e.g., Gen. 12:17–20; 20, 27, 34, 38), but in spite of all this the *Missio Dei* of extending blessing moves forward.

Migration intersects these stories in Genesis in multiple ways. Indeed, this narrative in which the *Missio Dei* is given is a book of migrations. To begin with, the patriarchs live a nomadic life. It is as migrants that they engage their God-given task to be his means of blessing the world. Abraham, the father of our faith (Rom. 4), is constantly on the move (Gen. 23:4; cf. 1 Chr. 29:14–15). The only plot of ground he owns is a space he acquired to bury his wife Sarah (Gen. 23). He and others after him go to Egypt looking for food (Gen. 12, 20, 42 – 47). This desperation parallels modern migration

---

7. For details see M. D. Carroll R., 'Blessing the Nations: Toward a Biblical Theology of Mission from Genesis', *Bulletin of Biblical Research* 10.1 (2000), pp. 17–34; cf. the sources of n. 2, *ad loc.*

stories, where people move and put themselves and their loved ones at great risk to feed their families. Perhaps this awareness explains, to some degree, the patriarch's willingness to lie in order to cross the border into Egypt and Sarah's acquiescence to the scheme (Gen. 12:10–16). Like today, these crossings are a complex mix of personalities, assorted motives and legitimate human need.

This perspective should awaken in the host culture a greater appreciation of perennial human realities – including migration – in which the people of God have always participated. It is enlightening to see the patriarchs, at their best, extending generous hospitality to strangers (Gen. 18:1–8; cf. Gen. 24; Job 31:32). Abraham offers food and drink, tangible expressions of God's blessings, to his three visitors. In other words, he is both migrant and host. Although this kind of hospitality has its roots in part in ancient cultures, it is also a core value that is expected of all who follow Yahweh, who himself sets the standard for open-handedness (Ps. 23).

On the flip side, immigrants can read the accounts of Genesis as their own. There is much in these stories that is similar to their experiences of want and their reception (negative and positive) by those to whose land they move. The pilgrimage towards maturity of belief of these biblical characters is also theirs. Immigrants of faith are called to be a blessing in their new lands, and the successes and frailties of those ancient migrants in their seeking after God in their struggles to survive have much to teach those who are on the move today. Immigrants, too, are called to obedience, faithfulness and hospitality. In sum, the *Missio Dei* applies to host and immigrant alike.

New Testament contributions
Reaching out to the outsider and marginalized continues into the New Testament. Hospitality, of course, is incarnated marvellously in the ministry of Jesus. A key passage in this regard is Matthew 25:31–46, which records Jesus' words about the final judgment to his disciples on the Mount of Olives. Several times he speaks about the 'stranger' in need (vv. 35, 38, 43) among the 'least of these' (vv. 40, 45). Although in the context of the Gospel of Matthew these individuals could very well be Christ's disciples, the moral imperative to bless the vulnerable stands. Not surprisingly, hospitality is required of every Christian (Rom. 12:13), especially of church leadership (1 Tim. 3:2; Titus 1:8; cf. 1 Tim. 5:9–10). To embrace the stranger, the author of Hebrews says, may be to welcome an angel unawares (Heb. 13:2). Hospitality, then, not suspicion and rejection, should distinguish the Christian encounter with the outsider. It is a concrete expression of the *Missio Dei*.

Welcoming the stranger into the missional community

Interestingly, and very importantly, in the Old Testament the *Missio Dei* is not left at the level of individual encounters with Yahweh or charitable acts; it is institutionalized in legislation in a community.

Societies organize themselves through legislation. Laws touch every realm of our life together – the economic, judicial, political and familial, and more. Of course, the shape these laws give to each society is context specific. Legislation is also an expression of the basic commitments that a people hold dear. It speaks volumes about the value given to individuals as persons and how they understand the proper ways to engage mutually in the countless settings of everyday existence. Said another way, legislation establishes a certain environment. Particularly telling is how it evaluates vulnerable groups and how it structures and sanctions their treatment. Vulnerable groups include women in general, widows, orphans, the physically challenged or seriously ill, the poor, racial and ethnic minorities, *and the immigrant*. Is there an atmosphere of care and grace, or is there instead suspicion, disdain and exclusion? Legislation, in other words, is a window into the soul of a society.

The nature of Old Testament law
Ancient Egypt was an imperial social construction of reality. It was a very stratified hierarchical society at whose pinnacle sat Pharaoh, who was a god. Its many deities and religious system legitimated this particular world. Israel suffered greatly there, as an exploited foreign labour force. In the first chapter of the book of Exodus the growth in the Israelite population triggers nativist sentiments of fear and repulsion. Throughout history this kind of negative emotional response has been a common human reaction to the presence of a large number of outsiders. It has also been customary to put teeth into this reaction through laws which are designed to limit and control this population of strangers. Egypt puts draconian measures in place (the killing of the male babies). They remove the straw for the manufacture of bricks, which makes the work of the Israelites nearly impossible, and these bricks are supposed to be for Egyptian buildings! The Egyptians do not want the Israelites, but they need their labour. Cruel, counterproductive and irrational laws, to be sure, but typical.

Yahweh redeemed Israel from this place. In the narrative he leads them to the middle of nowhere and reveals to them a new law, a different model for how to structure their life. Theologically it is significant that this law was given after the release from Egypt. It was never intended to be a means to redemption. Instead, it was to be a blueprint for a society that would be an alternative to the oppressive regime and culture of Egypt. It was to be the context in and through which they were to incarnate their mission to the world.

Accordingly, the law of God deals with every aspect of Israel's life. To the dimensions listed earlier are added other elements, like dietary and clothing guidelines, which were to serve as unique cultural markers. Permeating all of this was a comprehensive religious system. This law was rooted in the person and demands of Yahweh. The Ten Commandments, which preface two of the law codes in the Pentateuch, begin with the demand that Israel have no other god or make any images (Exod. 20:1–6; Deut. 5:6–10). These are not simply exigencies of religious segregation; they have immense societal significance. The god of Israel was unique. He had defeated the gods of Egypt and put the lie to the society that they sanctioned. Yahweh would create and sustain a very different society (Exod. 19:4–6).

If the law is a reflection of the heart of God, then surely it has relevance even today. But if so, how? This has been a topic of theological debate for two millennia. Permit me a very brief answer. It is true that the law was designed for an ancient theocracy in a far-away land, but the lessons we seek are not to be found in efforts to replicate that legislation in the modern world. Deuteronomy 4:5–8 teaches that these laws were a testimony of the wisdom of Israel before the nations and a pointer to Yahweh. The faith and values that are the foundation of Israel's law are what endure across the centuries and in every context.

Christopher Wright labels Old Testament law a 'paradigm' – that is, the law is a concrete exemplar of God's design for every nation always, even as it was to be visible in the life of his people at that time and in that particular place. In several publications Wright has presented a helpful graphic of a series of interlocking triangles that represent what he calls the paradigmatic, the typological and the eschatological interpretations of the biblical material. The three tips of the basic triangle of God, humanity and the earth are reflected in the Old Testament in the relationship of God, Israel and its land; this arrangement is a type of God, the church and its *koinōnia* in the messianic community of the New Testament, and a pointer to the eschatological future of God, a redeemed humanity and the new creation. He has utilized the jubilee legislation of Leviticus 25 to illustrate how this scheme of the principles found in the law works across the canon and in the life of the people of God in these various dispensations. I would suggest that the theme of immigration is another helpful example of this missional paradigm of a redemptive community.

Mission and immigrants in Old Testament law
Let us begin by setting the framework for immigration legislation in ancient Israel. At that time, there were nothing like the governmental programmes,

dedicated institutions or safety nets for the needy that we now take for granted. Charitable help was extended primarily through the extended family, although temples sometimes served as dispensaries of food for the poor and as a source of work and funds. Foreigners were at a disadvantage, because they were separated from their kinship network. In times of need, such as at childbirth, or when they were sick or experienced crop failures, natural disasters and war, foreigners would have had to turn to the Israelites for assistance.

Another major difficulty confronted immigrants in ancient Israel. Because Israel was primarily an agrarian economy, most of the population lived as peasant farmers in small rural villages. In an agrarian economy, access to land is vital. The problem for foreigners was that land was supposed to be passed down through the male heir. Once again, kinship was key. As outsiders, they were ineligible for the most part to own land and could survive only if they were hired by land-owning Israelites.

Sojourners, then, were vulnerable people, dependent on the mercy of the native-born. If, as was pointed out above, a nation's laws reflect the heart and values of its people, what does Israel's law say about their basic commitments? If Old Testament law is rooted in the person of God, how did he expect Israel to respond to the needs of the foreigners in their midst? What, if any, were the law's provisions for immigrants?

To begin with, the law classifies immigrants with others who were especially at risk in that society: the poor, widows and orphans. While widows and orphans faced a precarious existence due to the lack of a mature male to do the intense physical labour required to work that land, the poor and the sojourner lacked the resources to provide for their families. Because of their liabilities, these four groups are often treated together.

Several laws facilitated means for them to acquire food. They were to be given access to the edges of the fields at harvest time (Lev. 19:9–10; Deut. 24:19–22.). This explains the presence of Ruth, who was both a widow and an immigrant, in Boaz's fields (Ruth 2). A special tithe of produce was to be collected every three years and stored in towns to provide sustenance for them (Deut. 14:28–29; 26:12–13).

At the same time, there were laws directed specifically at immigrants.[8] Foreigners can suffer prejudice in the judicial system and be exploited for their labour. This is as true today as it was in ancient times. Fittingly, the law stipulates

---

8. In *The Immigration Crisis: Immigrants, Aliens, and the Bible* (Wheaton: Crossway, 2009), James K. Hoffmeier argues that these laws were applicable only to legal immigrants. I find this neither persuasive nor provable.

that immigrants were to receive the same impartial treatment as the native-born in legal proceedings (Deut. 1:16–17; 24:17–18; 27:19). They were not to be taken advantage of in their work. They were to be given a fair wage and paid on time (Exod. 23:12; Deut. 24:14–15), and they were to be allowed to rest from their labour on the Sabbath (Exod. 20:10; Deut. 5:14).

Israel was also supposed to invite immigrants to take part in its religion. This was a culture defined and regulated by its religious festivals and rituals. They were at the core of Israel's identity. To permit participation in this part of its life would have been especially sensitive. Nevertheless, in addition to the Sabbath, foreigners could take part in the Day of Atonement (Lev. 16:29), the Passover (Exod. 12:45–49; Num. 9:14), the feast of Weeks (Deut. 16:11), the feast of Tabernacles (Deut. 16:14) and Firstfruits (Deut. 26:11). The fundamental command in Leviticus 19:18 to love the neighbour, which is cited by Jesus (Matt. 19:16–19 and par.), is applied directly to the love of the sojourner in verse 34. That is, the love of the immigrant is the test of the love of neighbour. It is also inseparable from acceptable worship. To fast for Yahweh without extending help to the outsider (and other needy persons), the prophet says, is hypocritical and offensive to God (Isa. 58:7).

There would have been expectations placed on the outsider as well. One can assume, for instance, that sojourners would have had to learn the language of Israel to be able to work and to participate in its religious life. To be involved in that religious world would have meant a religious and cultural conversion. The sojourners were also to attend a periodic public reading of the law. There they would have learned more about their new context and how to act within it (Deut. 31:8–13; cf. Neh. 8). The inclusion of immigrants, in other words, would have been a mutual process of integration.

Circumstances today around the globe confirm that it is hard for host cultures to accept foreigners and accommodate them into their world. Not only must emotional reactions to strangers be overcome, a myriad of pragmatic details for incorporating the newcomers, with all of the potential impact on budgets and infrastructures, also have to be dealt with. Making these modifications functional and palatable to everyone is difficult. There must be interior motivations and/or legal measures to secure these adjustments. What reasons did God give Israel for welcoming the stranger?

Yahweh gives his people two primary motivations. First, he appeals to historical memory. Israel must not forget the marginalization and oppression they had lived through in Egypt. That socio-economic, racial and political memory was to be a living incentive for the people of God not to repeat that treatment of foreigners in their own land (Exod. 22:21; 23:9; Lev. 19:34; Deut. 24:17–18). To forget would open the door to unacceptable attitudes and behaviour towards outsiders; it would be to become the kind of people from which they had been redeemed.

The second motivation is more foundational. Deuteronomy 10:12–22 teaches that the God of Israel loves Israel, but that he also loves the foreigner. His love for immigrants is not an abstract love, an expression of sympathy only. It is tangible; he provides them with food and clothing. Of course, God accomplishes this blessing through the actions of his people. So they, too, are to love foreigners (vv. 14–19; cf. Deut. 24:14–15). This passage mentions that life in Egypt and thus joins both motivations together in a powerful statement of the divine commitment to these vulnerable people.

In sum, the people of God were, and are, to be marked by a gracious openness to the outsider. The motivations that were given to ancient Israel are still relevant. Host communities have usually forgotten their own histories of migration. Forgotten are the stories of hardship in travel to what is now home and their thorny reception by those who were already there. Buried are their forebears' experiences in immigrant ghettoes and the trials of finding jobs and housing and acquiring the language. Commonly the only vestiges of immigrant memory are family recipes from the homeland and a faded picture book. The very things that Israel was told never to forget – the socio-economic hardship and the ethnic abuse – are precisely what the host culture today does not remember. Christians of the host culture rarely connect the love of the stranger with the call to love the neighbour and to love and worship God. There is much here that demands reflection. How is it possible to engage in the *Missio Dei* if something so basic to faith and obedience is ignored?

At this point we return briefly to the point of Wright's diagram, with immigration as an illustration of the law's enduring legacy. The *Missio Dei* of being a blessing to all humanity is grounded in the universal framework of Genesis 1 – 11. With the call of Abram, this divine mission finds its expression in and through his descendants and is then institutionalized in the law. The law establishes, ideally, a welcoming community that is to live out the mission to be a blessing. The law offers a paradigm of how this can be worked out pragmatically even in modern societies. Not that they must replicate those ancient arrangements; rather, that law offers an example of systematizing divine favour towards immigrants in laws that deal with their sustenance, labour, protection and cultural accommodation. It surely in some fashion informed Jesus and the early church about how to respond to the needs of different kinds of people.

Mission and the 'other' in the New Testament
From the beginning of its existence Israel was a 'mixed crowd' (Exod. 12:38). In its history, people like the Moabitess Ruth and the Hittite Uriah migrated into

Israel and became a part of that society. Engagement with foreigners, then, was an ongoing reality.[9] Over time, and after centuries of war and occupation by a series of foreign powers, attitudes in Israel changed. By the first century AD, many Jews were zealous about their unique status as the chosen people. Jesus confronts this attitude head on by interacting with Gentiles. His dealings with the Samaritans would also have been surprising (Luke 17:11–19; John 4), and his employment of a Samaritan in a parable to explain the love of neighbour command of Leviticus 19 would have been especially irksome (Luke 10:25–37).

The welcome of the stranger is evident in the life of the early church, but it was clearly not easy or natural. The shift from a more circumscribed Jewish movement to one that was largely Gentile was complicated and emotionally charged. Peter is surprised at the coming of the Spirit upon the house of Cornelius (Acts 10 – 11), and not long afterwards a consultation in Jerusalem is convened to wrestle with the presence of Gentiles (Acts 15). Even after those deliberations, Paul must reprimand Peter for his prejudicial attitudes towards Gentiles (Gal. 2). The church at Antioch had a multinational leadership team (Acts 13:1), but several epistles reveal that problems with Judaizers plague local congregations. In Christ, however, the dividing walls have come down (Eph. 2). There is now 'no longer Jew or Greek . . . slave or free . . . male and female' (Gal. 3:28).

The realities of a multicultural, multiracial and multinational church today offer a unique opportunity for the church to fulfil its mission *within the church itself*, as well as be a model for and a prophetic voice to *society at large*. The church is a unique *polis*, whose structures and relationships should run counter to typical cultural reactions to outsiders. It should see these people as a gift from God. Immigrants are allowing the church to be the church, as it learns to incarnate an ecclesiology that more closely reflects God's design. The explosion in the number of immigrant churches in host countries around the globe and the revival of existing churches by the presence of these immigrants are a testimony to a sovereign and wonderful movement of God in the twenty-first century.

The people of God as immigrant communities
Much of the Old Testament speaks of the life of the people of God as a displaced community in other lands. The United Monarchy split into the

---

9. This interaction was not always positive for the foreigner: there are, for example, the complex reactions of Ezra and Nehemiah and the pressures to survive after the returns from exile (Ezra 9; Neh. 13). Discussion of these passages lies outside the purview of this essay.

Northern Kingdom of Israel and the Southern Kingdom of Judah after the death of Solomon (1 Kgs 12). The Northern Kingdom would be conquered in the last quarter of the eighth century by the Assyrians (2 Kgs 17), and Judah early in the sixth century by the Babylonian armies of Nebuchadnezzar II (2 Kgs 25). We have no biblical record of the life of the Israelites who were taken into exile by the Assyrians, but there are historical accounts and rich theological reflection from those who were taken by Babylon.

The experience under Babylonian and then Persian rule is one of the formative diaspora of the Jewish people. Entire books, such as Ezekiel, Daniel and Esther, reflect those circumstances.[10] They are resources for exploring the levels of cultural adaptation by God's people and the varied responses to them in those far-away places. On some occasions the reaction was one of violent rejection. Powerful passages, such as Psalm 137, express the deep humiliation and frustration of being a mocked and exploited foreign people. Ezra and Nehemiah touch on issues of integration as well, but they concentrate on returns to the land – one to establish a society that would follow the law closely, the other to rebuild the wall of Jerusalem. The physical move back to the land was not easy, and at those returns there were conflicts between those who came back and those who had remained and not gone into exile (see Ezra, Nehemiah, Haggai, Zechariah, Malachi).

These diverse and complex experiences are now being explored by immigrant pastors and theologians. They are trying to understand their changed identity in their new land and the purpose of their existence as individual believers and Christian communities through a diaspora lens.[11] These are creative deliberations on the *Missio Dei*, not by the majority or host culture, but by and for immigrants. Mission has often been the purview of those who have the means to go to other places or of a majority culture aiming to reach newcomers who have come into their context. This is different. These are the thoughts of a minority, who have been displaced or have voluntarily left their homelands to

---

10. Some critical positions place other prophetic material in this period (e.g., Isa. 40 – 66).
11. E.g., Luis Rivera, 'Toward a Diaspora Hermeneutics (Hispanic North America)', in M. Daniel Carroll R. and Jacqueline Lapsley (eds.), *Character Ethics and the Old Testament: Moral Dimensions of Scripture* (Louisville: Westminster John Knox Press, 2007), pp. 169–189. Other examples among many include *The New People Next Door*, Lausanne Occasional Paper 55 (Lausanne Committee for World Evangelization, 2004); S. Hun Kim and Wonsuk Ma (eds.), *Korean Diaspora and Christian Mission* (Eugene: Wipf & Stock, 2011).

come to a different place. Questions arise about what it means to be the people of God as a marginalized people, who are the target of discriminatory laws and attitudes within that context. In other words, the migration *did not originate in mission*; instead, *mission is born in* and *flows from* the circumstances of their migration. For instance, in the United States there is a flourishing of Hispanic theology and a wrestling with the meaning of mission as a Hispanic church. Korean diaspora communities around the globe are trying to process these challenges in their new lands. Examples of these processes could be multiplied.

It is important to note at this juncture that *all* Christians are 'aliens and exiles' (1 Pet. 2:11). Some argue that this descriptor in 1 Peter is specific to the addressees of that epistle and that it refers to their political and economic status in the Roman Empire. While it is possible that these Christians were living in peculiar circumstances, these words find an echo elsewhere in the New Testament. Other passages explain that every Christian is a foreigner in this world, with a different citizenship and calling (Phil. 3:20–21; Heb. 13:14). Baptism is a public statement of this new reality.

Two points flow from this. First, this new identity reveals the centrality of migration in the Bible. Migration is so fundamental to understanding the experiences of the people of God in Scripture and its teaching that it is *a key metaphor of what it means to be a Christian*. Therefore, Christians cannot ignore the reality of immigration and immigrants. To enter into this topic is to explore the nature of Christian faith and mission.

Second, Christians must think through carefully the Bible's teaching on citizenship and how the topic of immigration relates to it.[12] Is citizenship, as conceived today, a legitimate biblical category? This, of course, is a historical question (the answer could very well be 'no'). Nevertheless, the Old Testament does not make a seamless equation between the native-born and those who have come from elsewhere. A few laws make distinctions between them (e.g., Deut. 15:1–3; 23:3–8). This feature is not uncommon in immigrant legislation even today – that is, the interplay between acceptance and discrimination. Yet even within the Old Testament these strictures are left behind. One of the excluded groups was to be the Moabites, yet Ruth became part of Israel and that story is now utilized in the Jewish liturgical calendar (Shavuot, or feast of Weeks). Predictions of the future also point beyond these limitations (on which, see below). Of course, Old Testament law also provided a pathway into the

---

12. I am grateful for this helpful observation by Dr Richard C. Langer, who responded to the original version of this chapter presented at the Biola University conference.

community. From the side of New Testament realities, the coming of Jesus and the breaking down of barriers in the body of Christ should change perceptions about non-citizens.

It is not uncommon to hear Christians base their views on immigration on Romans 13:1–5. This passage is read as a decree to support the governing authorities, which means in relationship to the presence of immigrants, for example, that any undocumented immigration must be opposed as a breach of the laws of the land. Obedience to the law trumps all, and the defence of a cherished way of life is an obligation. One could ask these Christians all sorts of questions about immigration legislation. For instance, how well do they know the history of immigration and of immigration legislation in their country? How coherent are these laws, and are they fair and humane? Have these Christians factored in the possible immigration background of their own families? From a *Missio Dei* framework: How do higher loyalties to kingdom citizenship consciously impact their position? How do the virtues and the attitudes (even towards enemies) in Romans 12, the previous chapter – let alone the teaching of the breadth of the Scripture that we have briefly reviewed here – impact their view of foreigners? How should Christians of the host culture, who are resident aliens in the eyes of God and the world, respond to those sojourners who have come to live in their society and who, in some cases, worship as fellow believers and pilgrims in the church? And if a Christian stance on immigration should disagree with that of the authorities, what of the need to question them and existing laws in speaking the truth and doing the right thing, and to suffer at their hand for doing that (e.g., Acts 4:1–31; 1 Pet. 2:11–25, 3:8–18)? Hard questions all. Immigration in many ways can test the ultimate commitments of Christians and the church.

Immigrants can potentially have a better appreciation of the faith and the *Missio Dei*, or at least an important perspective on the biblical metaphor of the people of God as a migrant people. Theirs is not simply an appreciation of the theological meaning of the metaphor of being 'aliens and exiles'; that metaphor, that truth, is their life.

Eschatological hope and migration

The fourth dimension to be explored concerns the future. Not only are the creation and fall, the commissioning of the people of God to be a blessing and the establishment of welcoming communities elements for a missional ethics concerning immigration, eschatology factors in as well, as it does in the final triangle of Wright's scheme.

A few passages in the Old Testament look forward to the day when sojourners will find full inclusion in the people of God. Isaiah speaks of a future ingathering of Israel that includes the foreigner in the worship on Zion (Isa. 56:1–8; cf. 1 Kgs 8:41–43). Ezekiel speaks of sojourners inheriting land along with the tribes of Israel (Ezek. 47:21–23). Other passages predict the establishment of a kingdom in which the nations will seek Yahweh, and the coming of a Messiah who will reign over all (e.g., Isa. 2, 9, 11, 32, 42, 61; Jer. 33; Hag. 2; Zech. 9, 14). These hopes find initial fulfilment in the coming of Jesus and the founding of the Christian church. Jesus is that Messiah who opened the door to whosoever will follow him and gave his disciples the mandate to take the gospel to every people (Matt. 28:18–20; Mark 16:15; Luke 4:45–49; Acts 1:8). An earlier section of this chapter mentions that in Christ racial, ethnic and national differences are done away with in the church. One could mention other pertinent New Testament images, such as the church as one body with great diversity under the headship of Jesus (1 Cor. 12; Eph. 4; Col. 1:15–20), and the church as a single living building with him as the cornerstone (Eph. 2:19–22). Each of these demonstrates that the Messianic Age has arrived, although not in its fullness.[13] The fact that the awaited future of the universal, international kingdom is here should spur the Christian church to shape its attitudes towards outsiders, orient its treatment of those foreigners within the church and in society, and inform their political stance in accordance with that reality. The church should incarnate the future as an integral part of its participation in the *Missio Dei*.

In the book of Revelation, John has a vision of heaven in which he witnesses the four living creatures and the twenty-four elders singing of God's people, those 'saints from every tribe and language and people and nation' (Rev. 5:9). John also speaks of the new creation beyond the final judgment in which the nations will enjoy the presence of the Lord and the Lamb (Rev. 21:22 – 22:5). That is, the future of redeemed humanity is the mixing of all peoples in communion with and worship of the triune God. The Lord's table that is celebrated everywhere today looks back to the cross and Jesus' sacrifice for all peoples, even as it anticipates his second coming and the international flavour of that glorious end time. To ignore the multicultural dimension of that future is to misrepresent a key component of what the church celebrates when it gathers together to partake of the bread and wine.

The migration of millions today is a foretaste of what lies ahead. Then, diversity will not be feared as a threat, burden or curse; it will be the fulfilment

---

13. Christians, of course, hold various views concerning the meaning of the millennium and its relationship to the first and second comings of Jesus.

of God's goal for redemption of humanity. The church of the host culture needs to ask itself if and how it is walking in the light of that eschatological hope as it engages with the immigration debate and interacts with foreigners within its gatherings, in its neighbourhoods and in society in general. For the immigrants this vision can engender a strong hope in their final vindication. The climax of the *Missio Dei* should orient the church in the present.

Conclusion

A missional ethics approach to immigration does not permit the debate to be reduced to isolated social policy decisions based on certain deontological principles (e.g., citizens must obey the government; lawbreakers must be punished) or consequentialist calculations (e.g., a cost–benefit analysis of the impact of immigration on the national economy). It is also broader than a narrative ethics perspective. Narrative ethics rightly appeals to the contributions of a community's traditions (for the church this would include the Scriptures and Christian views about immigration in its history), practices (such as baptism and the Lord's table), the virtues it seeks and its exemplary individuals who embody these ideals. These classic schools of ethics have a part to play in immigration discussions by Christians, but a missional ethics repositions the issue.

Now immigration is indivisible from what Christians believe about the purposes of God. It is bound up with how they perceive and live out their Christian identity, both individually and corporately. This makes for a richer, more complex reflection that must be fully canonical, historically aware and brutally honest concerning its implications for the church as the church and for the church within the world.

This essay presents four themes that can inform a missional ethical perspective on immigration. We have attempted to focus on four key elements that cover the breadth of Scripture. To summarize briefly, the first was the image of God as the most appropriate place to begin the discussion. The second turned to the call of Abram in Genesis 12 to link the *Missio Dei* to the creation of a people – often a migrant people in the Bible – to be the means of bringing God's blessing to the world. The third explored how Old Testament law was designed to legislate that blessing into the life of a welcoming community, the ideals of which the New Testament develops in multiple ways for the Christian church. The fourth looked to eschatology and the component of the gathering of all peoples together in the ultimate fulfilment of the *Missio Dei*.

Clearly, immigration is an important dimension of the *Missio Dei*. The pragmatics of church policies and societal legislation will be difficult to iron out, of course. But anything less than a missional approach to these many challenges would be a disservice to immigrants and a disappointment in this unique opportunity to embody the *Missio Dei*.

© M. Daniel Carroll R., 2012

14. CONCLUSION

Andy Draycott and Jonathan Rowe

We will end this conclusion with reflections on the missio-ethical practice of Sabbath. In order to get there, and so enter into that rest, we will first narrate the journey the explorations collected in this volume have mapped. We deliberately invited fellow scholars to reach from their disciplinary specialism out to the horizon of missio-ethical practice. Since we did so for the good of the church, we should ask what good has been achieved or is indicated by this work. In other words, what promise is held out by these contributions for vigorous exploration in local churches into these and other subjects? Such a way of expressing the matter allows us the frank recognition that even in those areas upon which contributors have touched there remains much more scope for exploratory work. Moreover, the land is not only to be spied out, explored and mapped, but must then be inhabited daily with all the present interconnected challenges that academic reflection can help parse out, but cannot of itself disentangle and endure or overcome.

We suggest that part of the promise of the collection is encountered as discrete contributions are weighed in the light of the conversation represented by all. How does Jenson's concern for church family acceptance in contentious matters of sexuality relate to Ruble's reading of silent power relations in evangelical discourse on mission? Do these affirm, challenge or sit alongside a missional and Latin American exegesis of servant leadership as expounded by Moser, or the migrant theology testified to by Carroll? How do Macaskill's reflections on hope explicate the hopeful creaturely fidelity of staying put in the garden as Brock's theology of creation challenges the typical missionary focus on sending in favour of a more grounded missio-ethical witness? In this light, what should one make of the challenge of staying put culturally in familial circumstances that go against the norms of Western Christians, for example, in the ways that Hordern highlights as he raises the issue of the Muslim 'Insider Movement'? What may be said about Draycott's and Chaplin's contributions – are they complementary, or do they offer competing visions? Is it necessary to decide between them? And, if concrete decisions are made, how may they be undertaken in that most delicate arena, our handling of money? Does the sharp, even countercultural, position outlined by Doherty jeopardize the plausibility of reciprocal friendship that de Graaff commends?

These are just some of the overlapping questions that can be framed by overlaying these explorations in an attempt to form a greater, that is, more detailed, intricate and complicated survey of the missio-ethical terrain. It is clear, in terms of the collection's introduction, that the *scope* of missional ethics is broad, involving living well in creation. Yet although one can discern in these explorations myriad potential overlaps – and, of course, many practical ramifications – they retain a clear and determined Christian *shape*. Opening with Wright's biblical theological reflection on the Trinity is a way of posing the gospel question to each subsequent chapter. Is the mission and ethic thread interwoven through the fabric of this discussion that of the gospel of Jesus Christ, glorifying the Father in the power of the Spirit? Is it clearly *God-shaped*? It is to Jesus, 'the pioneer and perfecter of our faith' (Heb. 12:2), that we look, to him whose blood 'speaks a better word' of peace and healing and reconciliation (Heb. 12:24). Indeed, missional ethics is *story shaped*, so that with Hebrews we can recognize the voice of one God and Holy Spirit speaking in the whole of Scripture, culminating in the events of Christ's gospel advent. As a *community-shaped* reality missional ethics attests the community formation mediated by Jesus' mediating priesthood, one that holds open the Sabbath rest of the gospel for those who believe (Heb. 4). Even so, that this rest is enjoyed in mutual love by Christians 'outside the camp' speaks to the never complacent or accommodated missio-ethical stance whose full hope is oriented to 'the city that is to come'. That orientation is rightly *other shaped*, even as upholding marriage, obeying leaders, living free from the love of money and entertaining angels unawares all point to a peculiar and never fully definable prescription for who the other is (Heb. 13). While missional ethics is also *shaped only in outline*, requiring that Christ's disciples work out together what it means in practice, the idea and practice of Sabbath rest has been a constant in the life of God's people through the centuries. For this reason, we would like to conclude by highlighting how many of this volume's concerns coalesce in the missio-ethical practice of Sabbath.

The fourth commandment instructs the people of God to observe the Sabbath day and keep it holy by refraining from work, an exhortation that repays examination from three angles. First, the Sabbath is a *moment to remember*. We remember that *God* created the world, recalling that while we work we do not create our world. So often, we find it easier to continue with our self-absorbed activity rather than stop and wait in faith, potentially missing the point of everything we have been created to be. It is for this reason that Jesus said, 'The sabbath was made for humankind, and not humankind for the Sabbath' (Mark 2:27). By Sabbath keeping we also remember that God has rescued his people. The commandment itself refers to the exodus deliverance. And the salvation from Egyptian oppression was a constant point of reference for prophets and priests as they sought to lead God's people in God's ways. As Christians, of course, we remember the rescue wrought by the death and resurrection of Jesus; the Sabbath is an opportunity to stop our frenetic activity and remember this great salvation.

It is also, though, *our present discipline*. The purpose of the Sabbath is to keep a day apart for God. On the one hand, the Sabbath involves not doing things: it is a rest from all the activity that so consumes our time and energy. This is not only personal rest, for it involves the whole household. There is a social and economic dimension to Sabbath that ensures others are not exploited, and it is salutary to think that if we create a society that forgets this, then we may end up as the exploited ones. On the other hand, Sabbath is not only a refusal to work, in principle an intrinsically worthwhile activity, it is a positive rejection of something negative: the Sabbath is an opportunity to say 'no' to idolatry. Idolatry is simply putting something else in the place of God, and although modern forms are not expressed in rituals to ensure the earth's fecundity, they are no less extensive or insidious.

Third, the practice of Sabbath observance is a *sign of our hope*. In novels and films the end is when everything becomes clear and the loose ends are tied up. The Sabbath rest declares that the end of the story in which we are players will come not as a result of our activity but because of God's action. For this reason, early Christians conceived the Lord's Day as the eighth day of the week, a day for celebrating God's new creation. Our resting is a sign, both to ourselves and to those around us, that our hope is placed firmly in *this* hope instead of our ability to overcome obstacles to the more efficient or effective use of time.

The Sabbath is a space in which to remember what God has done and what he will do, but it is a practice that requires discipline, even courage, especially since God does not seem to operate to our timescales. For this reason, the psalmist says not only, 'Wait for the LORD,' but also, 'be strong, and let your heart take courage' (Ps. 27:14). Waiting can be work; but it is neither the sort of work required legalistically to fulfil some imposed requirement, nor the self-absorbed work of frenetic activity. Instead, it is a sign to us and others of the goodness of God.

An anecdote from the life of William Wilberforce provides us with an example of the benefits of Sabbath. At one point in his political career he faced the prospect of becoming a government minister and, according to words he penned in his journal, he 'was for a little intoxicated, and had risings of ambition'.[1] Yet Wilberforce was convinced of the benefits of Sabbath rest and spent Sunday in quiet contemplation. By the evening he was able to write, 'Blessed be God for this day of rest and religious occupation, wherein earthly things assume their true size and comparative insignificance; ambition is stunted.' As for Wilberforce, our natural, fallen ambitions take their proper place when God takes his. Sabbath space that is set aside for God is also a place from which temptations can be confronted; and the nature of temptation is that discipline is required if it *is* to be confronted.

Sabbath rest is a moment to remember, a present discipline and a sign of our hope in God. It is both an ethical issue – something highlighted by its place in the Ten Commandments – and a part of the mission of the people of God. In many ways it encapsulates the church's call to be a living witness. Our ability to fulfil this charge will depend on God himself, as it always has. For while God's commands follow God's redemption, keeping the law is also a gift of God. This is clear in Deuteronomy 30:6, which declares that 'the LORD your God will circumcise your heart and the heart of your descendants, so that you will love the LORD your God with all your heart and with all your soul, in order that you may live'. For this reason we should conclude our consideration of missional ethics with prayer. Originally penned in 1691, the sentiments and aspirations of Richard Baxter's oration remain as relevant today as when they were first prayed.[2]

> Keep us, O Lord,
> while we tarry on this earth,
> in a serious seeking after you,
> and in an affectionate walking with you,

---

1. Robert Wilberforce and Samuel Wilberforce, *Life of William Wilberforce Vol. III* (London: John Murray, 1838), p. 3.
2. Reproduced in *Time to Pray* (London: Church House Publishing, 2006), p. 41.

every day of our lives;
that when you come,
we may be found not hiding our talent,
nor serving the flesh,
nor yet asleep with our lamp unfurnished,
but waiting and longing for our Lord,
our glorious God for ever.
Amen.

© Andy Draycott and Jonathan Rowe, 2012

INDEX OF SCRIPTURE REFERENCES

OLD TESTAMENT

Genesis
1 *244, 260*
1:1–2 *52*
1:11 *80*
1:20 *80*
1:24 *80*
1:26–28 *261*
1:28 *161*
1:31 *58, 80, 244*
1 – 2 *80, 81*
1 – 3 *80*
1 – 11 *270*
2 *244, 262*
2:5 *60*
2:7 *80*
2:8 *58*
2:10–14 *59*
2:15 *60, 261*
2:22–23 *80*
2:16 *262*
3 *81*
3:5 *262*
3:8 *80*
3:10 *80*
3:14–19 *262*
3:15–19 *262*
3:17 *80*
3:19 *81, 262*
3:20 *262*
3:21 *262*
3:23 *60*
3:23–24 *263*
4:1–2 *263*
4:8 *263*
4:14–15 *263*
4:16 *62*
4:23–24 *263*
5 *263*
5:29 *263*
6:5 *263*
6:11 *263*
7:11–24 *263*
9:20–23 *263*
10 *263*
10:5 *263, 264*
10:20 *263, 264*
10:31 *263, 264*
11 *123, 263*
11:1–9 *263*
11:6–9 *263*
12 *264, 276*
12:1–3 *37, 264*
12:1–4 *14*
12:3 *82, 162*
12:7–8 *264*
12:10–16 *265*
12:17–20 *264*
13:4 *264*
13:5–6 *264*
13:18 *264*
14:22 *264*
15:1–6 *264*
16:11–16 *264*
18:1–8 *265*
18:17–19 *171, 264*
18:19 *37, 40*
18:22–33 *264*
20 *264*
20:7 *264*
20:17 *264*

Genesis (cont.)
21:1–3 264
21:33 264
22:15–18 264
23 264
23:4 264
24 265
26 264
26: 25 264
27 264
29 – 30 264
31:5–13 264
31:42 264
32:9–12 264
33:10–11 264
34 264
35:11 264
38 264
41 264
41:16 264
42 – 47 264
45:4–8 42
47 264
47:10 264
50:20 264

Exodus
3:10–15 42
4:22 45
12:38 270
12:45–49 269
18:21 171
19:4–6 15, 37, 38, 267
20:1–6 267
20:2 83
20:10 269
20:12 172
22:21 269
23:9 269
23:12 269
35:30 – 36:1 52

Leviticus
16:29 269
18:12–14 164
19 271
19:9–10 268

19:18 269
19:34 269
20:11 164
20:12 164
20:17 164
25 267
26:12 165
26:45 83

Numbers
9:14 269
11 122
11:16–17 52
11:29 52, 123
27:1–11 164
36:1–12 164

Deuteronomy
1:16–17 269
1:31 45
4:5–8 20, 267
4:6 163
4:6–8 37, 38, 40, 204
5:6–10 267
5:14 269
6:4–9 171
8:5 45
10:12–22 270
10:14–19 270
14:28–29 268
15:1–3 273
15:4 246
15:7–15 40
16:11 269
16:14 269
21:18–21 160
23:3–8 273
24:14–15 269, 270
24:17–18 269
24:19–22 268
26:5 171
26:11 269
26:12–13 268
27:19 269
28 – 30 83
30:6 83, 281
31:8–13 269

32:6 45
32:18 45

Judges
3:10 52
6:34 52
13:25 52

Ruth
2 268

2 Samuel
7:14 98

1 Kings
8:41–43 275
11:1–8 165
12 272

2 Kings
17 272
25 272

1 Chronicles
29:14–15 264

Ezra
9 271
9 – 10 84

Nehemiah
8 269
9:20 52
9:30 52
13 271

Job
31:32 265
33:4 52

Psalms
1 70
2:7 98
8:5 208
22:1 44
23 265
25:5 83

27:14 *281*
31:9–24 *112–113*
37:34 *83*
38:15 *83*
95:7–8 *74*
103:13 *45*
104 *76*
104:27–30 *52*
110:1 *47*
115:1–7 *74*
115:2 *55*
127:3–5 *159, 162*
137 *272*

Proverbs
10:28 *82*

Song of Solomon
4:16 *62*

Isaiah
1:2 *45*
1:5–6 *236*
2 *275*
2:2–4 *229*
6:1–7 *42*
6:9 *230*
7:4 *221*
7–9 *221*
9 *275*
9:6–7 *221*
11 *275*
11:1–5 *52*
19:20–21 *42*
32 *275*
32:1 *221*
32:1–8 *221*
32:15–18 *52*
32:17 *229*
35:8 *228*
37:6 *221*
38:15 *83*
39 *220*
40 *85*
40:27 *228, 235*
40:27–31 *230*
40–55 *221, 230*
40–66 *84, 272*
41:8 *220, 222*
41:10 *221*
41:22–29 *226*
42 *275*
42:1 *229, 236*
42:1–3 *92*
42:1–4 *222, 223, 233, 234*
42:1–7 *52, 221, 222, 226, 228, 232*
42:2–4 *230, 233, 236*
42:4 *84, 227, 229, 234*
42:5 *224, 225*
42:6 *38, 235*
42:6–7 *224, 227*
42:8–9 *224*
42:8–12 *224*
42:10–12 *225*
42:13–14 *226*
42:18–20 *219, 221, 222, 228, 230*
43:10 *222, 226*
45:1 *233*
49:1–3 *229*
49:1–13 *222*
49:3 *226, 228, 230*
49:4 *230*
49:6 *14, 38, 222, 230*
50:4–10 *219, 222, 229, 230, 231, 235, 236*
52:11 *165, 228*
52:13 – 53:12 *219, 222, 223, 231*
53 *84, 86*
53:4–5 *236*
53:4–6 *235*
53:6 *47*
53:10 *223*
56:1–8 *275*
56:6 *222*
58:6–8 *38*
58:7 *269*
59:14–15 *225*
59:14–16 *221*
60:3 *38*
61 *275*
61:1 *229, 236*
61:1–2 *53*
61:1–3 *52*
61:3 *228*
63:11–14 *52*
63:15ff. *229*
63:16 *45*
64:8–9 *45*
65 *89*
65–66 *80*
66:19–21 *222*

Jeremiah
1:7–9 *42*
3:4 *45*
3:19 *45*
29:4–7 *42*
31:33 *84*
33 *275*
52:11 *221*
52:31 *221*

Ezekiel
36 *84, 86*
36:25–27 *52*
37 *84, 86*
37:1–14 *52*
37:15–28 *56*
47 *89*
47:1–12 *61*
47:21–23 *275*

Hosea
11:2 *45*

Joel
2:28–32 *52*

Amos
6:12 *23*

Micah
3:8 *52*

Haggai
2 *275*

Zechariah
7:7–12 *52*
9 *275*

Zechariah (cont.)
14 *275*

Malachi
1:6 *45*

NEW TESTAMENT

Matthew
1:21 *47*
3:17 *222*
5 *229*
5: 9 *46*
5:16 *46*
5:40–42 *247*
5:42 *252*
5:43–48 *46*
6:4 *46*
6:6 *46*
6:10 *100*
6:14–15 *46*
6:18 *46*
6:19 *247*
6:25 *245*
6:25–32 *46*
6:31–32 *247*
6:33 *106, 247*
7:21–23 *46*
10:17–20 *53*
10:34–39 *97*
10:37 *77*
11:5 *232*
11:12 *77*
11:28 *230*
12:1–17 *233*
12:15–21 *222*
12:17–21 *222*
12:21 *234*
12:22–27 *234*
16:24 *91*
17:1–5 *222*
19:8 *242*
19:16 *76*
19:16–19 *269*
19:27 *97*
19:29 *97*
25:31–46 *265*

25:40 *73*
25:45 *225*
28:18–20 *13, 275*
28:18–30 *50*

Mark
1:11 *222, 238*
1:12 *53*
1:15 *24*
2:27 *280*
3:33–35 *97*
7:31–37 *74*
8:36 *250*
10:23–27 *248*
10:29–30 *175*
10:45 *16*
14:61–64 *47*
16:15 *275*

Luke
1:1 *85*
1:67–69 *86*
2:30 *47*
2:51 *170*
4:14–21 *53*
4:18 *232*
4:18–19 *41*
4:24 *123*
4:45–49 *275*
6:23 *123*
6:35 *252*
7:22 *232*
10:25–37 *271*
11:2 *100*
14:26 *169, 175*
14:33 *248*
16:19–31 *248*
17:11–19 *271*
17:34 *170*
21:15 *53*
24:45–47 *43*
24:49 *41*

John
1 *194, 196*
1:3 *47*
1:8 *102*

1:18 *56*
1:43–46 *180*
1:47–51 *180*
2:20–22 *88*
3 *86*
3:16 *46*
3:16–17 *43*
3:17 *41*
3:34 *41*
4 *271*
4:23–24 *53*
4:34 *41, 55*
5:19 *55*
5:26 *55*
5 – 8 *41*
6:57 *55*
11:42 *41*
12:32 *102*
13 *196*
13:6–8 *196*
13:34 *56*
13:35 *39*
13–15 *196*
14:16 *41*
14:16–17 *53, 88*
14:25–26 *53, 88*
14:26 *41*
14–16 *53*
15:12 *196*
15:13 *56*
15:13–14 *196*
15:14 *196*
15:15 *196*
15:16 *196*
15:17 *56*
15:18 *231*
15:26 *41*
15:26–27 *88*
16:7–11 *88*
16:7–15 *41*
16:12–15 *53*
16:13 *18*
17 *27, 226*
17:17 *102*
17:18 *41, 43*
17:20–26 *54*
17:21–23 *54, 56*

INDEX OF SCRIPTURE REFERENCES

17:22 *55*
17:23 *102*
18:37 *16*
19:25–27 *169*
20:21 *41, 43, 46*
20:21–22 *53*
20:22–23 *41*

Acts
1:8 *222, 226, 275*
2 *53, 123, 124*
2:16–21 *123*
2:38 *24*
4:1–31 *274*
4:12 *47*
8:26–39 *105*
8:28–35 *223*
8:35 *222*
10:38 *41*
10 – 11 *271*
13:1 *271*
13:1–4 *41*
13:47 *222*
15 *271*
15:11 *47*
15: 16 *88*
16:6–7 *41*
20:21 *222*
26:23 *222*

Romans
1:4 *41*
1:5 *51*
2:16 *47*
4 *264*
8:9 *89*
8:13 *91*
8:15 *98*
8:18 *104*
8:19–23 *90*
8:21–23 *104*
8:22–23 *89*
8:26–27 *53*
8:32 *46*
9 – 11 *226*
10:9 *47*
12 *274*

12:1–2 *211*
12:3–8 *53*
12:5 *130*
12:13 *265*
12:18 *214*
13 *203*
13:1–5 *274*
14:9–12 *47*
14:17 *100*
15:16 *15*
16:26 *51*

1 Corinthians
1:5 *123*
1:23 *18*
1 – 4 *123*
2:6 *216*
2:13–16 *123*
3:7–9 *62*
7:39 *165*
8:4–6 *47*
9:22 *21*
10:31 *19*
11 *124*
12 *76, 275*
12:3 *53*
12:4–11 *53*
13 *90*
13:9 *125*
14 *123, 124*
14:1 *53*
14:3 *124*
14:5 *124*
14:11 *124*
14:13–17 *53*
14:24–25 *124*
14:32 *124*
15 *90*
15:51–52 *90*

2 Corinthians
1 *123*
1:5–6 *88*
1:22 *90*
1 – 5 *88*
3:2–3 *226*
3:6 *88, 89*

3 – 5 *89*
4:10 *88*
5:10 *47*
5:17 *89, 90*
5:19–20 *227*
6:14–18 *165*
6:16 *87*

Galatians
1:4–5 *46*
1:15–16 *222*
2 *271*
2:9 *222*
2:20 *46, 111*
3:2 *88*
3:5 *88*
3:14 *88*
3:28 *100, 271*
4:28 *226*
5:22 *229*
5:22–23 *53, 90*

Ephesians
1:3–14 *39*
1:4 *40*
1:4–5 *98*
1:10 *40*
1:12 *40*
1:20–23 *47*
2 *271*
2:12 *91*
2:14–16 *48*
2:16 *99*
2:19–22 *275*
3:14 *99*
4 *275*
4:3–6 *53*
4:11–12 *53*
4:28 *250*
5:2 *39*
5:21–33 *175*
6:10–18 *53*

Philippians
2:5–8 *223*
2:2–4 *43*
2:6–15 *43*

Philippians (*cont.*)
2:14–16 *43*
3:10 *88*
3:15 *18*
3:20 *106*
3:20–21 *273*

Colossians
1:3–8 *125*
1:15 *226*
1:15–16 *48*
1:15–17 *47*
1:15–20 *50, 275*
1:20 *48*
1:24 *88, 231*
2:1–25 *229*
2:15 *47*
3:1 *111*
3:5 *91*
3:17 *19*

1 Thessalonians
1:3 *39*
2:13 *115*
4:9–10 *39*

2 Thessalonians
1:5–10 *47*
2:13–14 *39*

1 Timothy
2:5 *132*
2:12 *150*
3:2 *265*
4:3–4 *244*
5:9–10 *265*
6:10 *244*

2 Timothy
1:12 *19*

3:5 *104*

Titus
1:8 *265*
2:13 *47*

Hebrews
1:2 *47*
1:2–3 *50*
1:3 *99*
2:9 *230*
2:10 *47*
2:11–12 *98*
2:14 *48*
4 *279*
5:9 *47*
7:25 *47*
9:14 *41, 46*
11:6 *249*
11:13–16 *106*
12:2 *279*
12:6 *111*
12:10 *110*
12:24 *279*
13 *279*
13:2 *124, 265*
13:14 *273*

James
5:13 *230*

1 Peter
1:1–2 *39*
1:2 *53*
1:10–12 *86*
1:15 *40*
2:5 *87*
2:9 *15, 222*
2:11 *273*
2:11–12 *20*

2:11–25 *274*
2:12 *40, 204*
2:19 *230*
2:19–25 *231*
2:24 *47*
3:8–18 *274*
4:1–4 *18*
4:10–11 *117*
4:13 *88*

2 Peter
1:20–21 *52*
3:13 *80*

1 John
3:1 *46*
3:11 *56*
3:23 *56*
4:7 *56*
4:9 *41*
4:9–11 *46*
4:11 *39, 56*
4:12 *56*
4:13–16 *124*
4:14 *41*

Revelation
1:5 *47*
3:14 *47*
5:9 *275*
5:9–10 *47*
7:10 *47*
11:18 *60*
17 – 18 *91, 263*
18 *228*
21:1 *80*
21 – 22 *90*
21:22 – 22:5 *275*
22:1 *61*
22:17 *51*

INDEX OF NAMES

Abraham, William J., 95, 105
Ackroyd, P. R., 220
Adams, James Luther, 114
Adeney, David H., 142
Adeney, Miriam, 151, 152
Alexander, T. Desmond, 89
Allen, Catherine, 149
Alves, Rubem, 226
Aristotle, 29, 104, 183, 184–186, 187
Ashcroft, John, 203
Athyal, Saphir, 152
Augustine, 28, 107, 109, 169, 188, 249

Ballesteros, S. Torres, 234
Banner, Michael, 18, 25, 209
Barrett, Lois, 20
Barth, Karl, 40, 59, 66, 72, 98, 99, 100
Barton, John, 23
Bauckham, Richard, 88, 90
Baxter, Richard, 281–282
Beale, G. K., 59, 60, 64, 66
Beaton, Richard, 233
Bennett, Jana Marguerite, 97
Berger, Peter, 234

Beuken, W. A. M., 223
Biggar, Nigel, 119–121, 122, 124, 125, 129, 205–206, 207–208, 209
Bittles, Alan, 166
Blocher, Henri, 59, 60
Blum, Lawrence, 22
Bock, Darrell L., 145
Bockmuehl, Markus, 86
Bonhoeffer, Dietrich, 182
Bosch, David J., 14, 16, 181
Bowen, Roger, 132
Braude, Ann, 153
Bretherton, Luke, 203
Brock, Brian, 24, 27, 205, 279
Brown, Malcolm, 241
Brown, Rick, 157, 168, 176
Brown, W. P., 60, 81, 82
Bruce, F. F., 222
Brueggemann, Walter, 224
Burnside, Jonathan, 160, 163, 165, 171, 203
Bush, Luis, 145

Calvin, John, 99, 252
Campbell, Douglas, 87

Campese, Gioacchino, 260
Carmichael, Amy, 151, 152
Carroll R., M. Daniel, 31, 259, 264, 278
Carson, D. A., 234
Chaplin, Jonathan, 30, 116, 119, 202, 203, 209, 279
Childs, B. S., 221, 230
Chrysostom, 61, 245, 247, 255
Clark, Stephen, 203
Clifford, Richard J., 225
Conrad, Edgar, 220–221
Cooper, David E., 67, 68, 71, 75
Costa, Ken, 242–243
Croatto, José Severino, 218–219, 226, 231
Cumming, Joseph, 157
Cunningham, Harold, 212

Daniel, Ben, 260
Darwall, Stephen, 224
De Graaff, Guido, 29–30
De La Torre, Miguel, 260
Deiros, Pablo A., 234
Dille, Sarah J., 226
Doherty, Sean, 30–31, 279
Douglas, James D., 152
Draper, Don, 174
Draycott, Andy, 28, 279
Dussell, Enrique, 218, 236–237

Elliot, Elisabeth, 151, 152
Escobar, Samuel, 24, 148, 237
Evans, Bob, 151

Fletcher-Louis, Crispin, 60
Flett, John G., 17, 36, 40, 54
Forrester, Duncan, 240
Freston, Paul, 203

Gathercole, Simon, 89
Goldingay, J., 221, 233, 236
González, Antonio, 237–238
Graham, Billy, 142, 143, 151
Green, Chris, 203
Green, Stephen, 242
Grenz, Stanley J., 54
Griffiths, Brian, 242

Griffiths, Paul, 108, 109
Groody, Daniel G., 260
Guder, Darrell, 20
Gunton, Colin E., 54
Guroian, Victor, 60, 65

Halverson, Richard, 141, 142
Hanby, Michael, 25
Hanciles, Jehu, 260
Hardy, Thomas, 131–132
Harinck, Douglas, 87
Harrison, Robert, 58, 68–69, 73
Hartenstein, Karl, 40
Hauerwas, Stanley, 104, 124, 209, 241
Hay, Donald A., 242
Hays, Richard B., 95, 104, 120
Hellerman, Joe, 101
Henry, Carl F. H., 143, 144, 151
Hilary of Poitiers, 256
Hill, Wesley, 95, 111
Hoffmeier, James K., 268
Hooker, Morna, 84
Hordern, Joshua, 29, 279
Hunter, John Davidson, 65

Jackson, Darrell, 262
Jackson, Timothy, 214
Jeckyll, Gertrude, 71
Jennings, Willie James, 63, 72
Jenson, Matt, 28, 116, 278
Jung, Joanne, 126–128

Kane, J. Herbert, 143, 144
Kato, Byang, 148
Kierkegaard, Søren, 189–190, 191, 192
Kim, S. Hun, 272
King Jr, Martin Luther, 125, 213
Kivengere, Festo, 151
Koole, Jan L., 225, 236
Koser, Khalid, 258
Küng, Hans, 211

Lau, Lawson, 145
Lessing, G. E., 72
Lewis, C. S., 195
Lewis, Rebecca, 157
Lindberg, Carter, 246

INDEX OF SCRIPTURE NAMES

Lohfink, Gerhard, 105
Long, D. Stephen, 124
Luther, Martin, 68, 73–74, 108, 125, 190, 245–246, 248–250, 251, 252, 256

Ma, Wonsuk, 229, 272
Macaskill, Grant, 27–28, 84, 278
McConville, J. G., 221
MacIntyre, Alasdair, 21, 24, 160, 241
McIlroy, David, 203
McQuilkin, J. Robertson, 145
Martyn, J. Louis, 87
Meilaender, Gilbert, 183, 188–189, 191
Melugin, Roy F., 228
Mesters, Carlos, 219
Middleton, J. Richard, 64–65, 66
Migliore, Daniel L., 182
Milbank, John, 20, 205
Miranda, José Porfino, 218
Moberly, R. W. L., 125
Moser, Nathan, 30, 116, 278
Motyer, J. Alec, 236
Myers, Carol, 163

Netlund, Harold A., 260
Newbigin, Lesslie, 35–36
Nickelsburg, George, 86
Nida, Eugene, 235, 238
Noort, Gerrit, 262
Nuñez, Emilio A., 237
Nussbaum, Martha, 171, 172
Nygren, Anders, 191

O'Donovan, Joan Lockwood, 252
O'Donovan, Oliver, 14, 81, 95, 96, 102, 109, 118–119, 161, 195, 203, 207
Okin, Susan Moller, 160, 161, 167, 172–173
Old, Hughes Oliphant, 118, 119, 124, 128
Olford, Stephen, 151
Ord, Toby, 255
Ott, Craig, 260

Pachau, L., 40
Packer, J. I., 97–98, 99
Padilla, René, 143, 144, 148
Pao, David W., 222
Pickett, Kate, 252

Pieper, Joseph, 183
Pierce, Bob, 151
Pixley, Jorge, 218
Plato, 29, 183–184, 186, 187

Rah, Soong-Chan, 260
Ramachandra, Vinoth, 26
Ramsey, Paul, 162
Rankin, Jerry, 150–151
Rawls, John, 160, 172
Rice, Jonathan, 138–139
Richard, Pablo, 219
Rigali, Norbert J., 238
Rivera, Luis, 272
Rivera-Rodriguez, L., 219
Robert, Dana, 149
Robinson, Marilynne, 111
Rosell, S., 230
Rowe, Jonathan, 22, 137, 163, 164
Roxburgh, Alan, 20
Ruble, Sarah, 28–29, 124, 131, 278

Sandel, Michael, 173
Schluter, Michael, 203
Schwartz, Daniel, 190
Seccombe, David P., 223
Sedgwick, Peter H., 241
Seneca, 29, 183, 186–187, 188, 189
Simonetti, Manlio, 245, 247, 256
Slessor, Mary, 151, 152
Smith, Don K., 146–147
Smith, James K. A., 107, 216
Spencer, Nick, 203, 207, 260
Stordalen, Terje, 59
Storkey, Alan, 203
Stott, John, 16, 133, 151
Stronstad, Roger, 114, 121–122, 131

Tanner, Kathryn, 241
Taylor, Clyde, 151
Taylor, William D., 237
Thiselton, Anthony, 124
Thomas Aquinas, 190, 254
Tizon, Al, 260
Toynbee, Polly, 201
Travis, John, 157, 168, 176
Turner, Philip, 103

Ulrich, Hans, 77, 132, 133

VanGemeren, William A., 229
Vanier, Jean, 61–62, 64, 76
Vicedom, George, 40
Volf, Miroslav, 54

Wagner, Peter, 143, 144, 148
Wallis, Jim, 120
Walls, Andrew, 25, 100
Walton, John, 231
Wannenwetsch, Bernd, 74–75
Waters, Brent, 161, 168, 169–170
Webster, John, 94
Wells, Samuel, 19, 205
Wilberforce, Robert, 281
Wilberforce, Samuel, 281

Wilberforce, William, 213, 281
Wilkinson, Richard G., 252
Williamson, H. G. M., 221, 223, 228
Wirt, Sherwood Eliot, 141
Wolterstorff, Nicholas, 203, 209
Wright, Christopher J. H., 14, 15, 26–27, 37, 40, 42, 45, 47, 52, 163, 211, 259, 267, 270, 274, 279
Wright, N. T., 19, 20, 212

Yong, Amos, 114
Young, Edward, 233

Zamora, Pedro, 227
Zizioulas, John D., 107, 108
Zoba, Wendy Murray, 149

related titles from IVP

The Mission of God
Unlocking the Bible's grand narrative
Christopher J. H. Wright

ISBN: 9781844741526
584 pages, hardback

Most Christians would agree that the Bible provides a basis for mission. Chris Wright believes that there is actually a missional basis for the whole Bible – it is generated by, and is all about, God's mission.

In order to understand the Bible, we need an interpretative perspective that is in tune with this great missional theme. We need to see the 'big picture' of God's mission and how all parts of Scripture fit into its grand narrative.

In this comprehensive and accessible study, Chris Wright begins with the Old Testament understanding of who God is, what he has called his people to be and to do, and where the nations belong within God's mission. These themes are followed into the New Testament. Throughout, Wright emphasizes that biblically defined mission is intrinsically holistic. God's mission is to redeem his whole creation from all that sin and evil have inflicted upon it, and the mission of God's people must reflect the breadth of God's righteous and saving love for all he has made.

Available from your local Christian bookshop or **www.thinkivp.com**

related titles from IVP

Power and Poverty
*Divine and human rule
in a world of need*
Dewi Hughes

ISBN: 9781844743124
256 pages, paperback

Dewi Hughes' conviction is that the suffering through poverty of such a vast number of people in our day is overwhelmingly the result of the misuse of power by others. Hence, the underlying theme of this wide-ranging, challenging study is that poverty has to do with the way in which we human beings use and abuse the power God gave us when he created us.

'In this volume, Dewi Hughes writes compellingly on a matter of compelling importance. We are grateful to him; but true gratitude must be shown by our willingness to tread the path of biblically informed discipleship. I am glad to commend this volume warmly.'
Stephen Williams, Union Theological College

'It is thoroughly biblical, comprehensive, and with a clear central focus on the person, teaching and work of Christ. Dewi Hughes builds on some of my own work in biblical ethics, and makes it much more accessible with lots of practical and up-to-date application.'
Christopher J. H. Wright, Langham Partnership International

Available from your local Christian bookshop or **www.thinkivp.com**

related titles from IVP

Joined-up Life
A Christian account of how ethics works
Andrew J. B. Cameron

ISBN: 9781844745159
336 pages, paperback

'*Finding our best humanity in Jesus Christ*' is the key theme of Andrew Cameron's fresh exploration, in which he seeks to understand ethics as springing from Jesus, and to show how identifying with Jesus Christ brings order and clarity to human life. '*In a world where everyone is an expert on right and wrong, this book tries to show how Jesus unifies the best of what you hear. He joins up messy lives.*'

Cameron's accessible, coherent and innovative analysis is divided into seven parts. Each part contains several self-contained chapters that address some specific aspect of Christian thinking about ethics and life, and each chapter is cross-referenced to other key chapters. The chapters may be read in sequence, or dipped into in any order.

Cameron offers a stimulating reappraisal of our cluttered, tumultuous lives and encourages us to see life through a different lens.

Available from your local Christian bookshop or **www.thinkivp.com**

related titles from Apollos

Transforming the World?
The gospel and social responsibility
Jamie A. Grant and
Dewi A. Hughes (eds.)

ISBN: 9781844743742
288 pages, paperback

Evangelical Christianity has long been plagued by a dichotomy between evangelism and social action. The debate about whether evangelicals should attempt to make this world a better place in tune with God's will as well as prepare people for life in a better world is the background to this stimulating volume, which seeks to demonstrate that there is no tension between the task of evangelism and the Christian's obligation to care for those in need. The issue should never have been one of 'either/or' but rather should always have been voiced in terms of 'both/and'. The Bible's teaching makes it plain that God's salvific work is both spiritual and physical.

The first seven chapters survey relevant material in the Old and New Testaments; the second seven explore the theme of world transformation from the perspective of social ethics, systematic theology and church history.

The contributors are David L. Baker, Tim Chester, M. Daniel Carroll R., Jamie A. Grant, Peter S. Heslam, Jason Hood, Dewi A. Hughes, I. Howard Marshall, René Padilla, Anna Robbins, David W. Smith, Melvin Tinker, Alistair I. Wilson and Christopher J. H. Wright.

Available from your local Christian bookshop or **www.thinkivp.com**

www.ingramcontent.com/pod-product-compliance
Lightning Source LLC
Chambersburg PA
CBHW061434300426
44114CB00014B/1675